HOME ECONOMICS
AS A PROFESSION

SECOND EDITION

Home Economics as a Profession

MILDRED THUROW TATE, Ph.D.

Writer and Consultant
Blacksburg, Virginia

Formerly Professor and Chairman
Department of Home Economics
Virginia Polytechnic Institute
and State University

McGRAW-HILL BOOK COMPANY

New York   St. Louis   San Francisco   Düsseldorf   Johannesburg
Kuala Lumpur   London   Mexico   Montreal   New Delhi
Panama   Rio de Janeiro   Singapore   Sydney   Toronto

Library of Congress Cataloging in Publication Data

Tate, Mildred Bertha (Thurow) 1905–
  Home economics as a profession.

  Includes bibliographies.
  1. Home economics as a profession.
TX164.T36   1973   640'.23   72-2667
ISBN 0-07-062916-1

HOME ECONOMICS AS A PROFESSION

1 2 3 4 5 6 7 8 9 0 K P K P 7 9 8 7 6 5 4 3 2

This book was set in Times Roman by Black Dot, Inc.
The editors were Walter Maytham and James R. Belser;
the designer was Nicholas Krenitsky;
and the production supervisor was Ted Agrillo.
The printer and binder was Kingsport Press, Inc.

1719780

CONTENTS

PART IV APPENDIXES

PREFACE

Home Economics as a Profession is addressed to all who are interested in exploring the broad and important field of home economics. It is the belief of the author that many home economics students select their careers with only a limited knowledge of the many facets of the field. Since professional home economists usually are better acquainted with their own speciality than with the total field, they inadequately advise youth on what home economics has to offer and the great diversity of occupations for which to prepare. Wide knowledge of the total field is necessary for wise career planning and to ensure an adequate supply of trained home economists for the various specialities.

This book is written as a text for a course in introduction to, orientation to, or perspective in home economics, and for general students and others who wish to gain a better knowledge of the field. The specific purposes are twofold: (1) to acquaint the reader with the many vocations and professions open to home economists, the training necessary, and the activities and interests of home economists engaged in the various fields of work; and (2) to provide a means by which the reader can gain some appreciation of both forces which have brought home economics to its present status and the existing organizations for the promotion of home economics.

The two chapters dealing with college orientation that were Chapters 1 and 2 in the first edition, have been placed in Part IV as Appendixes 1 and 2 in this revision. In many colleges and universities today, activities dealing with orientation are offered in areas other than the student's academic speciality. For colleges where general orientation is offered in the beginning courses in home economics, Appendixes 1 and 2 should be of help.

This book does not attempt to answer all questions concerning the general field of home economics. It proposes to examine the field, highlight its history, and give the reader an increased awareness of home economics and home economists. The chapters are designed to help the reader apply the information received. The Interest Checklists in the chapters on careers provide a tool with which to evaluate one's degree of interest in the field under consideration. Class discussions of the Interest

Checklists furnish further ways of making meaningful the work of home economists in the various professions. These checklists have been used by the author in the course "Introduction to Home Economics," which she has taught for several years.

At the end of each chapter are suggested activities for helping students to explore further in the field of home economics. A short reading list is included in addition to references used by the author. These readings have been selected from the many that appear in the published literature on the basis of subject interest, readability, and accessibility in the average college library.

Although the author is fully aware that there are some men in the field, home economics college students at the junior level are almost exclusively women, and it seemed preferable to refer to the student as "she" for purposes of the text.

In developing the materials for this book, the author has become indebted to many persons. Her chief debt is to the many home economics students of the Virginia Polytechnic Institute and State University with whom she explored home economics as a profession for many years. She wishes to acknowledge grateful thanks to the library staff of the university, to Mrs. Nancy Wakeman for invaluable help in securing many of the materials necessary for the writing of the original manuscript, to the Home Economics Division of the Federal Extension Service for its aid in revising Chapter 6, and to the several businesses, agencies, and institutions that supplied both materials and photographs.

MILDRED THUROW TATE

HOME ECONOMICS
AS A PROFESSION

PART 1 A LOOK AT HOME ECONOMICS

1 THE BEGINNINGS OF HOME ECONOMICS

Home economics did not come into being suddenly. Nor was it the idea of any one person or group. It represents the results of many people's search for solutions to problems affecting individuals and families. It might be held that Socrates was the first to advocate home economics. Xenophon, a Greek writer who lived four centuries before Christ, wrote a dialogue called "Economicus" which supposedly took place between Socrates and a young Greek. The dialogue discussed home and farm management and analyzed the means that led to success in such management. In fact the modern science of economics began as household economics, as shown by the fact that the original meaning of "economics" was the management of the household, or "home management" (1).

To understand the development of home economics as we know it today, one must be acquainted with three parallel forces: (1) the growth of education for women in the United States, (2) the application of scientific knowledge to the problems of the home or household by men and women of science, and (3) the related movements which contributed to the solution of some home problems and highlighted the need for leadership in this field.

EARLY EDUCATION FOR WOMEN

The early colonists who settled in America had little, if any, concern for the education of women. When they came to America, the educational traditions and practices in the European countries favored schools for leadership which were limited to a few selected men. The lives lived by women did not demand formal education.

Colonial homes represented a fairly independent economic unit. The girl participated with her mother in the household work and management, and through her father and brothers, she received first-hand information about the industries which were carried on outside the home. Her work in colonial days consisted mainly of keeping the home and raising the children. The woman was the nurse, the social worker, and in a sense the manufacturer of household goods. She did the spinning, the weaving, the preserving and canning. She was the butcher, the baker, and the candlestick maker. She made the soap, carded and dyed the yarn, and styled and made the clothing for the family. She was the laundress and, so far as her daughters were concerned, the family-life teacher. Education for homemaking in that day was in the home itself.

3

Fig. 1-1 Registration in the department or college of home economics officially stamps these students as home economics students. (Courtesy of the Virginia Polytechnic Institute and State University)

The earliest schools for girls in the colonies were the Dame Schools (4, 8). For a few pennies a week, a woman with some knowledge of the three R's took the children of neighbors into her home and taught them a little reading, spelling, and sometimes writing and accounting. In addition, the young girls were taught a little needlework and cooking. These Dame Schools flourished in America during the 1700s and in many places became the primary schools.

In addition to the Dame Schools, the so-called finishing schools for girls became rather prominent in New England during the 1700s. In these schools, girls were taught knitting, mending, and other housewifely duties, with much emphasis on being a good hostess and by all means a lady. In some areas of New England, girls were admitted rather early to the grammar schools.

In addition, many private schools developed for girls. In the private schools for boys, the schoolmasters frequently taught girls before and after the sessions for boys in order to supplement their incomes. Nathan Hale, who was master in a school for boys, wrote in 1774, "I have kept during the summer a morning school between the hours of five and seven for which I have received six shillings a scholar by the quarter." In all probability, these early-morning pupils were girls. Thus, education for women, until 1800, was confined to schools open from two to six months during the year, schools in which the curriculum consisted of catechism, spelling, reading, and writing, but rarely arithmetic. It was thought that the woman's mind was of the type to which arithmetic would be incomprehensible.

The development of the academies in the 1800s gave great impetus to women's education. These academies spread rapidly, and many of them were coeducational. Most of the academies were religious in tone but gave some attention to the practical and scientific, which brought on an enlargement of the curriculum for women.

Public schools for girls, however, were very few until the latter part of the 1800s. It is interesting to note that in 1826 the Boston High School for Girls was established (4). The town appropriated $2,000 to experiment with the feasibility of high school education for girls. Before the end of the school year, the school had become so popular that the applications for admission greatly exceeded the facilities of the school. Many parents were disappointed that their daughters could not get in. Not knowing how to meet this feminine demand for education, the city fathers of Boston closed the high school, and for a period of twenty-three years no attempt was made to reopen it.

As was true of the academies, the female seminaries began to appear in the early 1800s to provide *higher* education for women.* Many of these seminaries were to grow into colleges for women, but unfortunately, most of them did not recognize women's role as being different from that of men. One of the exceptions was the Mt. Holyoke Female Seminary, established in 1836 (19). Miss Mary Lyon, the founder, recognized that women would spend their lives in homes and that they had a right to the type of training which would make their lives more creative and useful. She emphasized training for home and family life and incorporated the latest scientific training for the women into the curriculum of her school.

Although the seminaries on the whole did little to further education designed to help women better play the roles they were destined to play as wives, mothers, and homemakers, they did demonstrate and preach the doctrine that women were endowed by their creator with the same intellectual faculties as men and could participate in and profit by the activities of the institutions of higher education.

During the latter half of the 1800s, three types of colleges developed for women, namely, (1) independent colleges for women with separate facilities, such as Vassar, Smith, and Wellesley; (2) women's colleges affiliated with universities for men, such as Sophie Newcomb Memorial College for Women, affiliated with Tulane; the college for Women of Western Reserve; Barnard College at Columbia; and Radcliffe at Harvard; and (3) coeducational institutions where women were on a level of equality with men.

---

* Between 1800 and 1850 many seminaries granted diplomas to women.

COEDUCATION

Coeducation was an important influence in women's education (23). The Southern and Eastern parts of the United States were, in their earlier history, prejudiced against coeducation, and in these areas the separate woman's colleges and the affiliated colleges developed. It was in the North, Middle West, and West that coeducation had its early development. After coeducation developed in these areas it spread eastward and very slowly southward to open the doors of institutions of higher learning to women.

Oberlin College* which was established in 1833, became a pioneer in coeducation by abolishing sexual discrimination in the admission of students.† After 1837, it attempted to provide the same opportunities for women as for men (22). In fact, it probably was the only college or university which was coeducational prior to 1850. Horace Mann, the great exponent of the public school system in America, championed higher education for women in the early 1850s. He scorned the idea that women were not sufficiently strong physically or well endowed mentally to do college work. When he became president of Antioch College in 1852, the college was opened to women on the same basis as for men.

After it was once conceived, coeducation spread very rapidly. By 1880, 51 percent of the institutions of higher education were coeducational, and by 1900, this was true of 72 percent. Thus it took about 200 years to open the doors of institutions of higher education to women. Most of this progress was made in the latter half of the nineteenth and the first quarter of the twentieth centuries. Today, the majority of the colleges and universities are coeducational.

HOME ECONOMICS IN PUBLIC SCHOOLS

Practical work in cooking and sewing developed early in the public schools. As early as 1798 in the Boston public schools, girls spent part of their time on needlework, which was taught by the regular teachers. Two of the earliest educators who thought that preparation for homemaking was the responsibility of the schools were Mrs. Emma Hart Willard and Miss Catherine Beecher (5). It has been said that Mrs. Willard discovered domestic science and art (home economics) as a school subject and that Miss Beecher developed it. Mrs. Willard believed that homemaking might be greatly improved through school instruction.

In 1822 Miss Catherine Beecher established a private school for girls in

---

* Oberlin College was first known as Oberlin Collegiate Institute.
† Blount College may have been the first to admit women. Women were admitted from its beginning in 1795–1796. However, no woman ever received a degree, and after 1808, no women appeared on the rolls of the college. Blount College was superseded by East Tennesse College, which later became the University of Tennessee.

Hartford, Connecticut. She soon saw the need for teaching "domestic economy" and did much to get the work into the schools. She wrote two of the earliest home economics books, *Treatise on Domestic Economy*, which was published in 1841, and *Domestic Receipt Book*, published in 1842. Miss Beecher advocated the use of practice houses, in which the students might live with the domestic economy teacher and learn housekeeping by practice. Although this was considered a revolutionary idea at the time, most colleges of home economics now have such houses.

Mrs. Mary Hemenway was another leader who did much to get domestic science into the public schools in Boston, and as a result, in 1872 the Massachusetts legislature passed an act making sewing and other industrial education subjects legal throughout the state. In a few years cooking, sewing, housekeeping, and laundrying were offered as school subjects. By 1890 some form of domestic science was taught in the public schools of the majority of the large cities of the country. Many of the classes were started as private enterprises, later to be taken over by the school boards of the various cities and made a part of general education.

In 1887 the Boston Normal School of Cookery was established (2, 11). It was the first school for training teachers of the new subject of domestic science. In 1887 the New York College for Training Teachers, which was later to become Teachers College of Columbia University, was established. One purpose of the school was to train teachers of domestic science.

RELATED MOVEMENTS

There were many factors and movements which contributed to the development and expansion of home economics as a field. As has been pointed out, some of the work included in home economics today had been found for many years in the curriculum for girls in many parts of the United States. In the first half of the 1800s philanthropic organizations interested in social problems, such as the churches and women's clubs, found the teaching of cooking, sewing, and home sanitation an invaluable aid in their work. They opened classes outside the schools and sponsored activities in house-keeping and homemaking for children and adults.

Kitchen Garden

The kitchen-garden movement, which began in 1877, was promoted by such women leaders as Emily Huntington and Grace Dodge (10, 15, 16, 21). It taught small children household activities or object lessons in household work by means of miniature toys. The program spread fairly rapidly and was organized into the Kitchen-Garden Association of New York. In 1884 the Kitchen-Garden Association of New York was incorporated into the Industrial Education Association in recognition of the fact that the household activities were part of the manual training movement.

The kitchen-garden and manual training movements emphasized the need for practical education in the schools and are largely responsible for the vocational programs in home economics in the elementary and secondary schools in the United States of today.

Kindergarten

The introduction of kindergartens into the United States was due to the efforts of Miss Elizabeth Peabody, of Boston (25). Many of the early kindergartens were private, but gradually they became a part of the public school systems, especially in the cities. The kindergartens were closely associated to home economics, since home activities formed a source of many of the materials used in these schools. Problems of proper food, clothing, hygiene and sanitation in the home, and child care had to be met by the kindergarten teacher. Thus the work in the kindergartens further highlighted the need for home economics training in the schools and as a part of the education of teachers.

New England and Rumford Kitchens

The New England Kitchen, which was set up in Boston in 1890, was perhaps the forerunner of the home and commercial demonstration work. The money for the center was given by Mrs. Quincy Shaw, a philanthropist who had financed kindergartens in Boston. The kitchen was set up to experiment with the teaching of nutrition, the direct effect of which was to study the food and nutrition of working men and their possible relation to the use of intoxicating liquor. Mrs. Ellen H. Richards was asked to develop the experiment, and she secured the services of Mrs. Mary Hinman Abel. An attempt was made to serve scientifically cooked food, which was prepared under exacting rules of sanitation and cleanliness and offered for sale for home consumption. The greatest possible nourishment for a given amount of money was to be demonstrated, and these preparations were to supplement the foods served in the home.

It was in the New England Kitchen that Mr. Edward Atkinson's "Aladdin Oven," by which he hoped to change methods of cooking and decrease the cost of preparing foods, was tested. The "Oven" was of great value in the cooking of cheaper cuts of meat and other foods which required long, slow cooking at low temperatures. It was the forerunner of the fireless cooker which had a much greater sale later on.

Caroline L. Hunt in *The Life of Ellen H. Richards* describes the Kitchen as an "interesting failure, but one with great value as an experiment in unknown territory" (14). Certainly the Kitchen did not persuade the poor of the advantage of low-priced and nourishing food. "Its death knell was sounded," to quote Mrs. Richards, "by the woman who said, 'I don't want to eat what's good for me; I'd ruther eat what I'd ruther'" (14). Although the New England Kitchen did not accomplish its goals, it paved the way for the establishment of the Rumford Kitchen and the Boston school-lunch program.

The Rumford Kitchen was a part of the Massachusetts Exhibit at the world's fair in Chicago in 1893. In the kitchen, lunches were served that listed the weight and composition of each dish in the meal. The walls of the small dining room were hung with charts and diagrams showing the composition of the foods served. Pamphlets were made available to the visitors for study. This was the first attempt to demonstrate to the public by simple methods certain facts and principles of nutrition. No doubt it did much to highlight the need for nutrition research and education. The Kitchen was open only two months, but during this time at least 10,000 persons were served and partly educated on the subject of nutrition.

Probably the most important outgrowth of the New England and Rumford Kitchens was a plan for serving school lunches in Boston (14). Before 1894, the serving of food at the noon hour in the high schools of Boston was in the hands of janitors, who found it very profitable. Feeling that the serving of school lunches should be placed in better hands, the school committee of Boston made a contract with the New England Kitchen for the services of Mrs. Ellen H. Richards, who assumed the responsibility of this undertaking. As a result of this experience Mrs. Richards became an authority on the subject of school lunches and was consulted on the subject by school superintendents and others interested in education in all parts of the country.

Cooking Schools

Cooking schools became popular in the latter part of the 1800s (4). As the courses designed to help the future homemakers developed in the schools, the mothers in the homes began to demand help in meeting their problems, and cooking schools developed in most sizable cities throughout the United States. Three of the better-known ones were the New York, the Boston, and the Philadelphia cooking schools.

The acceptance and influence of these cooking schools can be appreciated from the following statement made by Mrs. Sara Tyson Rorer, who founded the Philadelphia cooking school (5):

> The New Century Club had opened a school of cookery (1878) under the care of Miss Devereux, a pupil of Miss Parloa, and a Miss Sweeney, a pastry cook in Boston. A cousin, who was chairman of the Committee of Household Science in the New Century Club, called upon me to join the first class for the good of my family, which I did. I, at that time, was studying chemistry, or pharmacy, with the idea of occupying the first position of this kind given to a woman in Philadelphia. I was also doing some preparatory work for the medical course in the Woman's College. I had not matriculated. I entered the cooking class, and I became so interested, and I saw so many possibilities coming from a school of this kind, that I immediately gave up my other work and went into this heart and soul. In less than a year I had given a course of cooking lectures, pure and

simple, to the fourth year students at the Woman's Medical College, and I had the honor of illustrating the first course of lectures given by a woman in the Franklin Institute in Philadelphia. . . . I taught for the [New Century] Club for two years. A number of physicians in Philadelphia, realizing the importance of the work, asked me to withdraw from the Club and start an independent school. I did, and the first year I enrolled seventy-four practice pupils; I gave four demonstration lectures during the week, with audiences ranging from 1,000 to 5,000. There never was any drawback to any of the work after that. I named the school the Philadelphia School. It continued for twenty-five years.

These early cooking schools did much to influence the offering of foods and nutrition in the high schools and colleges of the United States. They demonstrated the practical value of learning to prepare and serve food at small expense and tended to make the public nutrition conscious.

These cooking schools were one factor in influencing the creation of magazines devoted to the solution of household problems and played an important part in their development. Some of the early home economics magazines and their dates of publication were: *Good Housekeeping,* 1885–; *Everyday Housekeeping,* 1894–1908; *New England Kitchen,* 1894–1895; *American Kitchen Magazine,* 1895–1903; *Home Science Magazine,* 1903–1908; *Boston Cooking School Magazine,* 1906–1914; *American Cookery,* 1914–.

Early Scientists

Many nineteenth-century scientists contributed to the development of home economics. Several of these have been mentioned in the preceding pages, but others must be added even to a limited list.

Brillat-Savarin in the year of 1825 wrote a book entitled *Physiology of Taste, or Transcendental Gastronomy* (7). This was a book on the art of eating written in a vein of amusing pleasantry. This has been called one of the classics of home economics. Brillat-Savarin was a French writer, but he spent some years in America.

Edward L. Youmans, a chemist, made significant contributions to home economics through his efforts to apply chemistry to the home (30). In 1857 he published a book entitled *Handbook of Household Science,* in which he presented a scientific study of food, air, heat, and light from the standpoint of the home worker. Dr. Youmans was perhaps the earliest person to think in terms of the science of the home, and he was an untiring advocate of specialized household education.

Benjamin Thompson, i.e., Count Rumford, was one of the earliest scientists to treat household problems (20). He was an outstanding physicist and devoted much of his time to the study of heat in relation to houschold problems. The problems he studied included the application of principles of physics to heating, ventilation, fuels, kitchen ranges, and utensils. Certainly he was the first household physicist, the first to apply scientific methods to the preparation of foods, and the first to speak of the science of nutrition.

Wilbur O. Atwater, a chemist, was for many years in charge of nutrition investigations in the Office of Experiment Stations in the U.S. Department of Agriculture (28). His writings reporting the results of research on foods and nutrition were widely disseminated in this country and abroad and added materially to the knowledge of these subjects. His efforts did much to stimulate graduate study in home economics.

In 1886 Charles and Carrie Thwing published the first book on the family (27). It was largely a historical and social study of the family; however, it did discuss family relationships, including the relations between husbands and wives, parents and children, and the rights of children.

THE LAND-GRANT COLLEGE

The land-grant colleges and universities are largely responsible for the development of home economics at the college and university level (12, 24, 26). The land-grant college was made possible by the Morrill Act, passed by the Congress in 1862. This act offered to subsidize the establishment and endow the operation in every state of colleges for the common people. The funds were to be raised by the sale of public lands—31,000 acres or the equivalent in land script for each senator and representative in Congress to which each state was entitled. The proceeds of the sales were to be invested so as to yield not less than 5 percent annually, and this money was to be appropriated by each state for the endowment of at least one college, wherein should be offered college-level instruction in three specific fields: agriculture, mechanical arts, and military tactics. Teaching of other sciences, as well as the traditional classics, was expressly authorized, in order to promote the liberal and practical education of the industrial classes in the several pursuits and professions of life. The land-grant colleges came as a result of several forces. Before 1862, American colleges and universities had, on the whole, been dedicated to teaching the classics and preparing men of the upper socioeconomic group for the professions of law, medicine, and the ministry. But certain things had been happening in the United States prior to this time which were to make education more democratic. The free grammar school movement had given all classes a taste of education. The admission of women to the grammar schools and the academies for women exerted pressure on the colleges to admit women. The lyceums and other programs for adults strengthened the felt need for education for the average person.

Another force was the change in the general living pattern. Although life for families had continued much the same for many years, the developing frontier, with its growth of landowners, the beginning of industrialization and the development of cities, and science, which began offering its findings to agriculture and industry, brought to leaders in the United States the need for a new type of education.

Just as agriculture and industry were demanding help in the solving of their problems, the families they represented also had problems with which they wanted help. Science and change had helped to create problems for these families; now science and education had to be called upon to help in solving them, and so families called for help. The field of home economics developed in response to this call.

As the land-grant colleges were developed, the admission of women was sought. The first to become coeducational was Kansas, in 1863; others that followed shortly were Minnesota in 1868, Iowa in 1869, Illinois and Michigan in 1870, Nebraska in 1871, and New York in 1872 (29). With the admission of women into the land-grant colleges, courses to meet their special needs and interests began to develop. College home economics courses date from 1873 to 1875, when academic work in this field was first introduced into the land-grant colleges in Illinois, Iowa, and Kansas. Each of these colleges vies for the honor of being the first college to have given courses in home economics at the college level, and perhaps all three are entitled to the honor of being first.

Kansas State University stakes its claim for being first on the basis that it offered the first credit courses. In the year of 1873–1874, Mrs. C. H. Cheseldine taught a course in sewing. In 1875–1876, in addition to this course, Professor William Kedzie, a chemist, offered a course of lectures on "Bread, its composition, changes in baking; meat, changes in cooking; and vegetables, their composition and value." In the same year, a credit course on milk, butter, and cheese was given, and some work was offered in the cookery of foods. In 1882 a department of domestic science opened at Kansas State College, with Mrs. Nellie Kedzie (Jones) as head.

The University of Illinois, then known as The Illinois Industrial University, was the first to have a "School of Domestic Science and Art" (4). As early as 1869–1870, the catalogue announced a "Ladies Department," and in 1873–1874, the catalogue announced a School of Domestic Science and Arts—but the instructor to offer these courses, Miss Lou Allen, was not employed until 1874. The purpose of this new School of Domestic Science and Arts was "to give to earnest and capable young women a liberal and practical education, which should fit them for their great duties and trusts, making them the equals of their educated husbands and associates, and enabling them to bring science and culture to the all important labors and vocations of womanhood" (4). In 1880 the position of Professor of Domestic Science was made vacant by the resignation of Miss Allen, and the work was allowed to lapse until 1900, when Miss Isabel Bevier became head of the department, a position which she held for twenty-one years.

Perhaps it would be enlightening to today's student to review what her college sister of 1875 had to take in order to get a degree in Domestic Science from the Illinois Industrial University. Below are the requirements for a bachelor of science degree as listed in the college catalogue of 1875–1876 (29):

first year
1. Chemistry, trigonometry, drawing (full term), British authors
2. Chemistry, designing and drawing, American authors
3. Chemistry, designing and drawing, rhetoric

second year
1. Botany, physiology, German or English classics
2. Foods and dietetics (simple aliments), botany and greenhouse, German or English classics
3. Foods and dietetics (compound aliments and principles of cooking, etc.), zoology, German or English classics

third year
1. Domestic hygiene, ancient history, German or French
2. Physics, medieval history, German or French
3. Physics or landscape gardening, modern history, German or French

fourth year
1. Household aesthetics, mental science, history of civilization
2. Household science, constitutional history, logic
3. Domestic economy, usages of society, etc., political economy, home architecture, graduating thesis or oration or essay

Although the above education did not give preparation for the fields in home economics as they are known today, it was a beginning. Such subjects as household aesthetics, mental science, foods and dietetics, and home architecture were almost unheard of when this catalogue appeared in print.

Iowa State University gave recognition to "household arts" from its opening in 1868, although a course carrying college credit was first offered in 1877. In 1871 a one-year "Ladies' Course," consisting of lectures on domestic economy, was given by the dormitory matron. The matron of the college, in connection with her work as steward of the boarding department, adopted the so-called Mt. Holyoke plan, which required each young woman to work under careful supervision for two hours per day in the dining room, kitchen, or pantry. In 1872 a course of lectures was offered to junior girls on matters connected with housekeeping. In 1873 the board of trustees of the college was induced to open a department of cookery and household arts, but it was 1877 before the first class of cooking was offered with a laboratory equipped for class use. Mrs. Mary B. Welsh was the first to be in charge of the new department of cooking and household arts.

From these early beginnings, additional courses in domestic science and art were developed in the land-grant colleges. As new land-grant colleges developed, these courses became a fundamental part of their curricula. Slowly these courses began to be offered in colleges other than the land-grant, and later the name "home economics" replaced that of "domestic science and art." By 1908 home economics courses had been established in seven universities and all but three of the land-grant colleges.

Home economics grew rapidly and somewhat like "Topsy." The land-grant colleges, with their lower entrance requirements and definite vocational aims, soon developed comparatively strong departments of home economics. Much of the work was practical, and in many instances the science requirements were weak. In the land-grant institutions which were universities, the tendency was to minimize the practical work in home economics and make the instruction largely theoretical in order to gain the respect for home economics that was reserved for the applied sciences. The fact that there was no uniformity as regards nomenclature or content of the courses offered in the different institutions applied not only to the land-grant institutions but to other colleges attempting to teach this subject and in great measure to the normal and secondary schools.

LAKE PLACID CONFERENCES

Probably no one single experience had as much influence in chartering the course of home economics as did the Lake Placid conferences. In the early 1890s a group of educators and far-sighted citizens met annually at Lake Placid, New York, to discuss problems of common interest. Among this group were Mr. and Mrs. Melville Dewey. Mr. Dewey, being secretary of the New York State Board of Regents, had reason to be interested in the emerging field of home economics. "Household science" in the schools had grown to the point that the New York State Board of Regents had decided to give it a place in the examination for college entrance, and in order to learn more about this new field, Mr. Dewey invited Mrs. Ellen H. Richards, a pioneer in applying science to the home, to his summer camp at Lake Placid to discuss these examinations.

In 1898, during one of Mrs. Richards's visits with the Deweys, she was invited to speak on domestic problems before the Lake Placid conference members. In the discussion which followed, it was suggested that a number of trained workers meet the following summer to confer on the subject. The following summer, at the invitation of Mrs. Richards and Mrs. Dewey, eleven persons met and held the first of the ten Lake Placid conferences on home economics. Mrs. Richards was chosen chairman of the group and acted in this capacity throughout most of the conferences.

The first conference directed its attention to the following topics: the selection of a name for this new field of education, the preparation of women for leadership, the classification of home economics literature, and ways of raising the standard of living of American families. Several committees were set up to carry on the work of the group between conferences. These committies dealt with courses of study for public schools, colleges, and universities, the training of teachers, simplified methods of housekeeping, mission work and kitchen-garden classes, and similar matters.

In the minutes of the first conference is the statement: "The invitation of the Lake Placid Club for an annual conference was accepted by unanimous vote, it being clear by the close of the week that nothing could be more practically useful to the cause which the delegates had so much at heart than such an opportunity as this would give for comparison and discussion" (18).

This little gathering of eleven men and women who met in the bathhouse of the Lake Placid Club in 1899 expanded to thirty members at their second meeting in July of 1900. At the second conference important discussions concerned courses of study for grade schools and domestic science in the high schools. The training of teachers was given much consideration, for at that time the only state normal school for the training of teachers for home economics was at Framingham, Massachusetts. Miss Marian Talbot, dean of women and professor of sanitary science at the University of Chicago, gave the findings on her survey of courses in home economics and related subjects in colleges and universities, which revealed that of eighty-nine institutions listing courses on domestic science, hygiene, nursing, domestic architecture, etc., only fifty-eight reported work in one or more lines, and only twelve offered domestic science or home economics courses. In four others, work was soon to be undertaken (18).

Each year the interest in the Lake Placid conference on home economics grew. By the tenth conference, in 1908, the membership had grown to 201, with 74 attending the conference. Each year the conferences included an ever-widening set of problems of interest to leaders in home economics, including not only teacher training but graduate study, research, family welfare, and curricula for various types of schools and colleges, as well as administration problems, equipment, and financing.

The tenth and last Lake Placid conference was held at Chautauqua, New York, in July 1908. At the conference Mrs. Richards said (17):

> Ten years ago one of the greatest needs of the country was the appreciation of what science might do for the housewife in her daily home keeping, in making her work both easier and more efficient. The obstacle to satisfying these needs seemed the woman herself. One of the darkest spots in our civilization was the ignorance of the fundamentals of health which should be a part of the education of every woman.
>
> The present aim of the Lake Placid Conference is to teach the American people, chiefly through the medium of schools, the management of their homes on economics lines as to time and energy. Once the essentials of the home life are settled, they must be made a part of every child's education and the small details necessary must become so much a habit of life that no occasion will find the members of the family unprepared. . . .
>
> These ten years have seen the establishment of the Carnegie Nutrition Laboratory; the publications of Chittenden, Sager, Fletcher and others; the establishment of a regular department of home economics literature; and a

great increase in the attention paid to household sanitation: these all show the beginnings of a fundamental education along progressive lines.

One of the major accomplishments of the tenth conference was the laying of the plans for a national home economics organization. The recommendation was made that a national organization be organized, that home economics groups be started in different states to work for rapid growth of the new organization, that members pay annual dues to the organization, that a journal be published, and that a name national in character be chosen for the new organization.

A committee on national organization was appointed and directed to report to the teaching section of the Lake Placid conference, which was to meet in Washington in December, on ways and means for carrying on the new organization. When the teaching section of the Lake Placid conference closed, the group reconvened on the following day to organize officially the American Home Economics Association.

Today, over a short period of approximately eighty-five years since the first courses in foods and clothing were offered in college, home economics has grown to the point where over half of the junior and senior colleges and universities in the United States admitting women have home economics offerings, with approximately 100,000 men and women enrolled in these courses (9). Also, home economics has become the largest professional endeavor for women in the United States, with the exception of elementary education, and embraces a wide variety of offerings. The American Home Economics Association, which formally recognized home economics as a profession, was formed in 1909, and in this period of over sixty years, its membership has grown from less than 100 to approximately 33,000 with an additional 14,000 student members (21).

SUGGESTED ACTIVITIES

1. What is the history of home economics in your state? How did home economics begin? Who were the founders? Where did they get their training?
2. When was home economics introduced into your college? Who was the first head or director of home economics? What were the first offerings?
3. Do you have home economics research at your institution? If so, when was it started? What have been the main types of investigation? What contributions has home economics research in your state made to the furthering of knowledge? How many home economists are engaged in research?
4. Where is the home economics extension work in your state located? When was the extension work started? Who is the director of the extension work for women? How many home economists are employed by the extension service?
5. Which was the first college to admit women in your state? When were women admitted? What were the early offerings for women?

6. What is the history of women's education in your college? Did it develop along with education for men? If not, why?

7. When was home economics introduced into the high schools of your state? How many high schools offer home economics today? Is there any home economics in the elementary schools?

REFERENCES

1. Andrews, Benjamin R., *Economics of the Household*, pp. 2–3, The Macmillan Company, New York, 1935.

2. Baldwin, Keturah E., *The AHEA Saga*, pp. 5, 95, American Home Economics Association, Washington, 1949.

3. Bane, Juliet Lita, *The Story of Isabel Bevier*, pp. 31–34, Charles A. Bennett Company, Inc., Peoria, Ill., 1955.

4. Bevier, Isabel, *The Home Economics Movement*, pp. 10, 31, 44–51, Whitcomb & Barrows, Boston, 1918.

5. Bevier, Isabel, *The Home Economics Movement*, pp. 50–51, Whitcomb & Barrows, Boston, 1918.

6. Blow, Susan Elizabeth, *Kindergarten Education*, J. B. Lyon Company, Albany, N.Y., 1904.

7. Brillat-Savarin, Jean, *Physiology of Taste, or Transcendental Gastronomy*, Lindsay and Blakiston, Philadelphia, 1854.

8. Cubberley, Ellwood P., *Public Education in the United States*, pp. 25–26, Houghton Mifflin Company, Boston, 1919.

9. *Digest of Educational Statistics, 1968*, p. 73, Office of Education, 1968.

10. Dodge, Grace H., and others, *What Women Can Earn*, pp. 111–114, Frederick Stokes Company, Philadelphia, 1899.

11. Donham, S. Agnes, *The Eastern Massachusetts Home Economics Association*, p. 7, The Eastern Massachusetts Home Economics Association, Boston, 1956.

12. Eddy, Edward Danforth, Jr., *Colleges for Our Land and Time*, pp. 60–62, 90–91, 122–123, 160–161, 219–220, Harper & Brothers, New York, 1957.

13. Graham, Abbie, *Grace H. Dodge, Merchant of Dreams*, The Woman's Press, New York, 1926.

14. Hunt, Caroline L., *The Life of Ellen H. Richards*, pp. 215–216, American Home Economics Association, Washington, 1942.

15. Huntington, Emily, *How to Teach Kitchen-garden: Object Lessons in Household Work*, Doubleday, Page & Company, New York, 1901.

16. Keech, Mable Louise, *Training the Little Homemaker by Kitchengarden Method*, J. B. Lippincott Company, Philadelphia, 1912.

17. *Lake Placid Conference on Home Economics: Proceedings of the Tenth Annual Conference*, p. 25, Lake Placid, N.Y., 1908.

18. *Lake Placid Conferences on Home Economics: Proceedings of the First, Second, and Third Conferences*, pp. 8, 25, 45, Lake Placid, N.Y., 1901.

19. Lyon, Mary, *Mount Holyoke Female Seminary*, Directors of the Old South Work, Boston, 1903.

20. Malone, Dumas (ed.), *Dictionary of American Biography*, vol. XVIII, pp. 449–452, Charles Scribner's Sons, New York, 1936.

21. "1969–70 AHEA Membership Totals," *Journal of Home Economics*, vol. 62, p. 262, 1970.

22. *Oberlin College Bulletin*, vol. 55, General Catalogue no. 7, July 1957, Oberlin, Ohio.

23. Ross, Earle D., *Democracy's College*, p. 5, The Iowa State College Press, Ames, 1942.

24. Ross, Earle D., *Democracy's College*, pp. 46–67, The Iowa State College Press, Ames, 1942.

25. Tharp, Louise, *The Peabody Sisters of Salem*, Little, Brown, & Company, Boston, 1950.

26. "The Land-Grant Institutions and Their Relationship to State and Federal Government," *A Report to the Commission on Intergovernmental Relations by the Association of Land-Grant Colleges and Universities*, p. 4, Washington, March 1954.

27. Thwing, Charles, and Carrie Thwing, *The Family*, Lee and Shepard, Boston, 1886.

28. True, Alfred C., *A History of Agricultural Education in the United States*, U.S. Department of Agriculture, Misc. 36, pp. 270–272, 1929.

29. True, Alfred C., *A History of Agricultural Education in the United States*, U.S. Department of Agriculture, Misc. 36, pp. 267–268, 1929.

30. Youmans, Edward L., *Handbook of Household Science*, D. Appleton & Company, Inc., New York, 1857.

ADDITIONAL READINGS

Craig, Hazel Thompson: *The History of Home Economics*, Practical Home Economics Pamphlet, New York, 1945.

Crockett, Mary Elva: "A Golden Jubilee in Kansas Home Economics," *Journal of Home Economics*, vol. 17, pp. 285–286, May 1925.

Davenport, Eugene: "Home Economics at Illinois," *Journal of Home Economics*, vol. 13, pp. 337–341, August 1921.

Gesell, Arnold: "Nursery School Movement and Home Economics," *Journal of Home Economics*, vol. 17, pp. 369–371, July 1925.

Gibbs, Winifred S.: "The Development of Home Economics in Social Work," *Journal of Home Economics*, vol. 8, pp. 68–73, February 1916.

Gilchrist, Maude: *The First Three Decades of Home Economics at Michigan State College* [*1896–1926*], School of Home Economics, Michigan State College, East Lansing, 1947.

Green, Myron, "Home Economics in the Restaurant Business," *Journal of Home Economics,* vol. 18, pp. 138–142, March 1926.

Henderson, Grace: *Development of Home Economics in the United States,* The Pennsylvania State University College of Home Economics Publication 156, University Park, 1954.

"Home Economics in the Advertising Agency," *Journal of Home Economics,* vol. 18, pp. 455–458, August 1926.

Rose, Flora: "Pioneers in Home Economics," *Practical Home Economics,* vol. 25, part 1, pp. 79, 116–118, February 1947; part 2, pp. 154, 184, 194, March 1947; part 3, pp. 224–225, 262, April 197; part 4, pp. 288, 310, 324, May 1947; part 5, pp. 348, 380, June 1947; part 6, pp. 418, 484–486, September 1947; part 7, pp. 510, 541, October 1947; part 8, pp. 590, 622, 633, November 1947; part 9, pp. 674, 692–693, December 1947.

"The Ellen H. Richards Research Fund," *Journal of Home Economics,* vol. 8, p. 81, February 1916.

White, Edna N.: "The Merrill-Palmer School," *Journal of Home Economics,* vol. 13, pp. 545–548, November 1921.

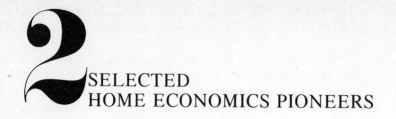

SELECTED HOME ECONOMICS PIONEERS

To understand home economics fully, one must have an intimate knowledge of the values and motivations of the early home economists who gave substance and direction to the new field of study. These pioneers believed so completely in the worthwhileness of the type of education now called home economics that they devoted their talents, energy, and, often, money to provide it for future generations. Each attacked the problem from a slightly different background and hypothesis; this brought about a rich and varied profession. Space permits the consideration of only a few of these unique leaders, whose teaching, research, and writing laid the foundations of home economics as a field of study in the schools, colleges and universities, and adult education programs of our land.

ELLEN HENRIETTA SWALLOW RICHARDS

The "patron saint" of home economics is Ellen H. Richards. She, more than any other person, may be called the founder and guiding light of home economics, and her life might be called "home economics in action." She gave the leadership which culminated in the American Home Economics Association and was its first president (7).

She was born on a New England farm in 1842. Early, under the tutelage of her mother, she learned to master the housekeeping arts which in later years she valued so highly that she sought to have them embodied in the curricula of the schools.

At sixteen years of age, she entered an academy in Westford, Massachusetts, where her education consisted of a little mathematics, a few compositions, some French, and much Latin. After finishing the academy she taught Latin. Always there was an open book beside her. At that time, there were few doors open to ambitious women, for New England had no colleges to which women were admitted. In speaking of this time she wrote to a friend, "I lived for over two years in Purgatory, really, and I didn't know what to do. It seemed best for me to just stay and endure it. . . . I was thwarted and hedged in on every side; it seemed as though God didn't help me a bit and man was doing his best against me. . . ." (7, p. 21). But better times were coming for her. In September of 1868, she entered Vassar Female Institute, which had just been founded, and somewhat over a year later she was admitted as a senior.

While at Vassar her grades were very high, and she received much recognition for her academic ability. Her great interest in knowledge and world affairs is shown in the following excerpt from a letter to her mother. In her home town in 1868–1869, many of the staid people were concerned as to what would happen to a young woman who had a scientific education. She wrote her mother (7, p. 33):

> People have a curiosity to know what monstrosity is to arise from my ashes, do they? I feel much like saying, confound their base ideas of true education. But I will only say, tell all such interested individuals that my aim is now, as it has been for the past ten years, to make myself a true woman, one worthy of the name, and one who will unshrinkingly follow the path which God marks out, one whose aim is to do all the good she can in the world and not to be one of the delicate little dolls or the silly little fools who make up the bulk of American women, slaves to society and fashion.

After graduating from Vassar in 1870, she longed to study further in chemistry, but there were no science schools open to her. She attempted unsuccessfully to apprentice herself to commercial chemists in Boston. In 1870, she made application to the Massachusetts Institute of Technology, which had been founded in 1865. Although the faculty recommended the admission of Miss Swallow as a special student in chemistry, it was *"Resolved:* That the faculty are of the opinion that the admission of women as special students is as yet in the nature of an experiment, that each application should be acted on upon its own merits, and that no general action or change of the former policy of the Institute is at present expedient." In January of 1871 Miss Swallow enrolled at MIT as the first woman ever to enter any such strictly scientific school in the United States.

Having been admitted to MIT as a special student, she was determined to make good and to make herself indispensable, so that she would be welcomed on the campus. The following statements show how conscious she was of this need (7, pp. 43–44; italics added):

> I hope in a quiet way . . . I am *winning a way* which *others will keep open.* Perhaps the fact that I am not a Radical or a believer in the all powerful ballot for women to right her wrongs and that I do not scorn womanly duties, but claim it as a privilege to clean up and sort of supervise the room and sew things, etc., is winning me stronger allies than anything else. Even Prof. _____ accords me his sanction when I sew his papers or tie up a sore finger or dust the table. Last night Prof. _____ found me useful to mend his suspenders which had come to grief, much to the amusement of young Mr. _____. I try to keep all sorts of such things as needles, pins, scissors, etc., around and they are getting to come to me for everything that they want and they almost always find it and as Prof. _____ said the other day, "When we are in doubt about anything, we always go to Miss Swallow." They leave messages with me and come to expect me to know

where everything and everybody is so you see I am useful in a decidedly general way—so they can't say that study spoils me for anything else. I think that I am making as good progress as anyone in my studies too. They say I am going ahead because Prof. Ordway trusts me to do his work for him which he never did anyone else—the dear old man—I am only too happy to do anything for him. [Professor Ordway had a large practice as a consulting expert in technical chemistry.]

In 1873 Miss Swallow received the degree of bachelor of science in chemistry from MIT, and the same year received the master's degree from Vassar. She became very much interested in the public health work, which was just beginning, and devoted the next few years of her life to teaching sanitary engineering and analyzing the waters of the State of New York. After her experience as water analyst, she entered upon a large private practice in sanitary chemistry, including the examination not only of water but also of air and food and the testing of wallpapers and fabrics for arsenic.

In 1876 she became instructor in the woman's laboratory of MIT, and in 1884 she was appointed instructor in sanitary chemistry, a position which she held until the time of her death. She married Professor Robert Hallowell Richards, head of the department of Mining Engineering at MIT. Thus Ellen H. Richards opened one of the foremost scientific schools in the United States to women and, further, broke established custom by marrying and remaining on its staff.

Always being interested in homemaking, Mrs. Richards turned her extracurricular time to improvement of home and family life. Mrs. Richards's home always was an experimental laboratory where she experimented with house furnishing in relation to time and energy saving in keeping house, food as it affected the body, and the cost of using various types of equipment. Mrs. Richards did not turn the housework over to hired help, as was the custom of her class in the day. Instead, she made her house into a home for girls who were anxious to get an education and allowed them to work for their board and room.

One of these students said of Mrs. Richards later: "She had mastered the principles of scientific management long before they became the subject of discussion in the industrial world."

In addition to teaching at MIT, running a home, and carrying a private practice as a consultant engineer, she directed correspondence courses for women who could not go to college.

Mrs. Richards was firmly convinced, and even more firmly as time went on, that if women were finally to get control over the conditions of their own lives, a beginning must be made in childhood. She interested herself actively, therefore, in the introduction of science and home economics instruction in the public schools of Boston.

Her work in the New England and the Rumford Kitchens was an experiment in ways of improving the food habits of families. She developed the first school-lunch program in Boston and as a result of this experience and pioneer work became an authority on school lunches. She was consulted on the subject by school superintendents and others interested in education in all parts of the country.

Mrs. Richards in later life turned her attention to the development of standards for teachers in home economics and the bringing together of the various and sundry developments into home economics. She was the first president of the American Home Economics Association.

Mrs. Richards died March 30, 1911, but her influence lived on, and perhaps is more far-reaching today than ever (1). Her influence can be traced in schools, in colleges, and in other educational institutions, in scientific and popular societies, and in the lives of many individuals. In the headquarters building of the American Home Economics Association, Washington, D.C., the Ellen H. Richards room contains many of Mrs. Richards's possessions. Her life should be a challenge to any young woman desiring to be a home economist.

ISABEL BEVIER

Miss Isabel Bevier was the second president of the American Home Economics Association and a pioneer in home economics college administration (4). She, like Mrs. Richards, came into home economics through her interest in applying scientific knowledge to the improvement of the home. Miss Bevier was only five years of age when Ellen H. Richards was struggling to be admitted to MIT, so she grew up in an atmosphere somewhat more favorable to the education of women. Miss Bevier took her bachelor's degree in 1885 and her master's degree in 1888 from the university of Wooster. She majored in languages, a far cry indeed from science, but language was a very respectable field for women of that day. Her first college teaching was at the Pennsylvania College for Women, where she was to teach science. In order to prepare for this work, she took special training at the Case School of Applied Science in Cleveland. Just as Mrs. Richards was the first woman to enter MIT, Miss Bevier was the first woman to be admitted to Case Institute.

Her interest in science made it possible for her to work with Dr. Charles Langworthy, Dr. Wilbur Atwater, and others in the chemical study of foods. She had the opportunity to participate in some of the earliest dietary studies conducted by Dr. Atwater.

It was at the University of Illinois where Miss Bevier began her real life's work, being a pioneer in teaching home economics to college students. She set out to develop a department of home economics based upon scientific principles. Dean Eugene Davenport later said of Miss Bevier (4, pp. 24–25):

> What was it that led or drove this farm girl along her zigzag course of preparation? Preparation for what? Nobody could have answered that question then, much less herself. She belongs to a worthy company of

pioneers. She worked with pioneers of science, not content to follow beaten trails along the margins of a goodly prospect, but intent upon exploration for themselves. So she caught the spirit of the trail maker, and it led her all of the way.

The true qualities of the pioneer are shown in the following statement, made by the president of the University of Illinois, under whom Miss Bevier served (4, pp. 25–27):

> What I wished was a University department [of home economics] which could command the respect of other University departments and at the same time make an impression upon the home life of the people. . . . I wanted a departmernt which was really scientific and knew what it was talking about and could attract students to the fundamental principles upon which the comfort and healthfulness and attractiveness of the home must rest. . . . Miss Bevier succeeded beyond my expectations. . . .

It is difficult for the student of today to realize that in 1900 the name "home economics" had not as yet been coined. Insight into Miss Bevier's personality can be gained from her account of the naming of the department at the University of Illinois. Miss Bevier says of this experience (4, p. 35):

> The naming of the new educational child was entrusted. . . . to Dean Davenport, Vice-president Burrill, and me. . . . The three of us wanted science as the basis and approach to the subject; but it was Dean Davenport who said, "I believe there will be some day a science of the household. Let's get ready for it and develop it." So the child was called "household science," and thus due warning was given that neither a cooking school nor a milliner's shop was being opened at the University.

Miss Bevier did much to elevate the courses being offered in land-grant colleges above the level of pure practice. Her desire to put these courses on a high academic level is shown by the following statement (4, p. 39):

> Planning the work in food proved to be a real undertaking. In those days, where to begin was a great question. Nine land-grant institutions had courses in "domestic economy" in 1900. . . . But, judged by their cata- logues, the work seemed to me to be on the cooking-school basis. . . . I sought for another classification and finally decided to use the method I was familiar with in the teaching of chemistry—namely, to take the classes of foods and study one class until the student knew something about it. Proteins, fats, and carbohydrates were the classes we decided to begin with. . . . Cooking seemed to me so inadequate that after much thought I

chose "selection and preparation of food" for the title of the first semester's work in foods and "economical use of food" for the second semester's work.

Putting home economics on a sound scientific and academic basis was not easy. This approach was opposed by those who felt that the practical side of education was all that was important, but Miss Bevier pushed on. Soon applied art was added to the curriculum, and in 1908 an experimental house, now known as a home-management house, was established.

Research was started early to furnish answers to the questions asked in the classrooms and throughout the state about the daily processes and products of the home. Miss Bevier met each new challenge with the same scientific approach. With the passage of the Smith-Lever Act of 1914, extension work was established, and soon the Smith-Hughes Act of 1917 brought the need to train teachers of vocational home economics into the department. Emergencies such as World War I and the influenza epidemic of 1918 called Miss Bevier and her staff into service. These situations, met courageously, brought wider vision to home economists and were incorporated into the expanding programs of home economics (6).

Miss Bevier not only knew when to take up a cause but she was equally wise in realizing when to turn over a piece of work to someone else. In 1920, against the protests of the officials of the University of Illinois and many others, Miss Bevier decided to put the leadership of the department of home economics into younger hands.

"It was characteristic of Isabel Bevier that when she felt she had built an enduring institution and guided it through the most vigorous years of her life she was willing to leave it to others for future development" (5).

MARTHA Van RENSSELAER

Martha Van Rensselaer, a pioneer in home economics extension work, was born in 1864 in Randolph, New York (17). After graduating from Chamberlain Institute in 1884, she taught for ten years in the public schools in western New York and from 1894 to 1900 was school commissioner in Cattaraugus County. She often combined the traveling and inspection work of this position with instruction at teachers' institutes. In 1900 she was called to the State College of Agriculture at Cornell University for an untried educational adventure, the development of extension work for rural women. When the success of this project made necessary resident instruction in subjects pertaining to rural homemaking, courses in homemaking were offered.

In 1903 Miss Van Rensselaer gave the first credit course in home economics at Cornell University, and in 1908 a department of home economics was established. Dr. Albert R. Mann said of her, "Miss Van Rensselaer seemed without limit in her capacity for sustained, arduous work, mental and physical. . . . Clarity and tenacity of purpose and of ideals kept her course always toward higher attainments. Martha Van Rensselaer revealed unmistakably the characteristics and qualities which mark greatness" (14).

In commenting on Miss Van Rensselaer's work in extension, Dr. Liberty Hyde Bailey said, "At the opening of the century there was no organized public extension work as we know it today. The colleges of agriculture were beginning to expand, . . . broadening their basis of research. . . . It was soon seen that it was not sufficient to help the man on the land. The woman must be helped as well; and here came Martha Van Rensselaer as one of the pioneers" (2).

The first effort to reach the farmers' wives was a reading course which was followed by the organization of clubs. The first bulletin in this reading course was entitled *Saving Steps*. The reading course grew, the clubs grew, requests arose from localities, students came to receive resident instruction, and classes of many kinds developed. Home economics college teaching and extension work grew together. Miss Van Rensselaer had the ability to meet all kinds of people effectively. She brought good staff members to the college, teachers who were broadly based and rooted in the advancement of women and the integrity of the home (14). She conceived of home economics education as a means by which women's minds could be trained, their capacities released, and their deepest desires satisfied through growth in understanding and directing their own normal social functions (20).

She gave of her time and talents to many enterprises during her lifetime, including being a member of the executive staff of the U.S. Food Administration during the greater part of the First World War, homemaking editor of the *Delineator* from 1920 to 1926, and, from 1929 to 1932, assistant director of the White House Conference on Child Health and Protection. She was active in the Lake Placid conferences and later in the American Home Economics Association, of which she was a charter member and president from 1914 to 1916. In 1923 she was chosen as one of the twelve greatest women of the United States by a committee appointed by the National League of Women Voters.

Her vision of what home economics was destined to be is shown in the following statement taken from one of her addresses as president of the American Home Economics Association in 1915 (22):

> The old methods of homemaking have not satisfied women's ability. Education of the past has not pointed out the home as a laboratory for the science and art of the school, and woman has looked outside for her professional experience. Home economics unlocks a vast and interesting laboratory and the result of the use of that laboratory is greater efficiency and a higher type of civilization, for "good citizenship is but an expansion of home ideals."

ABBY L. MARLATT

Miss Marlatt, a pioneer home economist in research and teaching, was born in 1869 in a home adjoining the grounds of Bluemont College, in Kansas, which later was to become the Kansas State University (the land-grant college). She received both her bachelor's and her master's degrees from this institution, majoring in chemistry. While she was working for her masters degree she began to work out some answers to questions asked in the kitchen laboratories, among them that of how long and at what temperature one should cook a beef roast to have it rare or well done. Mrs. Nellie Kedzie Jones, first home economist at Kansas State University, says of her, "I remember Abby Marlatt sitting by a kitchen range in which we had persuaded an ironworker to cut a hole through which we could put a long chemical thermometer into a huge roast. She cooked many roasts and recorded the temperatures of several stages of rareness in the prime western beef. No one called it research in that day" (9).

When Abby Marlatt was called to Utah, she was the second of a number of young women sent out from Kansas State University to organize "departments of homemaking" in other land-grant colleges. Her firm belief in the importance of such work to college girls and her personal interest in its success made her classes popular from the very start. She was to be the founder of home economics work at other schools and colleges, especially that of the University of Wisconsin. The story is told that when she went to Wisconsin she was given a free hand to develop the department of home economics, but with this went little money and space. She had been asking for a home economics building, and the matter was to come before the legislature. Having received a gift of maple syrup from a member of the finance committee, she invited the whole legislative finance committee to come to the University of Wisconsin to eat pancakes with maple syrup prepared and served by a class in home economics. Everyone accepted. Among the pancakes served, one the size of the griddle was carried in by the dean of the college and placed before the chairman of the finance committee. Funds for a home economics building were voted at that session of the legislature.

Miss Marlatt did not permit any obstacle to stand in her way of helping homemakers. For example, the story has been told that she was advertised as a speaker at a special club meeting at Baraboo, forty miles from Madison, Wisconsin, in the days before automobiles. The carriage which took her to the train arrived after the train had left. When she inquired as to how she was going to get to Baraboo, the only answer she got was, "All I know is a special train." Her response was, "Please get it ready as soon as possible." The trainmaster was sympathetic but insisted on pay for the extra train. Miss Marlatt wrote the check, the train was soon ready, and she was riding—the only passenger. When the conductor came and said, "Tickets, please!" she responded, "Why, man! I own this train!" She was on time at the meeting.

During the First World War Miss Marlatt was called to Washington by the United States Food Administrator, Herbert Hoover, later to be President. There she cooperated with the states in food conservation work; she was later active in defense work in her own state.

Her interest in research and her understanding of home economics is shown in the following statement (15):

> The University of Iowa has made a great step forward. There, in its child welfare station, a home economics worker is in charge of the nutrition of children. In the medical college there is a chair held by a nutrition woman, a former professor of home economics at Illinois. The home economics work began in the kitchen; now it is recognized as of full professional rank in the school of medicine. Medicine began in the barber shop. Which can call the origin of the other in question?

Miss Marlatt was always a prodigious worker, a good organizer, and an able administrator. She became a nationally recognized leader in home economics. Her interest in and vision for home economics are ably expressed in the following statement, which she made in 1914 (16):

> Higher education has been so long dominated by the study of the humanities that we now find opposition when there is an attempt to increase the number of the subjects which are supposed to give moral and intellectual discipline, to elevate and humanize the student. . . . Are food, clothing, shelter and family, when studied through Greek and Roman history cultural but when studied in relation to our city slums or country villages utilitarian and therefore uneducational? . . . There is no other profession which so bristles with unsolved problems. . . .

MARY TILESTON HEMENWAY

Mary Hemenway was born in 1820, the daughter of a wealthy New York shipping merchant. A pioneer in home economics education in the public schools, her own education was acquired in private schools in New York and at home. She said that she was reared principally on household duties, the Bible, and Shakespeare (13). In 1840, she married Augustus Hemenway, a successful merchant of Boston, where she lived the remainder of her life. After her own family was reared, she devoted her wealth and energies to the development of numerous educational and philanthropic projects.

Outstanding among these was her work in home economics. Her efforts to introduce home economics into the public schools of Boston were a very important landmark in the development of home economics. As early as 1835, parents in Boston had petitioned the school board for the teaching of needlework to girls. Some instruction in needlework followed, but the efforts during the next thirty years were haphazard and furnished very poor results. In 1865, as a result of the insight she had gained through welfare work with soldiers' families after the Civil War, Mrs. Hemenway requested that a class of older girls in the Winthrop school receive instruction in more advanced needlework at her expense. She agreed to send a dressmaker and seamstress to the school for the instruction, as well as to supply all of the materials. The results of this undertaking were very satisfactory, and in 1873 the work was taken over by the city.

It was also through Mrs. Hemenway's influence that cooking was introduced into Boston schools. From 1883 to 1885 she supported a summer-vacation school, then a new thing, under the direction of Miss Amy M. Homans in the Tennyson Street Schoolhouse for teaching girls the skills of housekeeping. Girls from the kindergarten age through the grammar grades were given useful employment and opportunity to play, and were taught kitchen gardening, knitting, embroidery, clay modeling, and simple needlework, and in 1885, a model kitchen was established in the basement of the schoolhouse where the older girls were given lessons in cooking. Later, girls from nearby schools were allowed to have cooking lessons during the school year.

The cooking laboratory was named School Kitchen Number One. Mrs. Hemenway paid all of the expenses of the school kitchen from 1885 to 1888, when it was taken over by the city. This was the first venture of its kind in the United States.

As there was no textbook suitable for the use by the pupils, Mrs. Mary A. Lincoln, head of the Boston Cooking School, prepared at Mrs. Hemenway's request the *Boston School Kitchen Text Book*, and as long as the kitchen was supported by Mrs. Hemenway, she gave a copy of the book and a diploma to each girl who completed the course.

Mrs. Hemenway's work was not confined to Boston, for she established cooking schools in several places, including two schools in the South. She pioneered in many educational ventures for women. One of her major projects after the establishment of the Boston Normal School of Cookery was in the field of physical education for women. She furnished free instruction in gymnastics to women teachers in Boston and promoted conferences on physical education which finally led to the introduction of gymnastics into the Boston schools.

With the increase in the school kitchens, the need for trained teachers for them was the next problem, because at that time there was no training school in this country for training teachers of cooking. To meet the situation Mrs. Hemenway established, under the direction of Miss Amy M. Homans, the Boston Normal School of Cookery in 1887, later to become the Mary Hemenway Department of Household Arts of the State Normal School at Framingham, Massachusetts.

Miss Katherine Stone, formerly secretary to Mrs. Hemenway, says, "Mrs. Hemenway has been called the mother of public school household arts, a title which may justly be claimed by her" (21). It is certain that home economics in the public schools of this country owes much to the efforts and support of Mrs. Hemenway and her colleagues.

CATHERINE ESTHER BEECHER

Catherine Beecher, a pioneer in women's higher education and home economics, was born in 1800, the oldest of nine children. She was a member of the illustrious family of Beechers, being a sister of Henry Ward Beecher, Edward Beecher, and Harriet Beecher Stowe. Catherine Beecher says that she was trained to industry by her mother, who was "remarkable, not only for her intelligence and culture, but for a natural taste and skill in domestic handicraft" (8), and by the fact that at sixteen she had to take over her large family of brothers and sisters on the death of her mother.

Her early education was in private schools and was typical of the education for girls at that time—the primary studies, and drawing, painting, and music. This was interrupted at the time of her mother's death, but at nearly twenty, she again took up the study of the piano and drawing, and about a year and a half later she began teaching in a private school for young ladies in New London, Connecticut. Largely by independent study she had gained a knowledge of mathematics, Latin, and philosophy.

In 1823. her plans for marriage were shattered by the sudden death of her fiance, Professor Alexander Metcalf Fisher of Yale College, and she decided to devote her life to women's education and, as she said, "to find happiness in living to do good." In 1821 at Hartford, Connecticut, she opened a small private school for young ladies. Success at once attended this venture, and the school was known for its advanced curriculum and its excellence of teaching (8).

She spent much of her time and energy on "the securing of professional advantages of education for my sex equal to those bestowed on men." She helped develop colleges for women in the East and West and sought to develop public opinion that would provide for ". . . American women a liberal education . . . by means of endowed institutions on the college plan of organization . . . to include all that is gained by normal school, and also to train women to be healthful, intelligent, and successful wives, mothers and housekeepers" (8).

She advocated publicly the branch of knowledge now known as home economics and introduced it into the schools which she founded. She wrote two of the earliest home economics books: *A Treatise on Domestic Economy for the Use of Young Ladies at Home and at School* (1841), and *Miss Beecher's Domestic Receipt Book* (1846).

Dr. Benjamin Andrews, commenting on Miss Beecher's books, said (3):

> The first [book] is a broad discussion of household problems; the second, a book of practical procedures. Both books went through edition after edition for forty years. . . . The first chapters of the *Treatise* deal with the

responsibilities of the American woman and her social and national opportunity through school and home. There follows the argument justifying domestic economy as a subject of study, which still rings true and carries conviction to the reader, and then the successive chapters on various aspects of the household. . . .

Sound, well considered, practical, the discussions present household management as a calling at once dignified and worthy of the best that women can give. . . .

Miss Beecher's plan of a practice house, in which the students might live with the domestic economy teacher and learn housekeeping by practice, is now finally realized in our higher schools of home economics. . . . Her books were the beginning of domestic education.

Thus, Miss Beecher was one of the early forces which created in this country the opportunity for higher education for women and promoted the belief that a part of this education should help prepare the woman for her responsibilities as a wife, mother, and citizen of the community.

HENRIETTA WILLARD CALVIN

Henrietta Calvin, a pioneer in college administration, public school supervision, and government service, was born in Illinois in 1865, the daughter of a banker. After receiving her preliminary education in the Illinois public schools, she attended Washburn College during 1880–1881 and was graduated from Kansas State University with a bachelor of science degree in 1886. Soon after graduation she was married to John H. Calvin, who had graduated from the same college two years earlier. In 1887 Mr. and Mrs. Calvin and their baby son went to New York City, where Mr. Calvin enrolled in the law school of Columbia University. While Mr. Calvin studied law, Mrs. Calvin read law and political science with her husband, made a home for a rapidly growing family, and at the same time studied widely in such subjects as dietetics, pediatrics, child care, health, and home nursing (18). All of these subjects contributed to the synthesis of the theoretical and practical knowledge that homemaking required and that Mrs. Calvin was later to use as a professional home economist.

When her husband died in 1898, Mrs. Calvin found that, in addition to the task of rearing a family of four boys and one girl, she must become the breadwinner. She became librarian in the children's room of the city library in Topeka, Kansas. After a short time there, she obtained a similar position at Kansas State University. In 1903 she became professor of domestic science and head of the department of domestic science, a position which she held until 1908. From 1908 to 1915 she was successively professor of home economics at Purdue University and professor of domestic science at Oregon State College.

In 1915 she accepted the position of home economics specialist with the U.S. Bureau of Education and served in this capacity for seven years, doing much to stimulate the growth of home economics in the public schools by studying the needs of home economics teachers and providing them with materials for teaching.

In 1922 she left the Bureau of Education to become director of home economics in the public school system of Philadelphia, a position she held until her retirement in 1936.

In a tribute to Mrs. Calvin, Margaret Justin has provided some interesting information (10). She writes, for example, of Mrs. Calvin's first job in the library at Topeka: "Mrs. Calvin often told of leaving the youngest, a tiny baby, in the care of the child who was only five and the Lord, day after day, as she went to her work, where she would spend nine hours earning a living for her brood.

Of her life at Kansas State University, Miss Justin says:

> A familiar sight in the morning was the Calvin carriage delivering its load of children to the primary and grade schools before the driver made her way to the campus, where she undertook her professional duties for an eight-hour interlude between her continuing duties as homemaker, housekeeper, and mentor for her family. Arduous as her load was, there was nothing in her attitude of the martyr or of self-pity.
>
> Her professional contribution was noteworthy. Her keen mind and vivid imagination, her versatility and adaptability made possible her effective work in these diverse home economics posts. Her practical experience as a wage-earning mother of a family of five impelled her to relate courses and lessons to ways of meeting everyday problems in living and to the application of basic principles to new situations. She was alert to the possibilities of extending the services of the college out in the state and had a major share in the development of the farmer's institute program in Kansas, out of which the extension program evolved.
>
> Mrs. Calvin pioneered in another regard when she arranged for summer school offerings through which the inadequate preparation of many teachers of home economics could be strengthened.
>
> Mrs. Calvin shared with other pioneers in home economics certain attributes: ability, high courage, deep conviction, and certitude of objectives. Beyond and above that possessed by most people she had enthusiasm, zest for living. and a merry heart. The world is better because she lived.

SARAH TYSON RORER

Sarah Tyson Rorer, probably more than anyone else, is associated with the development of foods and dietetics in the United States.

Mrs. Rorer was born in 1849 in Richboro, Pennsylvania, the daughter of a manufacturing chemist. As a young student she decided to specialize in science. No doubt this interest was kindled by the many hours which she spent in her father's laboratory among the beakers and retorts during her childhood. After she graduated from the East Aurora (New York) Academy, she started to prepare herself to be a dispenser of drugs, or as the job is known today, a pharmacist.

She, like Mrs. Richards and others, early found it possible to combine homemaking and a professional career. In 1871 she was married and for the next eight years spent much of her time caring for her home and two sons. In fact, it was the delicate health of one son that crystallized her interest in proper feeding.

In 1878, she entered the New Century Cooking School. Mrs. Rorer says of this experience, "In 1878 a group of intellectual, wealthy women formed the third Women's Club of Philadelphia. . . . They started a New Century Cooking Club. . . . I joined the first class, and finished what was then called 'the full course.' It constituted two practical lessons a week for three months and a course of twenty-four demonstrated lectures" (19).

Soon, Mrs. Rorer was the head of the New Century Cooking School. In 1879, after the principal of the school was dismissed for refusing to give a course on diet for the sick to the students and nurses of the Woman's Medical College and Woman's Hospital, and after replacements from New York and Boston had proved unsatisfactory, Mrs. Rorer was asked to take over the direction of the school, where she stayed for three years, after which she founded the Philadelphia Cooking School. According to Mrs. Rorer, this was a success from the beginning, and she says of this experience, "I could practice dietetics here unmolested. I formed a faculty for the school. The chemistry class under Dr. Leffman was always the most popular of all" (19).

At the request of several Philadelphia physicians, and with their financial help, she started a diet kitchen in the Philadelphia School where physicians could send a prescription and get in return food well-prepared for special diseases. Soon she started a doctors' class, in which experimental work could be done. As a result of this work she was invited by the medical school of the University of Pennyvania to lecture to the fourth-year medical sfudents. Her interest in foods and dietetics continued throughout her lifetime.

Not only did she teach and experiment with foods but she wrote many articles and books on foods and diets. Early in her career, she contributed articles to, and served as associate editor of, the *Dietetic Gazette,* which was published under the auspices of the American Medical Association. In 1886 she became editor and part owner of *Table Talk.* (*Table Talk* was published from 1885 to 1920 in Philadelphia and Cooperstown, New York. In 1916 it absorbed the *National Food Magazine*.) In 1893, she launched the magazine *Household News,* which was absorbed by the *Ladies' Home Journal* in 1897. Mrs. Rorer then became editor of the food and domestic science section of the *Ladies' Home Journal,* a position she held until 1911. From 1886 to 1905 Mrs. Rorer wrote and published sixteen or more books.

In addition to teaching, writing, and maintaining a home, she was greatly in demand as a lecturer. Mrs. Rorer's quick and keen mind, plus her courage and honesty, made it possible for her to foresee and champion many new developments in foods and nutrition. For example, sixty years ago she championed the cause of margarine, contending that it was a healthful, palatable substitute for butter. She was alert to developing what she considered "neglected foods, such as corn; in her world's fair kitchen she demonstrated nearly 200 recipes for corn. Seventy years ago, not only did she caution against the overcooking of green vegetables but she urged their use both raw and cooked, especially with starch vegetables. She preached the use of whole-wheat bread and the substitution of fruits for the heavy desserts of the day.

Mrs. Rorer trained many of the early dietitians and instilled into many of the young doctors a respect for proper diet. She says of herself, "I was considered a very severe teacher by my pupils. It was not because I wanted to be severe, but because I wanted to send out pupils who knew how to do things. I believe in the education of hands and brains, working together" (19).

The editor's note to an article written by Mrs. Rorer, called "Early Dietetics," which appeared in the *Journal of the American Dietetic Association* in November 1934, reveals much about this outstanding woman (19):

> Editor's note—The *Journal* has the honor to publish a paper from the pen of a woman who has been a pioneer in the dietetic profession in America. Mrs. Rorer is a true scientist, and has made her craft a fine art. She has had, as well, the happy faculty of being a real leader and teacher and is idolized by her friends and former pupils. At the mellow age of eighty-five, she presented the following reminiscences before the Pennsylvania Dietetic Association, of which she is an honorary member. . . . Mentally alert and inspiring, after her long and distinguished career, she was the "life of the party" at this meeting.

EDNA NOBLE WHITE

Edna Noble White is a twentieth-century pioneer in the study of child development and family life in higher education. Miss White was one of the early graduates from home economics land-grant colleges in the United States, receiving her degree from the University of Illinois in 1906. After teaching in public schools, she was called to the home economics staff of the Ohio State University and soon was made dean of home economics.

In 1916, Mrs. "Lizzie" Merrill-Palmer of Detroit died, leaving her fortune for the establishment of "a school for motherhood and home training." There were no landmarks to chart the course of such a school at that time. Hitherto, training for homemaking and motherhood had been interpreted chiefly in terms of practical work for girls in cooking, sewing, and housekeeping. The board of directors entrusted with this sum of money wisely selected a woman with great vision to pioneer this task—Miss White was invited to become the director of the Merrill-Palmer School and for twenty-seven years developed it and guided its destiny.

When Miss White began the work at Merrill-Palmer she started along familiar paths, with units in homemaking and classes in nutrition. Then she started a nursery school, combining the best in principles and practices that the United States and England had to offer. As the new plan grew she called to her aid specialists in each field to interpret these new ideas in concrete forms.

In a memorial to Miss White published by the Merrill-Palmer School is the following statement (12):

> As first director of the new school, she became a leader in education for home and family life and a primary organizer of the new field of child study and research, and in many ways liberalized the field of home economics. Among the ideas she originated were the use of the nursery school as a laboratory for studying children at an advanced level, at first chiefly for college women in home economics, but soon in such fields as psychology, physical growth and nutrition, child development, sociology, and education. She saw it also as an important medium for parent education. The idea of an interdisciplinary staff for such centers of human development and human relations study at the Merrill-Palmer School was also hers. Her energies were fruitfully exercised and applied not only at this primary center of her work, but on the national scene as well.
>
> A woman of wide horizons and large vision, she was aware of the universality and essential unity of home and family life among all peoples, and thus of the possibility of bringing a measure of improvement to human society everywhere through such an educational center.

Her interests in improving family life carried her into many activities in this country and abroad. In recognition of her outstanding work, before she died in 1954 she was granted honorary degrees from four universities, and she received many other awards.

SUGGESTED ACTIVITIES   1719780

1. As you read these thumbnail sketches of pioneer home economists, what factors in their lives seem to stand out? Are there certain traits that they all have in common?

2. What motivated them to become home economists? Do you think that these motivations were typical of women of their day?

3. Do you know home economists today who seem to have personality traits and motivations in common with these pioneer home economists? How are they being expressed today?

4. What inspirations have you received from reading about these pioneers? Do you feel that the young women of today are as concerned about opening

educational opportunities for women as were these pioneers? Are they as concerned about family welfare? What frontiers are open today for enterprising and intelligent women to conquer?

5. All of these pioneers had different types of education. Why can home economics use people with different types of education and interests?

REFERENCES

1. Andrews, Benjamin R., *The First Home Economics Publication of the Ellen H. Richards Memorial Home Economics Fund*, American Home Economics Association, Washington, 1913.

2. Bailey, Liberty Hyde, "As Pioneer in Agricultural Extension Work for Women," *Journal of Home Economics*, vol. 24, p. 763, September 1932.

3. Baldwin, Keturah E., *The AHEA Saga*, p. 2, American Home Economics Association, Washington, 1949.

4. Bane, Juliet Lita, *The Story of Isabel Bevier*, pp. 25–39, Charles A. Bennett Company, Inc., Peoria, Ill., 1955.

5. Bane, Juliet Lita, *The Story of Isabel Bevier*, p. 67, Charles A. Bennett Company, Inc., Peoria, Ill., 1955.

6. Bevier, Isabel, *Home Economics in Education*, J. B. Lippincott Company, Philadelphia, 1924.

7. Hunt, Caroline, *The Life of Ellen H. Richards*, pp. 1–91, American Home Economics Association, Washington, 1942 (reissued March 1958).

8. Johnson, Allen (ed.), *Dictionary of American Biography*, vol. II, pp. 125–126, Charles Scribner's Sons, New York, 1929.

9. Jones, Nellie Kedzie, "Abby L. Marlatt," *Journal of Home Economics*, vol. 35, pp. 483–484, October 1943.

10. Justin, Margaret M., "Henrietta Willard Calvin: A Tribute," *Journal of Home Economics*, vol. 39, pp. 563–564, November 1947.

11. Huddleson, Mary P., "Sarah Tyson Rorer: Pioneer in Applied Nutrition," *Journal of the American Dietetic Association*, vol. 26, pp. 321–324, May 1950.

12. *A Living Memorial*, The Recognition Fund of the Merrill-Palmer School, Detroit, 1956.

13. Malone, Dumas (ed.), *Dictionary of American Biography*, vol. VIII, pp. 518–519, Charles Scribners Sons, New York, 1932.

14. Mann, Albert Russell, "As College Administrator," *Journal of Home Economics*, vol. 24, pp. 764–766, September 1932.

15. Marlatt, Abby L., "Achievements of Home Economics," *Journal of Home Economics*, vol. 14, p. 8, January 1922.

16. Marlatt, Abby L., "Home Economics and Higher Education," *Journal of Home Economics*, vol. 6, pp. 241–243, June 1914.

17. "Martha Van Rensselaer," *Journal of Home Economics*, vol. 24, pp. 761–764, September 1932.

18. *National Cyclopaedia of American Biography*, vol. 41, pp. 409–410, James T. White & Company, New York, 1956.

19. Rorer, Sarah Tyson, "Early Dietetics," *Journal of the American Dietetic Association*, vol. 10, pp. 289–295, November 1934.

20. Rose, Flora, "As a Home Economist," *Journal of Home Economics*, vol. 24, pp. 769–770, September 1932.

21. Stone, Katherine H., "Mrs. Mary Hemenway and Household Arts in the Boston Public Schools," *Journal of Home Economics*, vol. 21, pp. 7–13, January 1929.

22. Van Rensselaer, Martha, "Presidential Address," *Journal of Home Economics*, vol. 7, pp. 461–464, November 1915.

ADDITIONAL READINGS

"Anna Godfrey Dewey," *Journal of Home Economics*, vol. 15, pp. 357–370, July 1923.

Cooper, Lena F., "Florence Nightingale's Contribution to Dietetics," *Journal of the American Dietetic Association*, vol. 30, pp. 121–127, February 1954.

"Dr. Louise Stanley," *What's New in Home Economics*, vol. 18, p. 117, October 1954.

"Edna Noble White," *Journal of Home Economics*, vol. 46, p. 409, July 1954.

"Ellen H. Richards and the Flowers She Loved," *National Magazine of Home Economics Student Clubs*, pp. 3–4, November 1938.

"Eva M. Benefiel: An Appreciation," *Journal of Home Economics*, vol. 8, pp. 656–657, December 1916.

Fine, Benjamin, "Dr. Rose: A Pioneer in Nutrition," *The Teachers College Student Journal*, vol. 1, pp. 1, 6, December 1936.

"Gertrude L. Warren Retires," *What's New in Home Economics*, vol. 17, p. 70, February 1953.

"In Appreciation of Abby Lillian Marlatt," *What's New in Home Economics*, vol. 8, p. 10, 1943.

"In Memory of Ellen H. Richards," *Journal of Home Economics*, vol. 21, pp. 403–412, June 1929.

MacLeod, Grace, "Mary Swartz Rose," *Journal of Home Economics*, vol. 33, pp. 221–224, April 1941.

Norton, Alice P., "Marion Talbot," *Journal of Home Economics*, vol. 17, pp. 479–482, September 1925.

"The Editorship of *The Journal of Home Economics*," *Journal of Home Economics*, vol. 7, pp. 434a, 434b, October 1915.

"The Professional Services of Helen Kinne," *Journal of Home Economics*, vol. 10, pp. 174–176, April 1918.

Tyler, Dorothy, "A Study of Leadership in the Making of an Institution," *Social Forces*, vol. 10, pp. 594–600, May 1932.

3 WHO IS A HOME ECONOMIST?

Who is a *home economist*? As defined in the bylaws of the American Home Economics Association, "A home economist [is one] who shall hold a Bachelor's degree or an advanced degree with a major in home economics or in a specialized area of home economics from an accredited college or university in the United States or Canada."[*] Irrespective of the home economist's speciality, she will find that people expect certain things of her not expected of other graduates. Home economics graduates are looked to for leadership in family living. Not only are they expected to have high ideals and standards for their own family life but their friends and associates seek help from them in practically all matters concerning the home and family. These requests range all the way from aid in buying to help in counseling.

That homemakers look to home economists for help is to be expected, for one of the major goals of home economics is the improvement of family living. Home economics aims at helping individuals, families, agencies, and the government to make intelligent decisions concerning all aspects of family life and to improve the environment surrounding the family. These include the social, economic, aesthetic, managerial, health, and ethical aspects of family relations, child development, foods, clothing, and housing. That this always has been the purpose of home economics is illustrated by the creed of Ellen H. Richards (1), first president of the American Home Economics Association, who wrote in 1908 that:

Home Economics Stands For[†]

The ideal home life today unhampered by the traditions of the past.

The utilization of all the resources of modern science to improve the home life.

The freedom of the home from the dominance of things and their due subordination to ideals.

The simplicity in material surroundings which will most free the spirit for the more important and permanent interests of the home and society.

[*] See Article 14, Section 2 (1) (a) of the bylaws of the American Home Economics Association.
[†] For a discussion of the changes in the definition over the last sixty years, see Flossie M. Byrd, "A Definition of Home Economics for the 70's," *Journal of Home Economics*, vol. 62, pp. 411-415, June 1970.

What the home economics field covers may be more easily understood by examining the stated objective of the American Home Economics Association: "The object of this association shall be to provide opportunities for professional home economists and members from other fields to co-operate in the attainment of the well-being of individuals and of families, the improvement of homes, and the preservation of values significant in home life."*

Home economics as a field of study has not remained static. Its emphasis has shifted from one decade to another. However, improving family living has always been its integrative center (4). Dr. Earl J. McGrath says in his article entitled *"The Changing Mission of Home Economics":*

> Home economics is not a profession with a single distinct body of knowledge, skills, and ethics like the whole of the education enterprises. Home economics is an area of human interest and concern that encompasses and impinges on a number of occupations and other life activities. Its central mission has been and must continue to be that of *family service. . . .* From the beginning the preoccupation of home economics has been centered in the family as a milieu in which individuals grow and achieve their basic learning in preparation for a productive, rewarding, and satisfying life.
>
> Around this commitment to the family unit there have been a number of more specific purposes related to such matters as nutrition, dietetics, and institution management directed either to individual needs or to groups other than the family. Yet "family service" remains the integrative center of home economics, just as "patient care" forms the core of nursing.

Dr. McGrath makes clear that instead of the American society outgrowing home economics, contemporary society requires more from this field. This same thought is expressed by Dr. David D. Henry, president of the University of Illinois, when he says, "The traditional emphasis on family service, when reoriented to the predominate social order of our day, can be made to offer new hope amid the problems of Social despair" (3).

Home economics in most colleges and universities has three goals in relation to the students: it educates them (1) for improved personal development, (2) for richer and more satisfying family living, and (3) for professional specialization. Home economics attacks the problem of strengthening the family in the world of today by (1) educating men and women to become better family members and citizens and to establish better homes; (2) training leaders to work with homemakers and boys and girls, as well as family groups and other organizations, in improving themselves and

* "Proposed Revision for the AHEA Constitution and Bylaws," *Journal of Home Economics.* vol. 54, p. 247, March 1962.

their everyday family living; and (3) carrying on research to learn more about the factors which affect the welfare of the family, its members, and the home.

It has been said many times that to the captain who knoweth not the port for which he sails, no wind can be favorable. For those who are home economists, the port is very obvious—it is that of strengthening the family.

Home economists can be proud of the role they have chosen to play. The importance of education for family living carried on by home economists is ably stated by Dr. Theodore Blegen, formerly, dean of the graduate school of the University of Minnesota (14):

> The potential of home economics is virtually without limit . . . for the home is the focus of our lives, its front yard is the community, and the community reaches out to the world . . . history begins at home, as do charity and home economics and just about everything else in life that is good, including the faiths and freedoms we cherish.
>
> As one draws up even a partial list of fundamentals in our concepts of individual and social welfare, with the home as focus, the importance of education for family living seems so undeniable and great that . . . home economics can stand on its feet as an integral part of the education we want for the emerging adults of every generation. No problem in home economics is not a strand in the social web of our life. Every part of home economics can be treated in its relationship to the sweep of family and community living. . . .

Similarly, many educators and leaders pay tribute to the role of home economists. They realize that the future of our democratic land depends in no small part upon what is done to help the families in the United States to live better and become stronger.

IMPORTANCE OF HOME ECONOMICS

Home economics embraces twelve separate but interrelated fields, namely, (1) clothing construction, design, and theory; (2) child development and family relations; (3) communications; (4) food—its preparation, management, and technology; (5) family and community health and welfare; (6) housing; (7) household equipment; (8) interior design and decoration; (9) textile design, production, and management; (10) human nutrition and dietetics; (11) family economics and home management, and (12) education (7). These fields, taken as a composite, provide the foundation for good health, satisfying and successful living, psychological balance, and good management, which are all essential for the development of the whole personality.

Home economics is available to most college and university students who seek it. More than 450 colleges and universities in the United States offer a major leading to a bachelor's degree in home economics. Although the curricula vary in content and professional emphasis from one institution to another, each curriculum will include a fine balance of liberal arts, science, and home economics courses. Those institutions that do not offer an undergraduate major in home economics usually offer a specialization in one or more home economics areas such as applied art, child development and family relations, family economics and home management, food and nutrition, housing and household equipment, or textiles (9).

Home economics graduates—both men and women—work in a great variety of positions to meet the needs of people. They can be found in the Peace Corps, community service, nursery and day care centers, health and welfare agencies, extension, business and industry, communications, fashion and interior design, food careers in institutions and industry, dietetics, research, education, and innumerable other key positions.

Employment opportunities for home economics graduates are very good, and home economists usually earn a better-than-average salary. In addition there is a shortage of home economists. Each year, there are approximately 15,000 new or vacant positions open to home economists but less than 12,000 home economics graduates to fill them (9).

HOME ECONOMICS IS LIFE EDUCATION

Home economics appears to be well in advance of other fields in focusing attention on the problems, needs, and interests of its students. It faces the fact that most women in the United States marry, establish homes, and raise children. These homemakers will have problems to meet and types of leadership to render which are uniquely feminine. Many of these needs are associated with guidance and rearing of children, helping family members to live happily and well, nursing sick family members back to health, creating and maintaining a well-decorated and comfortable home, providing the family with well-prepared and nutritionally adequate meals, clothing the family members to meet their physical and personality needs, directing the use of the family income so as to provide the goods and services needed by the family, furthering the activities which will make the community a better place for the family, and at the same time keeping themselves well informed, in step with the world in which they live, well groomed, and likable. Also, these homemakers will be active in furthering community interests.

Research is beginning to reveal that the point at which most women, especially those who are college graduates, feel inadequate in meeting the problems and challenges of everyday living is in the area of homemaking. In 1948 a study was conducted by the American Association of University Women to find out how well satisfied the women college graduates were with their college education and what changes they would recommend after their subsequent experience had tested the value of what they had learned at college (11). The 30,000 women who participated in the study, two-thirds of whom were married, expressed two felt needs, namely, (1) that a college education should be broad enough to cover every important aspect of each woman's life, and (2) that a college education should give more specific skills and more practice in doing things. The majority mentioned the need for more training in homemaking, child care, and guidance. Many mentioned that they found their careers as homemakers after graduation were difficult and that they were often handicapped because of their lack of preparation for homemaking. In fact, the need for education in homemaking was mentioned by more members than any other type of education. One-fourth of all of those making general suggestions urged that home economics be made available to all women students so that they might not be unprepared for the "most important career of all." In 1965, a study of southern college women revealed similar findings (5).

Not only does a career in home economics make it possible to serve, it can be creative and exciting (11):

> Home economics is one of the most exciting fields for women and men today. . . . There is a dire shortage of home economists across the nation. . . . Salaries have been rising over the past four years at a faster rate than in any other profession, and graduates can choose the geographical location in which they wish to work.
>
> A general shortage of home economists has caused a sharp increase in recruitment by business and industry. Large firms are sending recruiters to college campuses to seek home economists, others go to the secondary schools seeking the more experienced home economists to fill merchandising, publishing service, and other positions. Cooperative extension recruiters are searching diligently for the qualified graduate, and science and technology recruiters seek those with adequate training for research and development programs. . . .
>
> Home economics has always been a rewarding field, but never have the challenges, the excitement of rapid development, or the opportunities for creative careers been so great. It is a wonderful field for the bright, able, and creative student.

Non-home economics students see the value of home economics training. In one university, in one year, 73 percent of the students enrolled in home economics courses were nonmajors (13). This should not be surprising, for home economics is not only an integral part of a liberal education for university students, it is also a uniquely integrating discipline in higher education.

Home economics combines the liberal arts and the technical, the scientific, and the artistic. Stated in other words, home economics applies the findings of the physical, biological, and social sciences to the solving of problems arising in the operation of a home and in the care and welfare of family members. It applies the knowledge of the arts in making living more creative and enjoyable, as well as more emotionally satisfying. Home economics recognizes that neither the so-called liberal arts nor the purely technical approach can ensure a well-rounded education. The average home economics curriculum is equally divided between the arts and sciences. A home economist must be versed in both because the problems of modern-day living call for a knowledge of both.

A former president of one of our state universities expressed this in the following words (12):

> I cannot conceive of any curriculum that could be made more nearly to meet the ideal educational requirements for college and university women as a group, by combining elements of a liberal as well as a practical education, than a good basic program in general home economics. Home economics has its roots in at least five different basic sciences and arts, and it uses the techniques and disciplines of all of these, as well as a few which it has developed for itself. It has bases in the physical and biological sciences for its food and nutrition, textiles, and equipment studies; in the social sciences for its family economics and management studies; in psychology for its child development and family relations studies; and in art and architecture for its clothing and interior design and housing studies. Studies in these fields provide the broad and basic foundations for a true university curriculum in home economics.

World leaders ask help from home economists in the improvement of their countries. They recognize that the development and leadership possibilities of any country are closely tied to the progressiveness of its families. They are concerned with improving the welfare of the family in the belief that from the family will come benefits to the wider community. Dr. C. B. Hutchins, formerly president of the University of California, verifies this. He says (2):

> Home economics has won respect and prestige for itself in a relatively short span of years because it has made material contributions to improving home and family living, to knowledge of food, shelter, and clothing, and to the application and spread of that knowledge throughout the land. It has trained thousands of leaders and teachers for work in the schools and in the field. It has begun to arouse the public to some awareness of the value of a scientific approach to the job of homemaking and of the need for more general training for that job. It has made it possible for many women to choose from numerous opportunities a way to earn a living in the food, clothing, and housing industries and public health and welfare services. And it is largely due to home economics education today that child guidance, child development, family life courses and nursery schools are becoming integral parts of our educational program. . . .

There will be no lessening of the need for individuals trained in home economics. On the contrary, in the visible future, the demands for both generalists and specialists in home economics will continue to grow in response to internationalism, population shifts, and welfare trends (15). The time has never been more right for home economics (16).

INCREASING NEED FOR HOME ECONOMISTS

The need for home economists has increased greatly. The services of professional home economists are needed and demanded more today than ever before in the history of this country. There are many reasons for this. There are more families today, and they need more help than in former years. The changes in family living conditions over the last decade have made decision making on the part of the homemaker more difficult in all aspects of life. For example, to be a good purchaser or user of income requires the ability to judge the relative value of all of the new and varied products on the market today. The greatly increased number of products and the expensive advertising systems back of them make it impossible for the average homemaker to judge the relative merit of these products. The home economist should have this ability.

The many organizations which compete for the loyalties and time of family members require that the homemaker have unusual ability to discriminate and organize in order to protect the mental and physical well-being of her family and herself. Should the homemaker give her time to the scouts, the church activities, the Red Cross, the polio fund drives, the parent-teachers association, the women's club, the garden clubs, the home demonstration clubs—to mention only a few of the organizations which compete for her time and energy.

The fact that the majority of the people in the United States (73.5 percent in 1970) live in urban rather than rural areas increases the homemakers' problems (21, pp. 16). The crowding, noise, soot and dirt, lack of space for living and playing, unsuitable living quarters, cost of living, and impersonal contact with people put additional strain upon living. To counteract these influences and maintain a good home require more help from the professional home economist.

Living happily and creatively in the family is more important today than ever before. In the past, family members were more dependent upon each other; this tended to hold families together. A man had to depend upon his wife to keep his clothes in order, to prepare his food, and to make a home for his aged parents. A woman had to have a husband to support her and to give her social status. Times have changed for both. The cleaner, the tailor, and the laundryman will take care of the man's clothing for a price. The restaurant will feed him. His aged parents can partly provide for their own care through social security. The woman can earn her own living and establish her own status. Thus the satisfactions from the relationships existing between husbands and wives are extremely important today. These relationships will determine whether the family is stable and whether the husband and wife will keep the family intact, as well as the emotional well-being of the children.

Homemakers are working outside the home in ever-increasing numbers today. In 1940, only 27 percent of all women fourteen years of age and over were employed, while in 1970, 43 percent of those 16 years of age and over were employed (19). This increase is even more striking where married women are concerned. Only 24 percent of the female labor force were married women in 1920; by 1940 this proportion had increased to 36 percent; however, by 1970, the percent of married women in the female labor force had risen to 63 percent (18, 19). Many married women, after having their children, return to the labor force, while others work throughout their married lives. The trend today is toward the employment of older women and married women with families. In 1940, more than one-half of the employed women were under twenty-five years of age, while 20 percent were over forty-five (21, p. 220). Today, only 25 percent of the employed women are under twenty-five years of age, and over 38 percent are over forty-five (21, p. 29, 212).

Francena Miller says that we must bury the myth that women cannot manage both family and community responsibilities. Many of them are already doing it, and more must be encouraged to extend their talents beyond the family (8). Some feel that women who do not choose to be employed are cheating themselves. "I think women are being thoroughly cheated! At least they are cheating themselves if they think that the prior commitment to motherhood automatically precludes them from active participation in a career. Since work has never kept men from being fathers, why should it keep women from being mothers" (20).

Home economics is the one field that trains women for a dual role—it prepares a young woman to be a superior wife and mother, but at the same time it prepares her for a career. Young women of today can no longer assume that they will not have to work at any time during their lives, and many will work most of their lives.

Not only do changes in modern society make the dual role for women necessary, but it makes it ideal for them. Women spend many fewer years in child rearing today than formerly. Over one-half of the women today are marrying before they are twenty-one years of age, and one-half of these will complete their families at twenty-six years of age (21, p. 60). Thus, over one-half of our young married women will have approximately forty-four years of life after the last child enters school, and approximately twenty-five years after the last child finishes high school. This gives to the homemaker many years of relative freedom from family responsibilities to devote to work. The woman's dual role, which home economics recognizes, better fits women for life than any other arrangement in today's world.

Many married women, because they are qualified for professional service, find great pressure being put upon them to enter or reenter the professional field. This is attested to by the following statement from a young married home economist (2):

> No doubt you will be surprised to learn that I am teaching again this year, with Johnny being only six months old. Our local high school was without a

home economics teacher, and the superintendent begged me to return to teaching. I finally decided that I could not let those young high school girls down when home economics had meant so much to me. Thanks to my good home economics training at _____ College, I am handling the two jobs very well, and Johnny seems to be thriving on it.

Women without jobs may feel lost and out of step with society. "In an action-centered society," writes Margaret Mead, "having no job to do creates a sense of uselessness which generates emotional disturbances" (11).

Home economics has been the great home movement in the world. It recognizes that the principles of science and technology apply to the home as they do to industry and agriculture, that art finds its natural expression in the home as it does in architecture and the fine arts, and that the family is the great molder of personality and builder of character and thus holds the key to the future of civilization.

Home economists must be equipped to give needed help to families at all times, applying the principles of the biological and chemical sciences, psychology, sociology, economics, physics, engineering, and the arts to the problems in the lives of individuals and families. The solutions to these problems should lead always to a better and more worthwhile way of life.

SUGGESTED ACTIVITIES

Students vary greatly in the extent to which they have had contacts with home economics and home economists before coming to college. If these contacts have been broad, students will be able to appreciate many of the opportunities open to them. Below are listed several statements which will help students to measure their knowledge of the field of home economics.

1. List all of the different types of work that you have known home economists to do. Why are home economists employed for these positions?
2. Try to name one home economist in each type of work in your state in which home economists are employed.
3. How were these home economists trained or educated for their present occupations or professions? What satisfactions do you feel they are receiving from the work they are doing?
4. List all of the fields of knowledge in which the home economics student takes courses while in college. How does each of these contribute to a well-rounded education? Why would a home economist have need for all of these types of knowledge?
5. Think of all of the decisions a student has to make during a day. On how many of these will she receive help through the study of courses and experience required or provided for in the home economics curriculum?
6. What are the types of leadership and service asked of women in a

community? For how many of these will the study of home economics better prepare them?

7. In what ways will the study of home economics better prepare a student for being a homemaker and mother? For being a career woman?

8. In what new occupations and roles are home economists found today in which they were not found twenty-five years ago?

REFERENCES

1. Baldwin, Keturah E., *The AHEA Saga*, p. 17, American Home Economics Association, Washington, 1949.

2. From a personal letter to the author.

3. Hansen, Doris E., "The Future Is Now," *Journal of Home Economics,* vol. 60, p. 84, February 1968.

4. Henry, David D., Letter, *Journal of Home Economics*, vol. 60, pp. 407–408, June 1968.

5. Hottel, Althea H., "Higher Education for Women," Lecture delivered before the Home Economics Division of the Association of Land-grant Colleges and Universities, Columbus, Ohio, Nov. 11, 1953.

6. Horn, Marilyn J., "The Rewards of Commitment," *Journal of Home Economics,* vol. 60, pp. 83–88, February 1969.

7. Hutchinson, C. B., "Home Economics Education for Living," *Journal of Home Economics,* vol. 41, pp. 353–354, September 1949.

8. *Job and Career Opportunities for Women in Home Economics,* The Institute for Research, Research no. 24, Chicago, 1969.

9. McFarland, Margaret B., "Child Development in Education for Women," *Journal of the American Association of University Women,* vol. 43, p. 220, Summer 1949.

10. McGrath, Earl J., "The Changing Mission of Home Economics," *Journal of Home Economics,* vol. 60, pp. 85–92, February 1968.

11. Mead, Margaret, "The Higher Education Survey," *Journal of the American Association of University Women,* vol. 43, pp. 8–12, Fall 1949.

12. *Meet the Young Home Economist,* American Home Economics Association, Washington, 1963.

13. Miller, Francena L., "Womanpower," *Journal of Home Economics,* vol. 60, p. 693, November 1968.

14. National Manpower Council, *Womanpower,* p. 18, Columbia University Press, New York, 1957.

15. Ness, Frederic W., "Letters," *Journal of Home Economics,* vol. 60, p. 410, June 1968.

16. *1965 Handbook of Women Workers,* U.S. Department of Labor, Woman's Bureau, 1965.

17. Pahopen, Jo S., "Shopping for a Creative Career in Home Economics," *What's New in Home Economics,* vol. 33, pp. 33–34, March 1969.

18. Pahopen, Jo S., "Twelve Disciplines in Home Economics," *What's New in Home Economics,* vol. 33, pp. 33–34, March 1969.

19. U.S. Bureau of the Census, *Statistical Abstracts of the United States: 1971 Edition,* 1971, p. 212, Washington.

20. Whitehead, Floy Eugenia, "Home Economics and Liberal Arts in Today's University," *Journal of Home Economics,* vol. 57, pp. 613–618, October 1965.

21. U.S. Bureau of the Census, *Statistical Abstracts of the United States: 1971 Edition,* 1971, pp. 212, 16.

ADDITIONAL READINGS

Bates, M., "Home Economist as a Leader in Business," *Forecast in Home Economics,* vol. 13, pp. 42–43, March 1968.

Budewig, M., M. Brown, P. Nolan, and S. Nosow, *The Field of Home Economics—What Is It,* American Home Economics Association, Washington.

Conafay, K. R., "Home Economist as a Leader in the Community," *Forecast in Home Economics,* vol. 13, pp. 20–21, May 1968.

Cox, S. D., "Home Economist Serves in the Rehabilitation of Blinded Adults," *Journal of Home Economics,* vol. 57, pp. 801–802, December 1965.

Dobry, A., "Occupational Programs in Home Economics," *American Vocational Journal,* vol. 44, pp. 56–58, October 1969.

Fleck, Henrettia, "Home Economist as a Writer," *Forecast in Home Economics,* vol. 15, p. 45, October 1969.

Fleck, Henrettia, "Looking to the Future," *Forecast in Home Economics,* vol. 13, p. 23, January 1968.

Fleck, Henrettia, "Reassessment of Careers," *Forecast in Home Economics,* vol. 13, p. 19, May 1968.

Funderburks, K. W., "Home Economics Moves out to Meet the Challenge of Social Change," *American Vocational Journal,* vol. 42, pp. 31–32, Summer 1967.

"Glamour on the Job," *Glamour,* vol. 58, pp. 54–55, December 1967.

Johnson, J., "Can Home Economics Meet the Challenge of Change," *Forecast in Home Economics,* vol. 13, pp. 64–65, January 1967.

O'Toole, Lelia, "Intercultural-International Dimension of Home Economics in Higher Education," *Journal of Home Economics,* vol. 59, pp. 650–654, October 1967.

Stovall, R., "Leadership Development in Home Economics," *American Vocational Journal,* vol. 42, pp. 28–29, May 1967.

4 FINDING A PLACE IN HOME ECONOMICS

The college or university offers many fields of study from which to choose. These fields can be grouped into large classes, such as the arts, the sciences, and the humanities. They may be broken down into many smaller subject-matter areas, such as chemistry, physics, biology, psychology, sociology, political science, economics, mathematics, philosophy, and art.

Another classification of broad areas of study would be that of the *applied sciences* and *arts,* such as home economics, engineering, agriculture, and medicine. Home economics, like engineering, agriculture, and medicine, is a large field made up of several smaller areas of study. These four applied fields may be called "integrating," or "coordinating," fields of study. They bring together and organize certain principles or facts from the sciences, from the arts, and from philosophy into a functional whole. Home economics differs from the other applied fields in its focus or purpose: it is the one field whose primary concern is the welfare of families and individuals.

Home economics uses principles from most of the arts and sciences to improve homemaking and family living. For example, the laws of heat, studied in physics, are applied to kitchen ranges, pressing irons, and toasters quite the same as to steam engines or electric furnaces. The expansion of air by heat is a principle of physics used in cake and bread baking. A knowledge of the growth and control of bacteria, obtained from the study of biology, is important to the home economist in the preparation and preservation of food and in home sanitation, just as it is to the doctor or health engineer in preventing and controlling diseases and infections. Chemistry is used by the nutritionist in learning the essential substances of foods and their use in the body, just as the metallurgist uses chemistry to work with metals and separates them from their ores. The textile scientist uses chemistry in making new fibers and in dyeing fibers.

The principles of economics are used by the home economist to help families plan for the spending of the family income and establish economic security. The home economist uses her knowledge of sociology in studying the interrelationships within the family and the family in the community. Information furnished by psychology concerning the behavior of individuals under varying conditions is used in helping parents provide a suitable home environment for the rearing of their children. The principles of art and design are used by the home economist in designing dresses and other apparel and in selecting a wardrobe or house furnishings. Similarly, the artist selects colors and line to create a picture, and the architect puts these together to create a well-proportioned and functional house.

This analogy could be carried on indefinitely, for the ways in which home economics uses contributions from the sciences, arts, and humanities are almost limitless.

GENERAL EDUCATION AND HOME ECONOMICS

Home economics recognizes the need for both *general education* and *professional competence* on the part of its students. General education is the philosophy that education should aim at the cultivation of the mind and its sensibilities. It hopes to develop socially sensitive individuals who see the connection between their profession and society's needs, who can appreciate and enjoy the variety of creative expressions in their universe, and who are able to examine their beliefs and values and reflect this examination in changed attitudes and behavior.

Home economics, with the family as its major field of study and service, proceeds on the basis that the most fundamental beliefs and the most lasting behavior patterns of individuals are acquired in the relationships of family members in their homes. No institution is more important to the nation and the world than is that of the family. Home economics leads the student to a better understanding of human behavior and the meaning of effective living in the family. Furthermore, it develops in the student the desire and the ability for more adequate decision making in the feeding, clothing, sheltering, and educating of the family. It endeavors to help the student to live more effectively in the community, the state, and the nation as a citizen, a homemaker, and a professional worker.

Home economics makes its contribution to general education in several ways. In all its courses, the fundamental concepts of general education are kept uppermost, so that the student catches the vision and develops the desire and ability to live effectively in the modern world. The student is introduced to courses in a wide range of subject-matter areas—from chemistry to philosophy and from art to engineering—in order to provide a background for understanding home economics phenomena and applying general information. Home economics combines with other fields of study in constructing educational experiences which help young people become aware of themselves as having a responsibility for intelligent participation in the affairs of the family and in the duties of citizenship. Thus, in the home economics curricula, the college student will find a wide range of courses required and suggested and many experiences and problems available to think and work through, for the home economist must have wide knowledge. The life of a family is complex, and its needs and problems are as great as life itself.

HOME ECONOMICS PROFESSIONS

Home economics furnishes careers with futures. The rapid technological strides made in the past decades have thrust the home economist into the limelight. She has become a liaison between the family and a changing society. Thousands of home economists in education, business and industry, and community services adapt and transmit new educational and research advances in order to improve family living (7). From test kitchens to textile laboratories, advertising agencies to hospitals, designers' studios to the classroom, the range of careers is as varied and exciting as any young career-minded girl could desire. Salary? Home economics graduates rank in the top three starting salaries for women in the United States (10). And if one likes to travel, home economists are in demand in the Peace Corps and foreign service. A college or university student majoring in home economics, by planning her course work carefully, can meet the requirements for several career specialities. Intensive study in one or more areas is excellent preparation for a number of jobs. Those students seeking a particular type of vocation—such as research, teaching, writing, or artistic expression—will be able to combine the prerequisites for these specialized techniques with a specific area of interest in home economics (10).

In addition to her specialized training, a home economist must be able to work with people of various living standards and backgrounds, and should have a capacity for leadership, with ability to inspire cooperation. Good grooming, poise, and a genuine interest in people are also essential traits.

Home economists are expected to have very good employment opportunities through the 1970s (17). The greatest demand will probably stem from the need to fill teaching positions in secondary schools and in colleges and universities. Increased national focus on the needs of low-income families may also increase the demand for home economists in welfare and extension service. Occupational home economics training will demand many specialized teachers. In addition, the need for more home economists in research is expected to increase with the continued interest in improving home products and services. Many business establishments are also becoming increasingly aware of the contributions that can be made by professionally trained home economists, and probably will hire more of them to promote home products and to act as consultants to consumers. Many home economists will be needed to replace those who die, retire, or leave the field because of family responsibilities or other reasons during the 1970s. Opportunities for home economists who leave the profession temporarily and return later will be good, it is predicted. In other words, the future appears to be *wide open* for the home economist (2).

There are two groups of people who are actively working in the field of home economics. The first includes all the women and men who have majored in some phase of home economics or a related field during college and who are now actively engaged in home economics work. These are called the professional home economists. The second group is composed of those who majored in home economics in college and who are now devoting their time to homemaking. These are known as home economists in homemaking. Many college students recognize that home economists do combine professional life and homemaking and are training themselves for both.

Professional home economists are found in many fields. It is estimated that over 1,000 career opportunities await the college graduate who majors in home economics (12). Students sometimes become confused when thinking about careers, because in most colleges and universities the home economics specialities are given as subject matter areas and the positions for employment are listed in terms of fields of service or work. For example, the subject-matter fields usually found in colleges or universities of home economics are as follows (21):

Child development	Household equipment
Family relations	Food and nutrition
Home management	Textiles and clothing
Family economics	Art related to the home
Housing	Family and community
Home furnishings	Education

In all probability, the home economics student will choose to concentrate in courses of one of the above interest areas, and she will be said to be majoring in child development, in food and nutrition, in textiles and clothing, etc. When she selects her career, she will select some field of work where she can apply her specialized knowledge. For example, she may major in child development and then choose to teach this area of subject matter in high school or in college. Or she may choose to use this knowledge in nursery school or welfare work. Or she may decide to become a designer for children's toys. On the other hand, she may major in food and nutrition and may choose to use her knowledge as a teacher, a researcher, a hospital dietitian, or a home economist with a utilities. Some of the various types of jobs a home economist may enter are as follows (7):

Career opportunities for home economists*

child development and family relations	
Teachers	Counselors (*cont.*):
Colleges and universities	Youth
High schools	Marriage and family
Nursery schools	Designers of children's play equipment
Parent-education classes	
Day care centers	
Schools for exceptional children	Social welfare workers
Mental health programs	Researchers
Youth groups	
Extension work	*food and nutrition*
Counselors	Teachers
Adults	High schools

* This is not an all inclusive list. It provides the student with some idea of the vast employment opportunities.

Teachers (*cont.*):
  Colleges and universities
  Adult classes

Workers in test kitchens

Workers for utility companies

Commercial foods service operators

Dietiticians

Demonstration workers

Food photographers

Food and nutrition consultants

Researchers

interior design and housing
  Interior consultants

  House planners

  Fabric designers

  Equipment designers

  Manufacturer's representatives

  Buyers

  Teachers

  Researchers

education
  Teachers
    Elementary schools
    Secondary schools
    Trade and special schools
    Colleges and universities
    Adult classes

  Educators
    Extension service
    Vocational education
    Public health
    Housing agencies
    Senior citizen programs

Educators (*cont.*):
  International service
  Red Cross
  Girl Scouts
  YWCA
  Peace Corps

Workers for utility companies and
dairy councils
  Home service
  Demonstration
  Consultation

Consultants

Researchers

textiles and clothing
  Fashion merchandisers

  Fashion designers

  Fashion coordinators

  Specialists for pattern companies

  Testers in sewing laboratory

  Textile designers

  Teachers
    High schools
    Colleges and universities
    Extension service
    Adult classes

  Communications workers

  Researchers

international service
  Peace Corps workers

  Teachers

  Consultants

  Product representatives

  Researchers

journalism	household economics and management
Magazine writers	Teachers
Television and radio broadcasters	Colleges and universities
	Adult classes
Workers in advertising	Extension service
Public relations representatives	Consultants
Publishing companies	Banks
Extension service	Welfare services
	Workers in housing corporations

Figures are not available on the exact number of home economists employed in the various occupations, but the following estimates were made in 1968 (14, 17):

Table 4-1
Employed home economists

occupations		number employed
Teachers		50,760
High school	33,000	
Nursery school and kindergarten	300	
Adult classes in home economics	14,000	
Supervisors in public school systems	460	
College and university teachers, administrators, and research workers	3,000	
Research workers in the home economics programs of the Agricultural Research Service of U.S. Department of Agriculture		140
Extension service workers		5,000
Dietitians, food service and food administration workers		30,000
Social welfare and public health workers		725
Home economists in business, industry, and associations		5,000–6,000
Others		1,500
Approximate number of home economists employed		92,000

In addition to these professional home economists in paid positions, there are thousands of others with home economics degrees who are serving as volunteers in many community and state enterprises which require their specialized training. They work with state nutrition councils, teach Red Cross courses in nutrition, serve as local leaders in extension programs, help with housing programs, aid the local welfare and health agencies, supervise play schools in neighborhoods or churches, and assist the homemaking teachers in the schools. Some are homemaking consultants for Girl Scout and other youth groups or advisers to schoolgirls who want to learn more about home economics careers.

For one to be happy in her profession or work, she must feel a certain amount of success. The following table gives the criteria for judging success in employment as reported by home economists. It will be noted that the two most important factors to home economists are that (1) they get personal satisfaction from what they are doing and (2) if they do good work, it shows.

Table 4-2
Criteria for judging success in employment as reported by home economists

criterion	percent of home economists reporting each criterion
1. Does my job offer me personal satisfaction?	44.4
2. Do my students or employees reflect the quality of my work?	41.7
3. Are my salary increments adequate in my situation?	25.0
4. Do I observe favorable student, employee, or family attitudes?	25.0
5. Am I given increased opportunity to develop the job and increased responsibility on the job?	25.0
6. Am I given the cooperation and respect of my colleagues?	25.0
7. Am I continually called upon for opinions, ideas, resources, and consultant help?	19.4
8. Am I receiving promotions in rank and title?	16.7
9. Is the job challenging to me?	16.7
10. Are there evidences of growth in the program?	16.7
11. Have I continued to grow as a professional person?	16.7
12. Do I have the respect and cooperation of my supervisor or the management?	16.7
13. Can I look at my job critically?	13.9
14. Is my tenure status satisfactory?	5.6
15. Am I receiving other good job offers?	5.6
16. Am I recruiting desirable personnel for employment in my field, by personal example or activity?	5.6
17. Do I organize to accomplish my work effectively?	5.6

Source: Charlyce King, "How Can I Judge My Success in My Job?" *Journal of Home Economics,* vol. 53, pp. 262–265, April 1961.

To find one's place in this very large field called "home economics" requires much study and thought. To do it wisely, one must have a thorough understanding of the opportunities in its various divisions and a good understanding of one's own interests and potentialities. Again, wise selection of a speciality requires that the student be able to answer many questions: What positions are open to the person who trains in foods and nutrition, in clothing and textiles, in applied art, in child development and family life, in communications, in home management, in household economics, in housing, in extension, in education, or in research? What specialized training is needed for each of the fields? Are certain personality characteristics more suitable for one field of work than for another? What are the opportunities for service in each of the fields? What salaries may one expect at the beginning, and what are the opportunities for advancement? Is it easier to combine homemaking and careers in some fields than in others?

In the following chapters, these and many other questions will be answered in reference to each of these special fields of home economics.

SUGGESTED ACTIVITIES

To get a better concept of home economics in college and in the state, the student is encouraged to seek the following information.

1. Is home economics a department or college in the institution? What is the difference between a department and a college? When was the home economics work introduced into the institution?

2. For what fields in home economics is training given? What are the academic requirements for each field?

3. How many home economists are employed by public and private agencies, by schools and colleges, and by businesses in the state? Where were these home economists trained or educated? The state home economics association will be able to help supply this information.

4. Check over the list of home economics alumnae from the college. In what fields did they take their major work? How many of them went into professions when they finished college? Into what fields did they go? How many are now employed, and in what fields of work?

5. Discuss with your course adviser ways by which a student may prepare for more than one field in home economics. In most colleges this is possible, providing the student starts in time to arrange her courses.

6. Interview a few professional home economists. What are their educational and experience backgrounds? How did they happen to choose home economics as their professional field? What is your estimate of them as home economists?

REFERENCES

1. Barney, H. S., and M. C. Egan, "Home Economists as Members of Health Teams," *Journal of Home Economics,* vol. 60, pp. 427–431, June 1968.

2. Bates, Mercedes, "The Home Economist as a Leader in Business," *Forecast in Home Economics,* vol. 13, pp. F42–F43, March 1968.

3. Botzum, J. S., "Preparing Tomorrow's Household Engineers," *Ohio Schools,* vol. 46, pp. 19–20, February 1968.

4. "Counseling for Home Economics: An Education and a Profession," *Forecast in Home Economics,* vol. 12, pp. 11–14, November 1966.

5. Dabry, A., "Occupational Programs in Home Economics," *American Vocational Journal,* vol. 44, pp. 56–58, October 1969.

6. East, Marjorie, "What Is Home Economics?" *Journal of Home Economics,* vol. 57, p. 387, May 1965.

7. *Forecast in Home Economics,* vol. 12, pp. F11–F14, November 1966.

8. *Forecast in Home Economics,* vol. 9, p. 1, November 1963.

9. "Graduate Opportunities for Home Economists, 1968–69, 1969–70," *Journal of Home Economics,* vol. 60, pp. 119–136, February 1968.

10. Hancock, E. P., "Fields and Future of Home Economics," *Journal of Home Economics,* vol. 58, p. 52, January 1966.

11. Hoffman, Doretta, "Challenges Facing Home Economics," *Forecast in Home Economics,* vol. 11, pp. F26–F27, February 1966.

12. *Home Economics Careers for You,* American Home Economics Association, Washington, 1964.

13. Hughes, R. P., "Development and Evaluation of a Curriculum Package on Preparation for a Dual Role," *Journal of Home Economics,* vol. 61, pp. 350–358, May 1969.

14. Johnson, Jack T., "Can Home Economics Meet the Challenge of Change," *Forecast in Home Economics,* vol. 13, p. F24, January 1968.

15. Mallory, Bernice, "Home Economics Today," *American Vocational Journal,* vol. 42, pp. 30–32, February 1967.

16. Morris, M. M., "What Is a Home Economist to Do," *Journal of Home Economics,* vol. 59, pp. 697–701, November 1967.

17. *Occupational Outlook Handbook, 1968–69 Ed.,* p. 207, U.S. Bureau of Labor Statistics Bulletin 1150, 1969.

18. Robertson, M. E., "Home Economics in the Service of International Cooperation," *Time Educational Supplement,* No. 2687, p. 1234, Nov. 18, 1966.

19. Rogers, Willie Mae, "Home Economics: Career Gateway," *NEA Journal,* vol. 57, p. 32, May 1968.

20. Spitze, H. T., "Utilizing HEIH Members on Research Teams," *Journal of Home Economics,* vol. 61, pp. 366–368, May 1969.

21. *Unfold Your Future in Home Economics,* American Home Economics Association, Washington, 1965.

22. Urvant, W. P., "Home Economics: Catalyst for Progress in Appalachia," *Journal of Home Economics,* vol. 59, pp. 53–54, January 1967.

ADDITIONAL READINGS

Adams, Evelyn, "Who Carries the Ball in Consumer Education," *Forecast in Home Economics,* vol. 13, pp. F8–F9, April 1968.

Burress, A. W., "Nursing-home Care: A New Field for Home Economics," *Journal of Home Economics*, vol. 58, pp. 673–675, October 1966.

Gray, E., "Training: Where, What, How and Why," *Times Educational Supplement*, Nov. 15, 1968, 2791:1012.

Hill, A. D., "Foreward from 50 Years of Experience in Home Economics Education," *American Vocational Journal*, vol. 42, pp. 38–39, March 1967.

McDermott, Beth, "Reaching the Consumer through the Creative Home Economist," *Forecast in Home Economics*, vol. 13, p. F-33, November 1967.

Meyer, M. P., "Career Development at the Graduate Level," *American Vocational Journal*, vol. 44, pp. 59–60, December 1969.

Moore, Ruth S., "Call to Larger Leadership," *American Vocational Journal*, vol. 43, pp. 22–23, February 1968.

Robins, John, "On the Employment Market," *Times Educational Supplement*, Nov. 15, 1968, 2791:1093.

PART **2** HOME ECONOMICS CAREERS

5 HOME ECONOMICS EDUCATION

Never before in the history of American education has the teaching of home economics been given such an important role as at the present time. In this world of sweeping social and technological change, those dedicated to helping individuals and families gain maximum satisfaction from living face a tremendous challenge. Home economics education today is no field for the meek. To meet the needs in home economics today, there is need for both high-quality and an ever-increasing supply of teachers.

Although some form of home economics education has existed in some schools for over 150 years, most of the work has developed since 1918. During the last fifty years, home economics education has grown and expanded until now home economics is a part of the curriculum in almost all high schools in the United States and in over 450 colleges and universities (1).

SECONDARY SCHOOLS

Teaching in high school is the path followed by the largest single group of professional home economists. In 1970, it was estimated that over 26,000 home economists taught in high school, and they were teaching over 3.4 million junior and senior high school students (10). The great interest in home economics at the high school level is indicated by the fact that membership in the Future Homemakers of America (FHA), a national voluntary association for junior and senior high school home economics students, totals over 603,907 members in 1,901 chapters. This organization has helped over 2 million young people in our schools. In addition to high school students, high school home economics instructors in 1970 taught over one million adults enrolled in evening and part-time classes (17).

THE HIGH SCHOOL TEACHER'S JOB

The work of a high school teacher will vary somewhat with the size of the school and the type of the community. In the small schools, one teacher may have pupils from the eighth through the twelfth grades, but in the larger schools, the work will be divided between two or more teachers. Home economics education in the high school has two major purposes: (1) homemaking and consumer education and (2) prepara-

Fig. 5-1 Teaching arts and crafts to high school students can be fun. (Courtesy of Radford College)

tion for gainful occupations utilizing home economics knowledge and skills (9). Home economics teachers have always been expected to help students to improve their homes and themselves, and this is still a major function. This has been done through the teaching of all aspects of family living in the classes. The subject matter taught and the experiences provided for the students in the classroom and laboratory have included elementary food preparation and meal planning; clothing selection, care, and construction; health and home care for family members; child care and development; consumer buying; time and money management; and family relations. To this has been added preparation for employment. In preparing youth for employment, efforts are made to help them acquire not only the necessary skills and knowledge, but also the personal qualities needed for success on the job (14).

Much more attention is being given today to social and cultural needs and conditions, especially in depressed areas. Leaders in this country have come to appreciate what home economics can do in helping to improve the conditions of needy families. This belief was expressed by Senator John Sparkman (9) when he said, "Think of the potential impact that a good basic education in home economics can have on the improvement of the standard of living and basic happiness of every American family. . . . We have only begun to scratch the surface in providing home economics for the disadvantaged and low-income families."

Classes are offered for both boys and girls. The teen-age girls are most interested in discussions and study dealing with their own personal problems, relations with boys, dating, clothing, food, entertaining, home management, buying, and home decoration. Teen-age boys prefer classes dealing with understanding themselves and their families, family finance, boy-girl relations, housing, child guidance, and clothing selection (2, 3, 12).

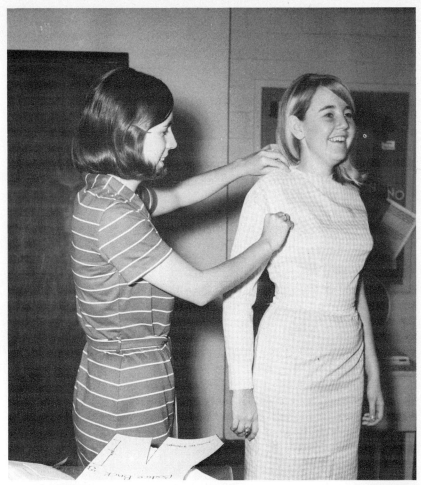

Fig. 5-2 Teaching students how to fit garments is an important step in teaching good grooming. (Courtesy of the College of Education, University of Kentucky)

The home economics teacher functions in many capacities as she works with students (7). Like other teachers, she must guide her pupil's learning, but she does many things over and above this primary duty. If she is a good teacher, she will show the relationships between her subject and every phase of living. She seeks to help the students use these learnings to grow toward increased maturity and to assume responsibilities in their parental homes.

The home economics teacher frequently acts as a counselor (12). Few teachers in the high school have more numerous and more varied opportunities for guidance.

Fig. 5-3 To select furniture wisely, one must understand the essentials of good construction. A home economics teacher is discussing the good and poor features of a chair with her students.

Girls and boys come to her for help with family problems, boy-girl questions, and grooming needs; they come to her to share their fun and to talk with as a friend. She has the opportunity to counsel on vocations and to discuss her students special abilities and aptitudes with them as well as their personal needs, both in the classroom and in private conversation. Again, the teacher can use her classes to help pupils develop attitudes of cooperation, consideration, and courtesy. In the informality of home economics teaching, the teacher may show an interest in the students personally without seeming to pry into their affairs. Finally, the chances are that the home economics teacher will be an adviser for one or more student clubs; for example, many home economics teachers sponsor local chapters of the Future Homemakers of America.

In most schools home economics laboratories are modern and attractive. They present the equivalent of an efficient, well-equipped, and well-designed home. The most modern household equipment and furnishings are put at the disposal of the home economics teacher. In fact, the home economics teachers usually are among the first to see and use new food products, textiles, and equipment.

Fig. 5-4 Home economics teachers share informal moments with students. (Courtesy of Radford College)

PERSONAL QUALIFICATIONS FOR TEACHING

Although the personalities of good home economics teachers are similar to those of good teachers in any field, the following attributes are especially important. The home economics teacher should:

1. Be patient
2. Have a pleasing personality
3. Know her subject
4. Be levelheaded at all times; think carefully before speaking
5. Like teen-age boys and girls
6. Be experienced, yet have a young approach
7. Understand high school pupils and their needs
8. Have a keen awareness of the basic needs of individuals
9. Have the ability to be friendly and at the same time hold the respect of students
10. Be well groomed and present a good appearance
11. Practice what she tries to teach
12. Have a pleasing voice, speak clearly, and use correct English
13. Be interested in family life and enjoy homemaking activities

Fig. 5-5 These home economics students are studying muscular coordination of children. (Courtesy of the College of Education, University of Kentucky)

14. Have the ability to inspire cooperation
15. Have the capacity for leadership
16. Be able to work with people of various living standards and backgrounds
17. Know something about employment opportunities in the community

The would-be teacher must know how students learn. Teaching is a matter of providing learning experiences, which include activities to be carried out, subject matter to be studied, and skills and techniques to be mastered. The teacher must be able to direct successfully the learning of students having different abilities, interests, and needs in order that they continue toward their fullest growth and development (5).

Since home economics is taught through the use, care, and management of the department, as well as through class discussions and special activities carried out by the pupils, the teacher must have the ability to select, plan, and carry through teaching activities in an orderly and meaningful manner. The successful teacher must have training and skill in teaching (11). Since teaching is also a matter of relationships between people, the teacher must know people of different age groups as well as the individual students with whom she works.

A good teacher must approach her subject with a scientific attitude and method. The scientific attitude is marked by the possession of intellectual curiosity, the willingness to test accepted beliefs, and the avoidance of personal or class biases.

A teacher of home economics must know how to budget money and to provide for equipment and furnishings, replacements and repairs, and materials with which to work. In addition, she must be able to maintain a department that exemplifies principles of good management, cleanliness, and attractiveness and one that is consistent with the needs and economic status of pupils and families in the community.

ACADEMIC QUALIFICATIONS

The academic requirements for teaching home economics will vary from state to state and from city to city. Also, they will depend upon the type of program offered. In general, a degree from an accredited college or university with a major in home economics education is required.

In every state, a certificate is required for teaching. To qualify for this certificate, the prospective teacher must have, at least, the equivalent of one-half year of education courses, including practice teaching, plus professional courses in one or more subjects commonly taught in the secondary schools (15, pp. 207, 186).

The curriculum required for teacher certification in home economics always includes general education, professional education, and home economics subject matter. Under general education will be English, social studies, natural science, health and physical education, fine and applied arts, and perhaps mathematics. Professional education is made up of courses in human growth and development, methods of instruction, curriculum organization, and student teaching. The home economics subject matter required will include family relationships and child development, housing, home management, equipment. foods and nutrition, clothing and textiles, family economics and consumer education, home care of the sick, and home art (16).

The specific requirements for any one state or city may be obtained from the dean or head of home economics or the dean of education in the university that the student is attending, or by writing to the appropriate state department of education or the superintendent of schools in the city or school division in which employment is sought.

In all institutions where home economics teachers are prepared, educators are employed to teach courses in methods of instruction in home economics. In addition, these educators plan the student teaching, work with supervising teachers, teach demonstration classes for students preparing to teach, follow up graduates, and make studies related to problems of teaching home economics.

The personal and academic qualifications for these positions are similar to those listed under high school teaching, with the addition of graduate study, which is usually done in education.

Where students do practice teaching, many colleges employ teachers who act as supervising or coordinating teachers. These teachers usually are members of the staff of the college and also of the high school where they work. Ordinarily, these positions are better paid than high school teaching, but a master's degree usually is required of the supervising teacher.

In most states there is a state supervisor with one or more assistants and several area supervisors of home economics education. Generally, these positions are held by successful home economics teachers who have returned to college for advanced degrees. Their responsibilities are to guide and coordinate the development of the home economics curriculum in education in the schools, set standards for home economics departments and buildings, see that the basic qualifications for teacher certification are met, and supervise and help teachers on the job. At all times they attempt to give leadership and raise the level of the home economics work in the schools.

In the Home Economics Education branch of the U.S. Office of Education, home economics education specialists are employed. Additional home economists work specifically with the Future Homemakers of America. These specialists consult with the states concerning program planning and curriculum development at both the secondary and college levels, with improvement of teacher education and supervision, and with strengthening and expanding studies and research in home economics education.

These state and federal positions offer opportunities for advancement for the young women who go into home economics education as a career. If the teacher has the ability to organize, lead, and work constructively with people, she will find advancement easy when the required graduate credit and experience have been gained.

ADVANTAGES AND DISADVANTAGES OF HOME ECONOMICS TEACHING IN THE HIGH SCHOOL

The opportunities for employment of home economics teachers are very good. At the present time there are over 33,000 teachers and supervisors employed in the schools of the United States (15, pp. 188–189). It has been estimated that in any one year, about one-third of these are replaced (15, pp. 188–189). To fill only these positions would require more than 11,000 new persons yearly. In addition to maintaining these existing positions, many schools need additional home economics teachers because of the growing student population, and for job training in vocational and technical schools. For many years there have not been enough qualified home economics

Fig. 5-6 A high school class in occupational foods services is planning a menu for the Copper Kettle, a small restaurant operated by the class. (Courtesy of Gloucester High School, Gloucester, Va.)

teachers to meet the demand. Salaries received by teachers in home economics are similar to those of other teachers, generally averaging from $5,500 to $10,000 for a nine- or ten-month period. Teacher's salaries are usually lower in towns and small cities than in larger cities and suburbs. However, higher educational and experience requirements are likely to prevail in large city school systems.

Home economics education and experience in teaching provide a good basis for work in many fields of home economics. Also, the promotions in home economics education itself are promising for the well-qualified teacher. Home economics teaching is very challenging for the young woman who enjoys working with people and helping them grow in understanding and maturity. The teacher gets her reward from teaching by seeing day in and day out the difference her work makes in the lives of people.

The teacher of home economics has a position of status in most communities and is looked to for information and help by the homemakers. In addition, home economics teaching is one field in which marriage is not a handicap; in fact it is an asset, for the home economics teacher can illustrate in her home the principles and skills she teaches in the school.

Most teachers have time available for travel and study, and many travel agencies plan programs especially for teachers. These not only are enjoyable but provisions usually are made by which the teacher can receive college credit or experience allowances toward promotions and increased salaries.

In some states, salary increases with experience in teaching have not been comparable with those received from business and other fields of occupation for the amount of education required. In most states, teacher's salaries have greatly improved during the last few years and are competing very well at the present time. One has also to consider that the materials with which to work and classroom and office space are furnished for teachers. Again, teaching offers certain types of security not found in other fields. No matter what the general economic conditions of the country are, children must be taught, and a state will discontinue most programs before it will give up its schools.

Some teachers object to the amount of routine work associated with paper grading, record keeping, and other clerical jobs, but in all professions and businesses, considerable paper work must be done by the person planning and directing the program. To some teachers, classroom and laboratory work become monotonous, while to others they furnish rewarding and stimulating relationships with students. Teaching requires constant study and preparation for success; the teacher who does not keep abreast of the times will soon cease being effective. This, however, is not exclusive to the field of teaching. In our competitive world, any professional or businessman or -woman who does not study and keep up with the times will soon be left behind.

OCCUPATIONAL TRAINING

Many home economics teachers are now giving occupational home economics courses on either a part-time or a full-time basis. These courses are designed to equip students for remunerative jobs in their community or elsewhere. A great many laboratory and on-the-job experiences are provided for the students to gain confidence in themselves and proficiency in the job. The students receive their on-the-job experiences mainly in cooperating businesses and industries. However, they receive class instruction, in addition, under the supervision of the home economics teacher. Upon completion of this training, they are usually employed by local businesses. However, they may take employment elsewhere, for there is considerable demand for persons with these skills and knowledge.

ADULT EDUCATION IN HOMEMAKING

In addition to teaching high school and elementary school students, home economics teachers work with adults. Adult classes may be on a full-time or a part-time basis, or they may be full-time for a short period of the year, as illustrated by summer programs. Changing conditions, new vocations, new findings of science, and the government's recent emphasis on improving the conditions of the low-income and other needy persons require continuous learning on the part of homemakers to keep

Fig. 5-7 These professional home economists are studying printout of microfiche in order to keep themselves up to date. (Courtesy of the College of Home Economics, Ohio State University)

abreast of the times. Also, many persons who saw no need for learning nutrition, food preparation, child guidance, time and money management, consumer buying, and clothing selection and construction in their youth see the worth of it when they are faced with these problems as homemakers. Too, many homemakers find it necessary to find employment and need to develop certain personal qualities and skills for the jobs available. The adult education classes usually are held after school hours or at night.

THE ELEMENTARY SCHOOL

Seldom is a home economics teacher employed solely for work with elementary school children. She does, however, work with elementary teachers in developing projects for the children (6, 18). She may act as a resource person to the elementary teachers or teach selected units herself. Elementary children need to learn to select their food and clothing, to work and play with others, to protect their health, to live happily in everyday intimate relationships with family members and friends, to keep themselves clean, and to improve their personal appearance. The home economics teacher has much to offer the elementary school child in these areas.

HOME ECONOMICS EDUCATION
IN COLLEGES AND UNIVERSITIES

In large colleges and universities, there are usually three groups of home economists on the staff, namely, administrators, subject-matter teachers, and research workers; and in the land-grant colleges and universities there are also extension specialists. There are about 450 colleges and universities in the United States granting degrees in various fields of home economics. In addition, there are many junior colleges and liberal arts colleges which offer some home economics courses but no degrees. The number of degrees granted in the fields of home economics in 1967–1968 were as follows: 12,657 bachelor's degrees, 1,517 master's degrees, and 83 doctor's degrees—a total of 14,257 (8). In Table 5–1, the number of men and women who received degrees in the various fields of home economics for the year 1967–1968 is shown (8).

It will be noted that the largest number of bachelor's and master's degrees were given in home economics education, with general home economics second.

If the institutions for which data are available are representative, there are between 3,000 and 3,500 full-time home economics faculty members on the staffs of the colleges and universities in this country (15, pp. 188–189). Many of these institutions employ additional staff members to carry on research and extension work.

College and university teachers instruct students in specific subjects. The usual teaching load is from twelve to fifteen hours of classroom work each week. However, the higher-ranking teachers may spend only six to eight hours a week in actual classroom teaching. Besides teaching classes, college teachers prepare tests and other materials for classroom work, check and grade students' work, advise students, and keep up to date with developments in their specialities. The increasing use of computers relieves college teachers, to some extent, of many routine tasks and

Table 5-1
Degrees in home economics conferred in 1967–1968

home economics field	bachelor's		master's		doctor's	
	men	women	men	women	men	women
Home economics education	4	5,233	0	550	0	12
General home economic	19	3,813	8	407	0	10
Clothing and textiles	9	1,014	3	117	1	8
Child development and family relations	11	905	17	154	15	13
Food and nutrition	20	778	11	144	3	11
Institution management or administration	110	193	9	19	0	3
All others	29	519	3	74	1	6
Totals	202	12,455	52	1,465	20	63

makes it possible for them to devote more time to preparing for classroom lectures, writing, and research. Some teachers work part time outside the college as consultants to business, industrial, scientific, welfare, or government organizations (19).

The influence of the home economics college teacher extends far beyond the classroom. Through lectures, TV and radio programs, and publications they reach many thousands who are not students (4). It is not uncommon for a bulletin or circular written by a home economist in a government agency or in a state university to be sent to 300,000 to 500,000 persons. In addition, home economics college teachers and administrators provide service for large numbers of people who visit university campuses and participate in workshops, conferences, study groups, and short courses.

Qualifications for College Teaching

To qualify for most positions in colleges and universities, applicants must have at least the master's degree, and increasingly, they must have completed all requirements for the doctorate with the possible exception of the dissertation. The doctor's degree is usually required for promotion or appointment to positions above the rank of instructor. Most four-year colleges and universities recognize four academic ranks, namely, instructor, assistant professor, associate professor, and full professor. In addition, there are many assistants who are carrying graduate study besides doing some teaching or service in the university.

It is difficult to give a picture of remuneration for college or university teaching since the pay rate varies from one institution to another and for different sections of the country. Usually, the larger institutions pay higher salaries; however, they often carry more assistants and part-time instructors who are also pursuing graduate study. In some institutions there is no base salary in relation to rank. Businesses, organizations, and individuals may supplement salaries in certain positions. The median salaries for college and university staff in 1968 were as follows (20, p. 125):

Table 5-2
Median university staff salaries—1968

staff rank	median salary for academic year	range for academic year*
Dean	$18,000	
Professor	16,000	$12,000–$35,000
Associate professor	14,000	10,000– 20,000
Assistant professor	10,000	7,500– 15,000
Instructor	7,500	5,000– 10,000
Public junior college	8,361†	
Private junior college	6,470†	

* These salary ranges are estimates based upon information received by author.
† These salaries are figures for 1966–1967 (15).

College and university salaries have been steadily rising, and no doubt will continue to rise for some time to come. The opportunities for employment for home economists in colleges and universities are excellent. For years there has been an extreme shortage of highly qualified home economists available for university teaching and research positions.

INTEREST CHECKLIST FOR
HOME ECONOMICS TEACHING

There are certain activities in which persons employed in education are engaged, and there are certain interests which they are likely to have. Following, are listed twenty-six activities or interests which are associated with home economics teaching, especially in the high school. In order to evaluate your interest in becoming a home economics teacher, place a check in the column at the right which best expresses the extent to which you would enjoy each activity listed on the left-hand side. Directions for scoring your responses are given at the end of the list.

activities	*degree of interest*		
	much	average	little
1. Help girls to improve their appearance including hair styles, clothes, and make-up	___	___	___
2. Chaperone a dance or a party for teen-agers	___	___	___
3. Supervise a group of teen-agers who are learning to cook	___	___	___
4. Lead a discussion on dating for high school students	___	___	___
5. Attend meetings with other teachers to plan activities for the school	___	___	___
6. Select furnishings for a college or a department to be used by homemaking students	___	___	___
7. Help a group of students organize a tea for their mothers	___	___	___
8. Help teen-agers select suitable patterns to improve their figures	___	___	___
9. Teach clothing-construction techniques to girls and women	___	___	___
10. Stage fashion shows, helping the girls to walk with grace and poise	___	___	___
11. Answer questions which homemakers have concerning food, clothing, equipment, etc.	___	___	___
12. Visit the homes of students and get to know their parents	___	___	___
13. Help girls or women redecorate their rooms, work out more efficient procedures for work, etc.	___	___	___
14. Sponsor a club for young people, helping them to plan programs and carry out their activities	___	___	___
15. Make out lesson plans for classes, and plan laboratory experiments on foods, clothing, etc.	___	___	___
16. Order supplies for laboratories	___	___	___

17. Counsel with teen-agers concerning their personal problems or needs   ____   ____   ____
18. Use new household and kitchen equipment for performing tasks   ____   ____   ____
19. Help families or individuals to solve problems related to selecting clothing, dieting, buying, etc.   ____   ____   ____
20. Go on hikes or outings with young people and cook out of doors   ____   ____   ____
21. Participate with other teachers in the extracurricular activities of the school   ____   ____   ____
22. Attend professional meetings and conferences of educators with similar interests and problems   ____   ____   ____
23. Participate in the activities of the parent-teacher association   ____   ____   ____
24. Have opportunities to grow intellectually and socially   ____   ____   ____
25. Be looked to as a leader in the community   ____   ____   ____
26. Help students prepare for jobs   ____   ____   ____
    Total score   _____

To score your responses, give a value of 2 for each item checked "Much" and 1 for each item checked "Average." If your total score ranges from 40 to 52, you indicate high interest in the home economics teaching field.

SUGGESTED ACTIVITIES

1. What are the requirements for certification to teach home economics in your state? Study these requirements and plan your course so that you can qualify for home economics teaching. The person responsible for home economics education in your college will be able to help you.

2. Invite a high school home economics teacher to talk to your class. Ask her to tell you about a typical day in teaching. Why did she choose to teach home economics? She could discuss with you some of the advantages and disadvantages of teaching.

3. If possible, have the state supervisor of home economics education speak to your class. She could tell you many things about teaching. You could discuss with her the opportunities in teaching, salaries paid, what is expected of a teacher, etc.

4. Find out as much as you can about the home economics teachers in your state. How many are there? How much education do they have? Where did they get their education? How long have they taught? What do they like most about teaching? Why did they choose to teach home economics? How did they get their first position?

5. Plan a trip to a well-organized home economics department in a high school. Observe the activities of the students and the teacher. Does the teacher seem to be enjoying her work? Do the students enjoy the classes? Is the department attractive?

6. Ask your teacher to arrange for a visit to an adult homemaking class. What are the interests of these women? How do these adult classes differ from the average classes for high school students?

REFERENCES

1. Amidon, Edna P., "Home Economics in Vocational Education," *American Vocational Journal,* vol. 40, pp. 18–20, May 1965.

2. Anthony, Hazel, "Boys in the Homemaking Department," *Journal of Home Economics*, vol. 48, pp. 327–330, May 1956.

3. Chachere, Nan Wells, "Why High School Girls Elect Home Economics," *Journal of Home Economics*, vol. 55, pp. 47–48, January 1963.

4. Harper, William A., "TV: New Force in Education," *Journal of Home Economics*, vol. 49, pp. 784–786, December 1957.

5. Hatcher, Hazel M., and Mildred E. Andrews, *The Teaching of Home Economics,* p. 4, Houghton Mifflin Company, Boston, 1963.

6. Hill, Mary M., "Planning for Nutrition Education in Elementary Schools," *Journal of Home Economics*, vol. 60, pp. 259–262, April 1968.

7. *Home Economists in Education,* pamphlet No. 4 in the "Home Economics Career Profiles Series," American Home Economics Association, Washington, 1963.

8. Hooper, Mary Evans, and Marjorie O. Chandler, *Earned Degrees Conferred: 1967–68: Part B—Institutional Data,* Office of Education, pp. 57–58, 150–155, June 1969.

9. Hurt, Mary Lee, "New Challenges for Home Economics Educators," *Journal of Home Economics,* vol. 51, pp. 771–755, December 1969.

10. *Jobs and Career Opportunities for Women in Home Economics,* The Institute of Research, Research No. 24, pp. 19–20, Chicago, 1969.

11. Lehman, Ruth T., "The Education of a Home Economics Teacher," *Journal of Home Economics,* vol. 48, pp. 88–90, February 1956.

12. McElroy, Joy, "The Role of Guidance in the Home Economics Classroom," *Journal of Home Economics,* vol. 58, p. 49, January 1966.

13. Midjaas, Ruth Whitmarsh, "From Research to Curriculum in Child Care," *Journal of Home Economics,* vol. 44, pp. 38–39, October 1952.

14. Nelson, Helen Y., "Occupational Home Economics Programs," *Journal of Home Economics,* vol. 60, pp. 435–440, June 1968.

15. *Occupational Outlook Handbook, 1968–69 ed.,* U.S. Bureau of Labor Statistics, 1969.

16. Simpson, Elizabeth J., "Challenges in Curriculum Development in Home Economics," *Journal of Home Economics*, vol. 60, p. 767, December 1968.

17. *Statistics Based upon Estimates by the Office of Education*, Office of Education, 1970.

18. Stone, Mary Louise, "Some Homemaking Projects Designed for Grade Classes," *Journal of Home Economics*, vol. 43, p. 116, February 1951.

19. *Unfold Your Future in Home Economics*, American Home Economics Association, Washington, 1965.

20. U.S. Bureau of the Census, *Statistical Abstracts of the United States: 1969 90th ed*, 1969.

ADDITIONAL READINGS

Boyer, Alan E., and F. Ivan Nye, "Family Life Education in Florida Public Schools,"*Journal of Marriage and the Family*, vol. 26, pp. 181–187, May 1964.

Brown, Muriel M., "Values in Home Economics,"*Journal of Home Economics*, vol. 59, pp. 769–775, December 1967.

Fenderburk, K. W., "Home Economics Moves out to Meet the Challenge of Social Change," *American Vocational Journal*, vol. 42, pp. 31–32, September 1967.

Force, Elizabeth S., "The Role of the School in Family-life Education," *Journal of Marriage and the Family*, vol. 26, pp. 99–101, February 1964.

Gauker, Norma S., "The High School Teacher as Counselor," *Journal of Marriage and the Family*, vol. 27, pp. 298–303, May 1965.

Job Horizons for College Women in the 1960's, pp. 10–14, 16–20, 41–46, U.S. Department of Labor, Women's Bureau Bulletin 288, Washington, 1964.

Johnson, V. S., "Home Economics in California's Junior Colleges," *American Vocational Journal*, vol. 43, pp. 43–50, April 1968.

Monts, E. A., and B. H. Peterson, "Graduate Teaching by Telephone and Radio," *Journal of Home Economics*, vol. 61, pp. 443–447, June 1969.

Osborne, Ruth Farnham, "Boys and Family-life Education," *Journal of Marriage and the Family*, vol. 23, pp. 50–52, February 1961.

Rible, Marilyn, "Have You Considered Graduate Work," *Journal of Home Economics*, vol. 60, p. 137, February 1968.

Swope, Mary Ruth, "How Short Is the Shortage," *Journal of Home Economics*, vol. 59, pp. 765–768, December 1967.

Wilkinson, Carol Ann, "Home Economics Enriches Elementary Classes," *What's New in Home Economics*, vol. 33, p. 16, November 1969.

6 HOME ECONOMICS EXTENSION

If a student is deeply interested in people and has a sympathetic understanding of them, if she has initiative and imagination and enjoys work that offers something new and different each day, her career may be in home economics extension. The person who chooses this career will be a coworker of approximately 5,000 other home economists who are employed by the Cooperative Extension Service. The agency was established by Congress through the passage of the Smith-Lever Act in 1914.

The extension home economist is as much an educator as the high school teacher; however, the students do not meet in the classroom or the laboratory. They are the homemakers and the young women and girls in the country, in the small towns, or in some cities, who wish to learn how to do a better job of homemaking, become better family members, or be better citizens in the community. Extension education is for use *now*. It involves people who differ in age, educational status, interests, levels of living, culture, and values.

Careers in Home Economics Extension:

I. Local, county, multicounty, or urban level
   A. County extension home economist
   B. 4-H club agent

II. State level
   A. District agent or supervisor
   B. Subject-matter specialists
      1. Food and nutrition
      2. Consumer education
      3. Clothing and textiles
      4. Family financial management
      5. Home improvement
      6. Housing
      7. Family-life and child development
      8. Home arts, health, and others
   C. 4-H club specialists
   D. State leader of home economics

III. Federal level
   A. Subject-matter specialists
   B. Administrator or program leader

COUNTY HOME ECONOMIST

Upon graduation from college, the home economist entering extension usually starts her career in a county. (Various titles are used, such as home agent.) She will be an off-campus member of the staff of her land-grant college and at the same time an employee of the U.S. Department of Agriculture. She will be appointed to her position by the state extension staff of a land-grant university in cooperation with local people of the county where she is to work.

The extension home economist usually has a whole county for her field of activity. She will travel from community to community, and often her class will be an informal meeting of homemakers or local leaders who in turn will teach others. Her office usually will be in the county-seat town, and will be the official headquarters for herself, her secretary, and any assistants she may have, as well as the agricultural and 4-H agents with whom she works.

Home economics agents in more than 1,000 counties throughout the country are also working with paid nonprofessional program aides in an expanded food and nutrition education program to help hard-to-reach poor families to improve their diets. The aides, who are usually indigenous homemakers, are hired, trained, and supervised by the home economist. The aides visit homes and teach the homemakers ways to improve their cooking, shopping, and meal planning, and also money management. The program aide concept was first tested in a pilot project in 1964; about 8,000 are now employed by the Extension Services in the United States, the District of Columbia, Puerto Rico, and the Virgin Islands.

WHAT DOES A HOME ECONOMICS AGENT DO?

The responsibility of the home economics agent is to carry on an education program for women and girls who are no longer attending school, as well as for girls nine to nineteen years old who may still be in school. One of her major responsibilities is to get the results of research in home economics to families in a form which they can easily understand and apply. The teaching which the home economics agent does is practical and timely; it is built around the problems, needs, and interests of women who live in the county and may belong to homemakers' clubs or other groups, or girls in 4-H and other youth groups. The subjects which they study may deal with nutrition, the buying and preparing of foods, the selection and care of house furnishings and equipment, planning spending for family wants, or the construction, selection, and care of clothing so that the homemaker and her family will be well dressed. The challenge is to help interested homemakers and youth achieve greater beauty, comfort, convenience, and efficiency in their homes. Family finance, home improvement, work simplification, and family relationships and child development will also be subjects for study, along with maintaining good health in the family.

Fig. 6-1 Home economists train paid paraprofessionals in nutrition education. (Courtesy of the U.S. Department of Agriculture, Federal Extension Service)

Working with others for community improvement is a regular part of the extension home economist's job. She works with homemakers, boys and girls, young men and women, and families as groups.

She knows that a program planned by the people to meet their needs is the key to successful extension work. In order to achieve such a program, the agent will get to know the people in her area and their wants and needs. Attention must be given to their major problems to make the best use of her time and services. The program takes into consideration the education of the people, the mores of the community, the general economic status of the families, and their sources of income. The extension agent must understand the goals of families in the community and help achieve these goals.

The home economics agent does not perform all this work by herself. She is the administrator and the teacher, but she calls upon many "hands" to do the work. Her major helpers in the county are the local leaders. In fact, her success as an agent will depend upon how well she discovers, stimulates, inspires, develops, and trains these volunteer leaders. A local leader is usually a homemaker in the county who has an interest in some specialty. The home economics agent will train the leaders, who go to others and teach what they have learned, serve as organization leaders, or serve in other ways. This strengthens community ties and activities and develops leadership

Fig. 6-2 Leaders trained by home economists teach young people in 4-H clubs and other youth groups about good buymanship and many other aspects of home economics. (Courtesy of the U.S. Department of Agriculture, Federal Extension Service)

ability in the volunteers, produces self-confidence, and helps people to do things for themselves.

Although much of the home economics extension work has been in rural areas, city women want help just as much as rural women with such matters as food for the family; time and energy management; efficient money use; clothing themselves and children; decorating rooms for beauty, convenience, and comfort; and aiding their children to make decisions.

The home economics agent uses many methods in teaching. Some of the teaching is done through individual contacts, whether in the form of visits to homes, office calls, telephone calls, or personal letters. Much of the teaching, however, is done through group contacts, which consist of workshops, leader-training meetings, conferences and discussion meetings, and tours. The home economics agent makes use of mass media for teaching. She writes and sends out bulletins, leaflets, and circular letters; writes news stories for county or local papers; gives talks on the radio or presents programs on television.

The home economics agent will cooperate with many groups in the county working for family betterment. Schools, the parent-teacher associations, Red Cross,

Fig. 6-3 Here an extension home economist shows on television how to prepare low-cost good food and teaches the general public about other extension programs available to them. (Courtesy of the U.S. Department of Agriculture, Federal Extension Service)

and the dairy council are examples of such groups. Her satisfaction comes from helping people develop their talents and abilities and from seeing improvements which she has helped bring about, as well as from the friendship of people and the confidence they place in her.

WORK WITH 4-H CLUBS

The county home economist also works with 4-H and youth in home economics in her county. Ordinarily she spends one-fourth to one-third of her time working primarily through leaders she has trained. There may be a full-time 4-H club agent who shares this responsibility, but usually this is a part of the home economist's job.

The 4-H program is a nationwide system of education for boys and girls. Nearly 4 million boys and girls are enrolled in more than 96,000 4-H clubs under the leadership of 500,000 volunteer leaders. Membership in a 4-H club is entirely voluntary. Individuals also can participate through television programs. There are more than 100 different projects through which they learn by doing.

The 4-H's stand for, "head, heart, hands, and health." They represent the fourfold training and development that club members undergo. In most states, the membership of a 4-H club varies from a minimum of five to one hundred or more, with an average from fifteen to twenty-five members between the ages of ten and twenty-one years. Members of a club live in the same neighborhood or come from the same school district, township, village, town, or city ward. As the home economists and leaders work with 4-H youth, they help them to develop leadership, improve their homes, broaden their interests, build up a pride in accomplishment and skills of group participation. This encourages them to be better citizens as they try to live up to the challenge of the 4-H club motto, which is, "To make the best better."

In addition to working with 4-H boys and girls, the home agent may work with other youth, or an older-youth program in the county. These programs help young people develop leadership, have wholesome recreation, and become interested in improving their communities.

THE TYPE OF PERSON NEEDED

Personal qualifications for extension work are similar to those of teaching and social work. The extension home economist should be sympathetic and understanding, like people, and have an appreciation of their worth at all income and educational levels. She needs to be patient, and have a sense of humor, imagination, orginality, and the ability to do things cooperatively with others. She needs to be able to lead and at the same time develop the abilities of others to assume leadership for themselves. An agent should be able to speak and write well and to teach effectively. She should be willing and able to continue learning. Good health and the ability to present a neat, well-groomed appearance are also important.

A bachelor's degree in home economics is necessary to enter extension. In addition, a well-rounded curriculum in home economics, psychology, sociology, economics, public speaking, art, journalism, radio and television techniques, housing, and extension methods is helpful.

STATE EXTENSION POSITIONS

To support and implement the work of the county home economist, each state maintains a staff at the land-grant university consisting of a state home economics leader, district agents, state 4-H club agents, and subject-matter specialists.

The *state home economics leader* assumes responsibility for the organization and functioning of home economics extension work in the state. This requires that she be a good administrator. In addition, she must thoroughly understand extension

Decide what you want
(GOALS)

Make a PLAN

Make your PLAN work!

Make a
Spending Plan

a

Decide what you want
(GOALS)

Make a PLAN

Make your PLAN work!

Make a
Spending Plan

b

Fig. 6-4 (*a*) and (*b*) Extension leaders help older youth make plans for creative and satisfactory living. (Courtesy of the U.S. Department of Agriculture, Federal Extension Service)

work and its relationship to other programs in the state and nation. Good leadership includes being able to win and hold the confidence of workers under her supervision. The leader is involved in helping to budget large sums of money necessary to carry on the total program. Finally, she must *know people,* for she has the responsibility of helping to select home economists who work in the extension service.

District agents are program leaders of the home economics program in various sections of the state. The district agent works with the county agents in organizing and carrying through successful programs. The district agent advises the county agents on many problems, including developing programs, understanding new policies, or handling personal problems. In addition, she helps to interpret the policies and wishes of the state office to the county staffs and to bring the needs of the county agents to the attention of the state staff.

Most states have from four to twenty *subject-matter specialists.* It is their responsibility to keep the county home economics agents informed on new developments and methods related to subject-matter fields which they represent.

For example, the state food and nutrition specialist will help the county home economist keep up with new information in food and nutrition, and ways to apply the new findings of research in their teaching. Usually, there also are subject-matter specialists in clothing, textiles, home art, housing, equipment. family finance, family relationships, child development and guidance, and household management.

Subject-matter specialists help the county workers in many other ways. They prepare kits of lessons for use by leaders. They help hold public meetings on their subjects, give talks on the radio and demonstrations on television, and write articles for newspapers and magazines. In addition they develop bulletins, leaflets, and pamphlets as well as illustrative materials to be used by the county workers.

The *4-H club specialists* help the county agents in their work with the youth programs. They help in training leaders and aid with project work, camp organization, and other group activities. They give support in all programs relating to work with boys and girls. They write many articles and help prepare bulletins, leaflets, and illustrative materials for the county agents to use with the youth.

Qualifications for positions on the state level are similar to those at the county level. In addition, a master's degree and experience usually are required. For the district agents and 4-H club specialists, the advanced work may be in extension methods and organization, personnel work, group leadership, and community organization, while for the subject-matter specialist it may be in a specialized field.

ADVANCEMENT

Extension offers many opportunities for the willing, efficient worker to advance. The small-county worker who is outstanding may be promoted to a larger county. With additional training, she may be selected to be a district agent, state specialist, or to a 4-H position. She may advance to the position of state home economics leader. Furthermore, she will find opportunities in the extension service of other states. She may also qualify for a position in the federal government. Persons with extension experience also will have opportunities for employment in public relations work, in administrative positions with business and industry, with utility companies, or in foreign service.

ADVANTAGES AND DISADVANTAGES OF EXTENSION WORK

There are certain advantages in the extension field which students should understand before selecting a career. Work with extension offers continuous training while working, which in many cases may be equal to college course work. The work offers much variety and, for an enterprising worker, does not become monotonous. The county home economics agent works in a variety of situations. She has freedom in planning and organizing her work, and she can get the help that she needs from her supervisors and specialists. She has wide social contacts, and since she meets people in various stations of life, her own life takes on added interest. In most states, the Extension Service has good retirement policies. Many extension home economists continue in their profession after marriage.

Some may consider certain factors connected with extension as disadvantages. Because of the wide contacts of the extension agent, it is easy to get involved in too many community activities. Many groups in a community seek the help and cooperation of the extension agent. Although work time and night meetings are controllable by agents, some average one or more night meetings a week. Extension work also requires travel since the program is informal and not in a classroom. The continued expansion of work in a county will depend, to some extent, on the understanding and appreciation felt by the people for the work that is carried out.

WHAT THE POSITION PAYS

The salaries and operating expenses of extension personnel vary in states. Most states involve federal, state, and county funds in support of the work. On the whole, extension salaries are good. They usually are equal to or somewhat better than the prevailing salaries for teachers in the same areas.

Table 6–1 will give students some idea of the remuneration to expect as an extension worker.

Table 6-1
National average salaries of home economics extension personnel—1970

	high	low	average
Home economics agent—county	$21,714	$ 5,880	$ 9,831
4-H agent—county	17,539	6,200	9,412
State specialist	20,647	6,000	12,108
State leader of home economics	23,400	12,620	15,524

Source: U.S. Department of Agriculture, Extension Service.

INTEREST CHECKLIST FOR EXTENSION

Listed below are a number of activities in which extension workers engage. As you read each statement, check on the right-hand side the degree to which you would enjoy this activity. Scoring instructions are given at the end of the checklist.

activities	degree of interest			
	much	average	little	score
1. Demonstrate to leaders the use of a stove, food preparation, or the care of equipment or clothing.	_____	_____	_____	_____
2. Develop programs and see that they are carried out.	_____	_____	_____	_____
3. Work with individuals of different ages, from different types of homes.	_____	_____	_____	_____
4. Write articles for newspapers or magazines.	_____	_____	_____	_____
5. Discuss with people their home-making problems.	_____	_____	_____	_____
6. Organize a contest for young people's participation.	_____	_____	_____	_____
7. Give radio talks on things of interest to homemakers.	_____	_____	_____	_____
8. Appear on television programs.	_____	_____	_____	_____
9. Meet with other home economists in planning a meeting or carrying through a project.	_____	_____	_____	_____
10. Write reports of activities, keep accounts of expenditures, and make reports to supervisors.	_____	_____	_____	_____
11. Participate in committees that are planning meetings, developing programs, or studying problems.	_____	_____	_____	_____
12. Give talks to women's or men's groups in the community.	_____	_____	_____	_____
13. Train homemakers or teen-agers to give lectures and demonstrations to groups.	_____	_____	_____	_____

activities	degree of interest			
	much	average	little	score
14. Talk with individual homemakers concerning problems of house improvement, care of children, etc.	_____	_____	_____	_____
15. Plan and direct the work of others, including the training of a secretary and other paid helpers such as aides.	_____	_____	_____	_____
16. Work with other agents in developing joint programs and activities.	_____	_____	_____	_____
17. Teach homemakers or youth how to conduct meetings and prepare reports.	_____	_____	_____	_____
18. Travel to various communities, meeting with different people and working with them.	_____	_____	_____	_____
19. Interview prospective workers, discussing their qualifications for jobs.	_____	_____	_____	_____
20. Learn about new research findings and apply them to homemaking activities.	_____	_____	_____	_____
21. Answer questions about homemaking problems, make suggestions about new ways of doing things or new approaches to problems.	_____	_____	_____	_____
22. Help plan and conduct camps for young people.	_____	_____	_____	_____
23. Live in a rural area where you associate with rural people.	_____	_____	_____	_____
24. Compile material for leaflets, leader lessons, etc.	_____	_____	_____	_____
25. Work with supervisiors to gain new ideas and on-the-job training.	_____	_____	_____	_____
Total score	_____			

Please score your interest chart in the following way. Give a score of 2 for each item checked "Much," a score of 1 for each item checked "Average," and 0 for each item checked "Little." If your total score for the 25 items is above 28, you have many of the interests needed for extension work. If you score 45 or above, you exhibit great interest in the activities associated with careers in home economics extension.

SUGGESTED ACTIVITIES

1. Plan a visit to the extension service of your land-grant college. Talk with the director of the extension service, the state home economics leader, the subject-matter specialists, and the district agent concerning appointments for home economics graduates with the state extension service.

2. Invite the county home economist nearest your college to visit your class. She can discuss with you various activities in which she engages and procedures for preparing for extension work. You may wish to spend a day with her to see extension work at first hand.

3. Write to your state extension service for materials on career opportunities in extension. You can get information on suitable training, salaries in your state, procedures for applying for positions with extension, etc.

4. Ask your county home economist for the names of some of the local leaders in your area. Invite some of these women to your class so that they may tell you what extension work has done for them. Also they can tell you the accomplishments of homemaker groups in your area. This can give you some idea of what home economics extension work accomplishes.

5. If you have been a 4-H club girl, you will know something of the work. If not, talk with fellow students who have had several years in 4-H club work. What did they learn through 4-H activities? What did these contacts mean to them? Looking over the record books of outstanding 4-H members will give you insight into this work.

6. During the summer, visit a 4-H club camp in your state. Or better still, offer your services to the camp during a summer. You may be able to be a counselor, to help with the food preparation, to teach crafts, etc. At camp you will see one side of the 4-H club work for boys and girls. Also, you will have the opportunity to meet and talk with 4-H club members, home economists, and agricultural extension leaders, and see how they work together.

7. Most states have statewide meetings for members of homemakers' groups and 4-H clubs. By attending one of these conferences you would learn a great deal about extension work.

8. Arrange to join your local home economist when she trains leaders or paid assistants or does a TV show.

REFERENCES

1. Chronicle Occupational Briefs, *Extension Home Economist*, "Methods of Entry," Circular 192, Chronicle Guidance Publications, Inc., Moravia, N.Y., 1968.

2. Eddy, Edward Danforth, Jr., *Colleges for Our Land and Time,* Harper & Brothers, New York, 1957.

3. Home Economics Subcommittee of ECOP, *Extension Home Economics Focus,* MP81-5M-68, December 1967.

4. Kelsey, Lincoln Davis, and Hearne, Cannon Chiles, *Cooperative Extension Work,* Comstock Publishing Associates, 3d ed., Ithaca, N.Y., 1963.

5. *A People and a Spirit,* Report of the Joint USDA-NASULGC Study Committee on Cooperative Extension, Colorado State University Printing and Publications Service, Fort Collins, Colo. November 1968.

6. *Your Career as an Extension Agent,* U.S. Department of Agriculture, Federal Extension Service, Misc. Pub. 972.

7. Sanders, H. C.: *The Cooperative Extension Service,* Prentice-Hall, Inc., Englewood Cliffs, N.J., 1966.

7 CHILD DEVELOPMENT AND FAMILY RELATIONS

The interest of home economics in child development and family life is of long standing. It was one of the first fields to be concerned about the welfare of the family and is today the only field whose main purpose is that of *family improvement.* Most home economics students in colleges and universities study children and families irrespective of their major emphasis, and, in addition, many home economists are preparing for professional careers in this field. If you wish to work with children, youth, or families, positions in child development and family life may offer your best opportunities.

Home economists majoring in child development and family life would find employment in one of the following fields:

Positions in Child Development and Family Relationships

I. Education
    A. Nursery school
    B. Kindergarten
    C. Elementary school
    D. Schools for exceptional and handicapped children
    E. High school
    F. College
    G. Public and private agencies
II. Youth work
    A. Camp Fire Girls
    B. Girl Scouts
    C. 4-H clubs
    D. Recreational and leisure-time programs
        1. Community
        2. Governmental
        3. Private
        4. Church
III. Adult work
    A. Extension and homemaking teaching
    B. Parent education
    C. Community family-life programs
    D. Counseling or consultation
        1. Marriage and family counseling
        2. Child counseling
        3. Youth counseling
            a. With agencies
            b. With colleges
            c. Private practice

E. Social welfare
F. Personnel work
IV. Communications
   A. Journalism
   B. Radio
   C. TV
V. Research
   A. Private agencies
   B. Government agencies
   C. Colleges and universities

EDUCATION

The educational activities of home economists in child development and family relationships truly go "from the cradle to the grave." *Nursery school* teaching is a very popular career for those who enjoy working with young children (4, 11, 23, 31). The nursery school is an educational program for children between the ages of $2^{1}/_{2}$ and 5. It is designed for the systematic training of the social, emotional, physical, and intellectual faculties of small children.

The first nursery schools were established in England toward the end of the nineteenth century and later were introduced into the United States. By 1936, there were approximately 285 nursery schools in the United States, distributed among colleges, philanthropic institutions, and private and public schools. It is difficult to estimate how many nursery schools are in operation in the United States today. At the university level, most colleges of home economics, many departments of psychology and education, and many teacher-training institutions have nursery schools. There are many cooperative nursery schools in urban areas, and most communities of any size have both public and private nursery schools.

In Project Head Start, financed by the Community Action Program Funds, approximately three-quarter million four- and five-year-olds attend child development centers to prepare themselves for school entrance (25).

In a nursery school the children do not learn the three R's, but they learn to handle their bodies, to eat and enjoy many kinds of food, to relax and sleep at regular intervals, and to play with other children cooperatively and happily. Not everyone can be a good nursery school teacher; those wishing to teach in nursery schools must respect, enjoy, and have affection for children. They must be willing to gain a thorough knowledge of developmental levels, activities, and characteristics of children of nursery school age. They must acquire the type of perspective which enables recognition of normally desirable and undesirable behavior. They must develop the ability to bring out the best in children and to help them play and work with other children and adults happily and constructively. Nursery school teaching requires a dedication to children as the most important resource in the world (25).

The amount of education needed for nursery school teaching varies with the type of nursery school. A bachelor's degree with a major in child development and

Fig. 7-1 This preschool child is learning to set a table correctly in nursery school. (Courtesy of the Virginia Polytechnic Institute and State University)

nursery school education is a minimum that will qualify one for work in most community, church, welfare, public health, and private nursery schools. Also, this will be suitable for most nursery schools operated in hospitals, although some training in nursing techniques may be required in addition. For nursery schools located in colleges and universities, a master's or doctor's degree will be necessary. Many home economists have developed schools in their own homes or in cooperative neighborhood groups, and in this way they can carry on their career without leaving home (22).

In preparing for nursery school teaching, a thorough knowledge of children must be gained. Students should include psychology, sociology, and physiology in their courses, and, in addition, they should acquire a good grasp of child nutrition, children's clothing, child development, art and music for children, and some science. They must have knowledge of and experience with nursery school procedures and organization. They should have some knowledge of parent education. An understanding of household management, genetics, family relationships, and hygiene, plus a good general education, will aid the would-be nursery school teacher (38, 39).

Home economists trained for nursery school education may qualify for

Fig. 7-2 Preschool children are able to select food and serve themselves under wise supervision. (Courtesy of the Virginia Polytechnic Institute and State University)

kindergarten and elementary education with little additional work. The understanding of children acquired through nursery school study is invaluable in working with children in any age group. Students who wish to work with children from five to six years of age should add methods in kindergarten education to their courses. In the same way, a few additional courses in education will equip them to work with the elementary school child (13, 17, 21).

Working with young children is a very rewarding activity. One can watch not only the development of children's bodies but the awakening of their intellects and expansion of their personalities as well. Much of the training necessary for work with young children is also training for parenthood. There is no age barrier for directors or teachers in schools for young children, and the work tends to help one maintain a youthful outlook and perspective.

As in all fields, there are some disadvantages, such as suffering with children who become ill in school and meeting fairly strenuous physical demands. However, the rewards from the children in affection, admiration, and loyalty are a constant challenge to the best that is in a teacher.

In many communities, *schools for exceptional children* are being established.

Fig. 7-3 Constructing a jack-o'-lantern stimulates learning as well as develops skills on the part of nursery school children. (Courtesy of the Merrill-Palmer Institute)

The exceptional child is the one who differs from the normal child mentally, emotionally, physically, or socially. This includes children who are gifted, unstable, retarded, disturbed, blind, deaf, or crippled. A thorough understanding and appreciation of these differences and their meaning for normal living is required for working with the exceptional child. A teacher needs to have warmth, understanding, intelligence, humor, and objectivity when working with the child who is different. The satisfactions of doing this type of work result from the challenge and opportunity to "uncork" minds, to work to overcome handicaps, and to develop happy, productive persons. This work offers much freedom to experiment in a new and challenging field (8, 10, 27).

Family-life education in the high school offers many opportunities for trained home economists. These programs are of two types: (1) the teaching of child care and guidance and family relationships as a part of the home economics program in the secondary schools, and (2) teaching them as separate courses or units in marriage and family relationships. The purpose of family-life courses in high school is threefold: (1) to help students gain understanding of themselves and learn better ways of solving their own problems, (2) to encourage them to grow into maturity of understanding for marriage and parenthood, and (3) to help them become worthier members of their own families.

Fig. 7-4 Many types of materials are used with small children to stimulate their learning. Here, nursery school children are matching like numbers on dominoes. (Courtesy of the Merrill-Palmer Institute)

The family-life teacher in high school should have a thorough general knowledge of home economics. In addition, she should have special training in child development, family relationships, marriage, parenthood, sociology and other social sciences, adolescent psychology, genetics, health education, social arts, consumer education, sex education, and perhaps some knowledge of family law. From the standpoint of personality, the family-life teachers should be mature, objective, and normal in their point of view. They need to understand the decisions which young people are making and be able to help them in making these more wisely. They must enjoy working with young people and be able to see activities and problems from the student's point of view. They must be able to understand the points of view of both parents and teenagers. They need to know the community resources available to young people and help them make the most of these resources. For the home economist who chooses family-life teaching in high school, there are many rewarding challenges (19, 26, 30).

Most *colleges and universities* have teachers of both marriage and family-life education. The marriage-education courses usually are focused on dating, mate

Fig. 7-5 The nursery school teacher guides the learning of small children in many types of challenging experiences. (Courtesy of the Merrill-Palmer Institute)

selection, and preparation for marriage and parenthood. Education for family living tends to be broader and usually includes child development, family relations, home management, consumption problems, and family health and recreation. The home economist who wishes to prepare for college teaching must expect after finishing college to do graduate work leading to a master's degree and often a doctor's degree. This advanced training will include psychology, sociology, physiology, mental hygiene, eugenics, economics, parent education, and techniques of counseling. Some basic work in elementary psychiatry is helpful to the marriage and family-life teacher, for her purpose is not only that of imparting knowledge but also one of influencing attitudes and changing behavior (1, 2, 4).

The personal characteristics of the college teacher are similar to those for high school teaching. However, she will need additional knowledge of research as a basis for establishing course content and procedures (1, 3, 43).

Governmental services for children at both the state and local levels employ many home economists trained in child development, including health services, education, recreation, social services, protection against abuses of child labor, vocational counseling, and guidance. At the federal level most of these programs are administered through the Children's Bureau, the Office of Education, and the Public Health Service of the U.S. Department of Health, Education, and Welfare.

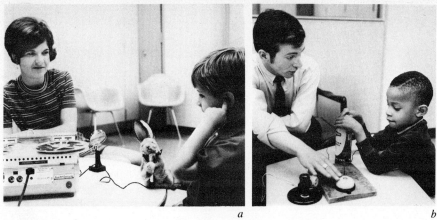

a   b

Fig. 7-6 (*a*) and (*b*) Students in family life and child development learn various types of testing. To obtain reliable results, testing requires much insight and skill on the part of the tester. (Courtesy of the Merrill-Palmer Institute)

YOUTH ACTIVITIES

If a home economist who is trained in family life prefers to work with youth, there are several fields from which to choose. The field directors with the *Camp Fire Girls* work with community groups and volunteer leaders. The Camp Fire program is designed to help girls seven to eighteen years of age participate in group activities, practicing democracy as they learn by doing. The qualifications for such a position are at least a bachelor's degree with training in child development, family relationships, homemaking skills, arts and crafts, health and physical education, plus a good general education.

The *Girl Scout* organization has positions as directors of girl scouting. They work with volunteer men and women to develop scouting in a community, train and supervise group leaders, direct or assist at summer camps, and work with other agencies in planning for the youth of a community. The qualifications for professional scouting are similar to those for Camp Fire work.

The *4-H club* program is extension's work with young people. Since the 4-H programs are carried on in all of the states and Territories of the United States, they furnish many opportunities for home economists. The 4-H club program is developed for boys and girls between the ages of ten and twenty-one years of age. Its extent may be indicated by the fact that there are over 2 million boys and girls enrolled in the 4-H clubs of this country. The purpose of the work is to help young people develop their talents for greater usefulness, learn to live and work with friends and family members, learn many of the skills associated with homemaking, develop leadership, share community responsibility, and try to build a stronger and healthier nation.

Extensions program for young men and young women, known as the YMW, is directed to young people approximately eighteen to thirty years of age whose interests and needs have matured beyond the 4-H club but have not reached the adult level. This program is a joint effort of all extension workers.

Many communities have *youth recreation* programs under the auspices of the YWCA or the departments of welfare, education, or public health (22). Others may be administered by churches, civic organizations, and private foundations. Provision for recreation and leisure time is a function of all youth programs and includes camping, tours, folk games, handicraft, sports, nature study, improvement of home grounds, field trips, and participation in community events that are both educational and recreational.

In all fields of work with youth, the personal qualifications necessary for success are concern for the welfare of others, regardless of race or creed, enthusiasm, initiative, resourcefulness, good health, belief in the individual and in the democratic process, and ability to help others set suitable goals and gain the inspiration to work toward them.

There are many advantages in youth-organization work. It is especially rewarding to those who are interested in serving and guiding youth. It offers an opportunity to work with all kinds of people, to help youth grow in character and wisdom, and to enjoy travel in various parts of this country and the world. The work abounds in prestige and dignity.

Disadvantages may be found in the fact that work with youth is demanding, and much of it must be done at times when those following other careers are enjoying their families. There are many opportunities for advancement, but their acceptance may require pulling up roots and moving away from friends, relatives, and the home town. However, many of these disadvantages may be found in other fields.

ADULT WORK

Today we find adults participating in educational programs in family living in numbers not even dreamed of a generation ago (6, 28, 31). They are enrolled in classes taught by the home economics teacher, the county home economist or family-life specialist of the state extension service, the community parent-education leader or family-life coordinator, or a representative of the PTA, the YWCA, the churches, or other civic groups. This interest in adult family-life education is understandable when the many factors which affect families today are considered. The help which the homemakers are seeking from family-life personnel spans life's problems from infancy to old age (20).

The family-life programs mentioned above offer unlimited opportunities to

Fig. 7-7 These children are doing screen painting in a summer camp. Home economists who have majored in child development and family life are in demand as camp teachers and counselors. This student is getting camp experience as she prepares herself for professional work. (Courtesy of the Merrill-Palmer Institute)

home economists trained in child development and family life. To qualify for such work requires at least a bachelor's degree in home economics with special training in personality development, adult education, counseling, and the group process, plus specialized training in child development and family relationships. There are many advantages for those who train for family-life work with adults. The career training provides excellent preparation for marriage and community leadership. It provides outlets for part-time work after marriage if desired, and employment is available in all areas of the country. Advancement is rapid for the well-qualified person, and the positions carry prestige. Opportunities for meeting a wide variety of people are provided, and salaries usually are good.

COUNSELING

A counselor is an adviser with specialized knowledge in one or more specific areas (9). The chief purpose of a counselor is to help people live more successfully by helping them interpret their needs and make plans for meeting them. The broad background of the home economist makes her especially suitable for counseling if she acquires the specialized training. Special counseling training is available in the departments of psychology and education in many universities (2, 42).

Many of the problems brought to family-life counselors concern needs and practices of children and youth, household management, money, family, marital or parent-child relationships, and family-community problems. Those hoping to go into counseling should expect to have graduate training; they should be familiar with the general teachings relating to marriage and family life to be found in biology, psychology, economics, law, medicine, and sociology. They must be able to interpret related sciences as they bear upon marriage and family living and be willing to keep up with the applicable research in all these sciences. In addition, knowledge of counseling procedures and the ability to adapt these to individual clients must be gained. An understanding, sympathetic, and friendly personality is necessary for success in counseling, as are a genuine interest in people, objectivity, and basic curiosity. Furthermore, the counselor must be able to put forward a good appearance and be easily approached (1, 3, 32, 43).

Most large business agencies and institutions have personnel specialists to interview and counsel employees or staff members. They are often the contact persons between the administration and the workers, interpreting the workers' needs to the leaders and the policies of the firm or institution to the workers (31).

Most colleges and many schools have departments of guidance and counseling. Usually these departments are responsible for the student testing programs. They also carry on personal, academic, and vocational counseling with the students. The requirements for this work are similar to those for work as a general counselor.

SOCIAL WORK

Students interested in raising the general level of living through their own and community resources will do well to investigate the opportunities for home economists in social welfare or public assistance agencies. Not only an understanding of children and family life but a broad background in foods and nutrition, family economics, home management, clothing and textiles, and housing make the home economist especially qualified to work with people in need. Most welfare agencies have home economists on the staff to consult with their social workers; the case worker looks to the home economist as subject-matter consultant in all aspects of family management. The home economist also helps to formulate policies on assistance.

Upon graduation from college many home economists trained in child development and family life enter the social welfare field as case workers. For promotion, however, graduate training in social case work with supervised field practice in a welfare agency is necessary. Many students prefer to get a few years of experience before doing graduate study in social work, and there are many scholarships available for capable people who wish to take advantage of the graduate training that is available (5, 18).

A new career development program for social work graduates is now in effect in the Welfare Administration's Bureau of Family Service. The program offers a two-year accelerated work-training internship leading to a professional career in public welfare administration. Starting salaries while in training are around $8,000 and upon completion of training the salaries range from $10,619 to $17,055 (18).

COMMUNICATION

Radio, TV, and journalism provide interesting careers for child-development and family-life majors who are able to write, speak, or dramatize (29, 34). Most radio and TV stations are seeking good family and children's programs that will interest and help their listeners. These may take many forms: interviews, plays, talks, demonstrations, forums, story hours, etc.

Many magazines carry family-life features regularly, and some have editors for their departments of family counseling or family aids. Many newspapers carry articles or columns regularly on feeding and care of children, training and guidance of children, or youth problems, and the question-and-answer department in newspapers and magazines is familiar to many readers.

The making of family-life films designed for use by adults or youth requires many family-life specialists. The production of pamphlets or bulletins on family life and child development is a part of the services of most educational institutions and agencies.

To enter the communications field, one should have, in addition to her basic knowledge of child development, family relationships, and marriage, training and experience in writing and journalism, photography, and voice and diction. Some training and experience in dramatics, plus technical training in the communications media to be used, are assets to the person wishing to enter these fields.

RESEARCH

In modern society, knowledge is becoming indispensable in every phase of family living. The home economist must study the family and its members in order to have the information necessary to improve family life; such research answers the needs of homemakers for information that will enable them to do a better job. Knowledge of ways to improve the activities of the home and the factors which affect these activities is necessary for training men and women for family life and marriage. The care and training of children in the modern world bring into relief many questions, the answers to which home economists are seeking (16).

Although the research programs carried on by home economists in child development and family life have lagged behind research in many other areas, most states have some research under way. In addition, many of the private foundations that are conducting research on the family offer employment opportunities for home economists (38, 40).

Anyone who wishes to do research in child development and family relationships should have a thorough knowledge of the family, the child, and marriage; and a good background in the social and biological sciences and in psychology. Also, one should know research methods and have supervised experience in research. Graduate study leading to a doctor's degree is necessary for advancement in research positions.

A career as a home economist who works with children, youth, and families can carry one into varied fields, many of which are mentioned in the foregoing pages. Whether one decides to be a teacher, a youth leader, a counselor, a writer, a radio lecturer, a TV dramatist, a researcher, or an administrator in child development and family life there are many rewarding opportunities open. As a homemaker and parent, training in this field is indispensable, and opportunities are always available in the community for part-time volunteer work in which one's special training and knowledge can be put to use.

WHAT THE JOB PAYS

The salaries paid to persons working in the fields of child development and family life vary greatly. The salaries paid to nursery school teachers are comparable to those of elementary school teachers; however, if the nursery school teacher is on the college staff, her salary will be commensurate with that of other staff members. Those who go into social work, teaching, or youth work will find that the salaries vary from one part of the country to another. In communications, one's income depends upon her ability to sell her services to the public.

CHECKLIST FOR INTERESTS
IN CHILD DEVELOPMENT AND FAMILY LIFE

Listed below are a number of activities associated with the child development and family-life field. After reading each item listed at the left of the page, check in the appropriate right-hand column your degree of interest in the work described. Instructions for scoring your responses are given at the end of the checklist.

activities	degree of interest		
	much	average	little
I. Education:			
1. Read stories to children.	————	————	————
2. Write stories and plays for children or youth.	————	————	————
3. Develop and direct games for children.	————	————	————

activities	degree of interest		
	much	average	little
4. Take care of children.	_____	_____	_____
5. Explain new ideas to children.	_____	_____	_____
6. Help a handicapped child achieve his goal.	_____	_____	_____
7. Discuss family and personal problems with associates.	_____	_____	_____
8. Study different types of families to understand their strengths and weaknesses.	_____	_____	_____
9. Plan family activities suitable to different families.	_____	_____	_____
10. Answer questions that associates have about their families and friends.	_____	_____	_____
11. Teach high school students how to make a good appearance, how to make friends, etc.	_____	_____	_____
12. Teach high school students how to select a suitable mate.	_____	_____	_____
13. Read books and research studies about family life and marriage.	_____	_____	_____
14. Direct a nursery school or kindergarten for children.	_____	_____	_____
15. Help college students make plans for marriage.	_____	_____	_____
Score for Section I	_____		

II. Youth work:

	much	average	little
1. Direct a playground for children.	_____	_____	_____
2. Train 4-H club girls, Girl Scouts, etc., for contests at fairs, etc.	_____	_____	_____
3. Judge contests where young people are participating.	_____	_____	_____
4. Lead discussions on youth problems, such as what to do on dates, where to go, etc.	_____	_____	_____
5. Plan parties for young people.	_____	_____	_____
6. Advise young people about their problems.	_____	_____	_____
7. Teach young people to dance or take part in social activities.	_____	_____	_____
8. Work with young people on arts-and-crafts projects.	_____	_____	_____
9. Supervise hikes and field trips for young people.	_____	_____	_____
10. Solicit funds for recreational programs for young people.	_____	_____	_____
11. Work with young people in remodeling a room, decorating a lounge, etc.	_____	_____	_____
12. Teach classes in swimming or other sports.	_____	_____	_____
13. Have young people to drop by your home for visiting, snacks, etc.	_____	_____	_____
14. Assist in or manage a summer camp for young people.	_____	_____	_____

activities	degree of interest		
	much	average	little
15. Attend planning meetings with young people.	_____	_____	_____
Score for Section II	_____		
III. Adult work:			
1. Give talks on family life before women's clubs, civic, and professional groups.	_____	_____	_____
2. Help church or civic groups develop programs on family life.	_____	_____	_____
3. Advise with parents concerning problems of their children.	_____	_____	_____
4. Help homemakers in low-income families live on a higher level.	_____	_____	_____
5. Help families get the type of medical or financial help needed.	_____	_____	_____
6. Work with a parent in helping a child overcome a problem.	_____	_____	_____
7. Organize and develop a recreational program for children.	_____	_____	_____
8. Work with persons of a different race or religion.	_____	_____	_____
9. Organize committees to carry through family-life projects.	_____	_____	_____
10. Help a family make out a budget for its family income.	_____	_____	_____
11. Help a community group plan family-life activities for their families.	_____	_____	_____
12. Coordinate the work for families in the various agencies in the community.	_____	_____	_____
13. Train leaders to work with adults and adult groups in family life.	_____	_____	_____
14. Counsel with parents or adults to help them meet their problems more adequately.	_____	_____	_____
15. Demonstrate better methods of handling children or meeting problems in the family.	_____	_____	_____
Score for Section III	_____		
IV. Communications:			
1. Conduct a story hour on TV for small children.	_____	_____	_____
2. Dramatize a child's story over TV.	_____	_____	_____
3. Write stories for children and illustrate them.	_____	_____	_____
4. Give a talk on the radio about how to meet some family problems.	_____	_____	_____
5. Interview couples or families on the radio or TV concerning family activities.	_____	_____	_____
6. Write stories for publication in magazines about children, families, or youth.	_____	_____	_____
7. Write a column in the newspapers on youth or family problems.	_____	_____	_____

activities	degree of interest		
	much	average	little
8. Read the articles on marriage and family relationship appearing in the magazines.	_____	_____	_____
9. Prepare crossword puzzles for children or youth.	_____	_____	_____
10. Direct children's plays or activities for the entertainment of others.	_____	_____	_____
11. Read the family advice columns in newspapers or magazines.	_____	_____	_____
12. Arrange displays of children's toys or books.	_____	_____	_____
13. Give a demonstration on how to make toys.	_____	_____	_____
14. Put on a play about family life using teen-agers.	_____	_____	_____
15. Select books for children or young people to read.	_____	_____	_____
Score for Section IV	_____		

To score your interest responses, give a value of 2 for each item checked "Much," and 1 for each item checked "Average." A score of 20–30 indicates considerable interest in any one area. A total score of 80–120 indicates high interest in child development and family life as a career.

SUGGESTED ACTIVITIES

1. Study the programs for children that are supported by private organizations in your community and then answer the following questions. Some of the organizations which should be studied are the churches, the civic groups, and women's clubs.

a. What is the purpose of the program?
b. What does it do for children?
c. What is the cost of the program?
d. For whom is the program designed?
e. How extensive is the program?
f. Are some children included in many programs and others not included in any?

2. Find out how many recreational programs for children and youth are in your community? How are they financed? Who are the leaders of the programs? What training have they had? Would you enjoy doing this type of work?

3. How many nursery schools do you have in your state? In your county? Do you have a Head Start Program? Do you have play schools and day nurseries in

addition to the nursery schools? Visit a well-organized nursery school to observe the activities carried on. What type of training do the teachers have?

4. Are there schools for exceptional or handicapped children in your locality? How could one trained in child development improve the conditions provided for these children?

5. Visit a counseling center for marriage or family life. Ask the counselor about some of her cases. What types of family problems are brought to her for help? How many of her clients are young people? How was the counselor trained for counseling? What are the advantages and disadvantages of counseling as a career as seen by the counselor?

6. Find out how many of the high schools in your state have courses in family-life or marriage preparation. If courses are not given, to what extent are these subjects taught in home economics classes?

REFERENCES

1. Albert, Gerald, "Advanced Psychological Training for Marriage Counselors—Luxury or Necessity," *Journal of Marriage and Family Living*, vol. 25, pp. 181–183, May 1963.

2. Albert, Gerald, "A Survey of College Counseling Facilities," *Personnel and Guidance Journal*, vol. 46, pp. 540–543, February 1968.

3. Allen, James E., "Training for Family Planning Counseling," *The Family Coordinator*, vol. 18, pp. 70–75, January 1969.

4. Bartuskava, Maria, "Nurseries in the Czechosland Socialist Republic," *Childhood Education*, vol. 42, pp. 92–95, October 1965.

5. Beck, Bertram M., *A Definitive Study of Your Future in Social Work*, Richard Rosen Press, Inc., New York, 1963.

6. Berger, Miriam E., "The Continuous Parent Education Group," *The Family Coordinator*, vol. 17, pp. 105–107, April 1968.

7. Beyer, Alan E., and F. Ivan Nye, "Family Life Education in Florida Public High Schools," *Journal of Marriage and Family*, vol. 26, pp. 182–187, May 1964.

8. Caldwell, Bettye M., and Julius B. Richmond, "Programmed Day Care for the Very Young Child," *Journal of Marriage and the Family*, vol. 26, pp. 487–488, November 1964.

9. Carkhuff, Robert, and Bernard G. Berenson, "The Counselor Is a Man and a Woman," *The Personnel and Guidance Journal*, vol. 48, pp. 24–27, September 1969.

10. *Childhood Education*, "Focus on Nursery School, Kindergarten, Primary, Intermediate," vol. 41, pp. 478–479, 484, May 1965.

11. Christianson, Helen M., Mary M Rogers, and Blanche A. Ludlum, *The Nursery School: Adventure in Living and Learning*, Houghton Mifflin Company, Boston, 1961.

12. Crow, Maxine S., "Preventive Intervention through Parent Group Education," *Social Casework,* vol. 48, pp. 161–165, March 1967.

13. Dager, Edward Z., Glen A. Harper, and Robert N. Whitehurst, "Family Life Education in Public Schools: A Survey Report on Indiana," *Journal of Marriage and the Family,* vol. 24, pp. 355–360, November 1962.

14. Dumphy, Cornelia, "Qualifications for Home Economists in Welfare Agencies," *Journal of Home Economics,* vol. 43, pp. 272–273, April 1951.

15. Dunlap, Richard S., "Employment and Compensation Practices for Counselors," *The Journal of Personnel and Guidance,* vol. 47, pp. 744–750, June 1969.

16. Duvall, Evelyn Millis, "Research Finds," *Journal of Marriage and the Family,* vol. 23, pp. 49–50, February 1961.

17. Eckerson, L. O., "Realities Confronting Elementary School Counseling," *Personnel and Guidance Journal,* vol. 46, pp. 350–354, December 1967.

18. "Federal Employment Opportunities for Recent Social Work Graduates," *Journal of Home Economics,* vol. 58, p. 385, August 1966.

19. Gauker, Norma S., "The High School Teacher as Counselor," *Journal of Marriage and the Family,* vol. 28, pp. 298–303, May 1965.

20. Greene, John T., "Family Life Education at the Church-Community Level," *Journal of Marriage and the Family,* vol. 13, pp. 100–101,141, Summer 1951.

21. Hawley, Alice Hadley, "Home Economics Experiences for the Elementary Level," *Journal of Home Economics,* vol. 54, p. 239, April 1962.

22. Highberger, Ruth, "Nursery Education in Home Economics," *Journal of Home Economics,* vol. 52, pp. 437–440, June 1960.

23. Henriksen, Grethe, "Danish Recreation Homes for Young Children," *Childhood Education,* vol. 45, pp. 457–459, April 1969.

24. Khan, Aftab Ahmad, "Child Development in Higher Education," *Childhood Education,* vol. 44, pp. 308–312, January 1968.

25. *Kindergarten Work as a Career,* The Institute For Research, Research No. 106, Chicago, 1964.

26. Kirkendall, Lester A., and Esther Handwerk, "Preparation of Teachers for Education in Marriage and Family Living," *Journal of Marriage and Family Life,* vol. 12, pp. 7–8, 19, Winter 1950.

27. Klaus, Rupert A., and Susan W. Gray, "Murfressboro Preschool Program for Culturally Deprived Children," *Childhood Education,* vol. 42, pp. 92–95, October 1965.

28. Kurtz, John J., "Family Life Education and Parent Education in Maryland," *Journal of Marriage and the Family,* vol. 28, pp. 531–532, November 1966.

29. McArthur, Arthur, "Missouri Specialists Take to the Air," *The Family Coordinator,* vol. 17, pp. 95–96, April 1968.

30. McElroy, Jay, "The Role of Guidance in the Home Economics Classroom," *Journal of Home Economics,* vol. 58, p. 49, January 1966.

31. Mandel, Nathan G., "Family Life Education in a Rural Community," *Journal of Marriage and the Family,* vol. 28, pp. 526–527, November 1966.

32. Moak, Franklin E., "The Anatomy of a Counselor," *Journal of College Placement*, vol. 25, pp. 49–52, December 1964.

33. *Nursery School Operation as a Career*, The Institute For Research, Research No. 214, Chicago, 1967.

34. Pennell, Ellen, "Home Economics on Television," *Journal of Home Economics*, vol. 45, pp. 253–256, April 1952.

35. Read, Katherine H., *The Nursery School*, pp. 20–21, W. B. Saunders Company, Philadelphia, 1955.

36. Rioux, J. William, "Economic Opportunity Act and Elementary and Secondary Act of 1965," *Childhood Education*, vol. 42, pp. 92–95, October 1965.

37. *Careers in Professional Social Work*, The Institute for Research, Research No. 43, Chicago, 1966.

38. Sperry, Irwin V., "Cooperative Research in Family Life," *Journal of Home Economics*, vol. 44, pp. 177–180, March 1952.

39. Stith, Marjorie, and Ruth Hoeflin, "Preschool Teacher Certification," *Journal of Home Economics*, vol. 59, pp. 371–373, May 1967.

40. Tate, Mildred T., "Family Life Research for Home Economists," *Journal of Home Economics*, vol. 41, pp. 182–184, April 1949.

41. Trapman, John E., "The Married Professional Social Worker," *Journal of Marriage and the Family*, vol. 30, pp. 661–665, November 1968.

42. Vermilye, Dyckman, and Glenda Hightower, "Financial Aid for Guidance and Personnel Graduate Study, 1969–1970," *The Journal of Personnel and Guidance*, vol. 47, pp. 473–476, January 1969.

43. Vincent, Clark E., "The Training of Professional and Subprofessional Personnel as Adjunctive Marriage Counselors: Opportunities and Dilemmas," *The Family Coordinator*, vol. 18, pp. 217–221, July 1969.

ADDITIONAL READINGS

Forbes, Grace S., "Some Observations on Family Life Education in India," *Journal of Marriage and the Family*, vol. 25, pp. 466–468, November 1963.

Force, Elizabeth S., "The Role of the School in Family-Life Education," *Journal of Marriage and the Family*, vol. 26, pp. 99–101, February 1964.

Home Economics Careers in Health and Welfare, American Home Economics Association, Washington, 1965.

Spencer, Lucille B., "Our Professional Attributes," *Journal of Home Economics*, vol. 54, pp. 537–540, September 1962.

8 CLOTHING, TEXTILES, AND APPLIED ART

The fashion business today is one of the leading industries in the United States; in fact, it is *the* leading industry in the city and state of New York, and it is still growing. Its influence is felt in every city of the world. It employs workers with every degree of skill, and pays salaries that range from minimum wage to the upper one-tenth of 1 percent of incomes in this country. Furthermore, it is one of the largest employers of women (2).

What opportunities are open to young women and men who major in clothing, textiles, and applied art? This question is difficult to answer, for the field of employment is very large and has many facets. The four major types of positions and their subdivisions are listed below. In each of these there are many types of jobs with varying requirements for success.

Positions in Clothing and Textiles

I. Designing
    A. Designer
        1. Fabrics
        2. Garments
        3. Accessories
    B. Fashion illustrator
II. Production
    A. Patternmaker
    B. Fabric buyer
    C. Draper
    D. Cutter
    E. Training director
    F. Stylist
III. Distribution
    A. Retailing
        1. Executive
            a. Owner of store
            b. President of store
        2. Buyer
        3. Merchandise manager
        4. Salesperson
        5. Personal shopper
        6. Consultant
            a. Bridal shop
            b. Interior decorating department

            c. College board
            d. Others
    B. Promotion
       1. Advertising agent
          a. Store
          b. Newspaper
          c. Radio
          d. Television
       2. Display manager
       3. Copy writer
       4. Illustrator
       5. Art director
       6. Account executive
       7. Fashion editor
       8. Fashion coordinator
       9. Training director
     10. Model
IV. Education
    A. Teacher
       1. College
       2. Technical school
       3. High school
       4. Adult education
    B. Researcher
       1. College or university
       2. Industry
       3. Government
    C. Reporter
       1. Journalism
       2. Television
       3. Radio

There are several terms that the professional in clothing and textiles must know, irrespective of his field of employment. These are "fashion," "style," "vogue," and "fad." *Fashion* is the accepted manner of dressing, living, entertaining, or traveling adopted by groups of people at a particular time. It is concerned not only with objects used by consumers of clothes, furniture, and household appliances but with systems of government and ideologies.

Style is much narrower in meaning than fashion. The style of a thing lies in the distinctive characteristics that make it different from others of its kind. In clothing, the word "style" refers to the silhouette, fabric, color, decoration, trim, or accessories used at a particular time or identified with a particular group of people. A style is a constant; it remains static. A fashion is a style accepted by a sizable number of people. It represents what people at a given time want, buy, and use. For instance, wide-skirted gowns worn over large hoops were a style of the 1860s. Debutantes, college girls, and young matrons in 1950 found gowns of this type appealing and romantic. Therefore, the style of the 1860s was again in fashion.

Vogue means a style that is extremely popular at a certain moment, and a *fad* is a minor style that is popular for a limited time but is never accepted by more than a few people. The person working in the clothing and textile field must be very sensitive to the trends that produce fashions, styles, vogues, and fads.

DESIGNING

Designing is a process by which something new is created. It culminates in original work. The individual, when designing, creates or adapts styles that become fashionable. There are two major positions in designing: the *designer* and the fashion *illustrator* (2, 8, 15).

Many young women express interest in becoming designers. It is one of the highest-paid positions in the clothing and textile field, but it is one of the most difficult to enter and be successful in (5, pp. 623–674). Often young men or women who have some talent in drawing feel that they will do well in designing, but they do not realize that a designer must be able to do much more than draw pictures. Talent, ability, courage, determination to work, and a knowledge of fabrics, patternmaking, and historic costume are essentials. Equally important are the knowledge of how to make a garment, hat, or shoe so that it can be worn and the ability to give an interpretation in line, color, and material that is acceptable for the time and market for which it is presented (8). To design, one must have a sense for nice clothes, a feel for fabrics—how they act and how they drape, a knowledge of fit, and an understanding of the figure (8).

A good designer makes what people want by working in advance of the season. This requires the ability to predict the colors, fabrics, silhouettes, and trims that will be accepted. This ability in designing is called *timing*. It is an awareness, an acute sensitivity to changes in public taste. Accuracy and timing ensure a degree of success to competent designers. The creation of a collection three or four times a year from beginning to end is demanding.

Fashion designing is a small, highly competitive field that is hard to break into. Yet, for people who love to design clothes, it is constantly exciting. In the clothing industry, designers may work in the area of fabrics, garments, or accessories. A designer may do her own illustrations, or these may be done by someone else. The *fashion illustrator* makes drawings that exemplify or interpret the design for a pattern or fabric. She draws the fashion illustrations found in the daily newspapers. She makes the sketches for the magazines, the advertisements, the booklets on fashion that you receive through the mail. She interprets the "new look"; illustrates the catalogs, and captures the fashionable silhouette (2). The designer may be employed by an advertising art studio that handles the art work for several firms or by the advertising department of a large department store. On the other hand, the employer may be a pattern company where drawings are needed of figures used on pattern

Fig. 8-1 Designing may become a very challenging career for those who are creative. (Courtesy of the Virginia Polytechnic Institute and State University)

envelopes, in pattern books, or on large posters. The designer may be on the staff of some fashion or trade publication or women's magazine.

Any student who is thinking of becoming a designer or fashion illustrator should consider, when planning her courses in college, the following (2, 8, 15):

1. A knowledge of fabrics or textiles is a necessity. This includes knowledge of the names, character, "hand," cost, and available colors of fabrics suitable for the types of garments to be designed. Thus a designer of coats must be completely familiar with the materials available for coats in the price range suitable for the factory, as well as the special qualities of these materials.

2. A thorough knowledge of clothing construction is essential in designing. One must know how garments go together, what lines look like in a garment, and the degree of difficulty the design presents in construction.

3. The designer of wearing apparel must understand the human body. This includes a knowledge of body structure, bones, muscles, and the effects of activity on clothing. To be worn, clothing must be constructed in such a way that the wearer can move his arms, walk, stoop, and sit comfortably without destroying the grace of the garment.

4. A thorough grounding in art fundamentals is essential in designing. Also, a knowledge of the principles of geometry and the use of drawing instruments is necessary.

5. The ability to forecast or predict the trends in style is essential. To do this, one must be keenly sensitive to social, political, and economic developments. One must be alert to what is happening in the arts—in music, painting, sculpture, the theater, ballet, and the movies. The sports world, international exhibitions, archeological findings, and similar events may dictate style, and the designer must be aware of them. To gain such knowledge requires an understanding of the social and political sciences, as well as of psychology and family life.

6. Designers must have the rare ability of selecting exactly the right fabric, weight, and color for each design. Designers work like composers. They must have something to say in color, silhouette, fabric, and theme that is acceptable and pleasing. Working in the various art mediums with textiles and patterns helps develop this sensitivity.

7. To succeed, designers must know people's needs and interests. They must be able to decide ahead of time whether women want long or short evening gowns and whether they will accept short or long coats, pencil-slim or full skirts. Furthermore, they must be able to design for the working girl, the teen-age girl, the society lady, and the housewife. Retailing experience, organizational work, or any group activity helps students to learn to know people.

8. Designers must ever be able to get new inspirations for designs. These may come by observing people in their everyday activities, by studying the native costumes of people of other cultures, by re-analyzing the costumes of the past, or by observing nature.

9. Designers must have experience; the only way to learn to design is to design. Not only must they have experience in designing but they should have as many experiences with clothing as possible. Home economics students can get experience through designing their own clothes, as well as those of relatives and friends. They can supervise a tailor or dressmaker who caters to special persons, or they can obtain a position with a small factory as an apprentice on a part-time or summer basis. They should get as much technical training as time will permit, including clothing construction, flat pattern and draping, costume

shop experience, fashion illustration, managing and producing of fashion shows, etc. In most colleges these experiences are available to the enterprising student.

10. Patience is a special need of a would-be designer. Often it is a long climb to the top, and one of lesser perseverance will fall by the way. Furthermore, those wishing to make a living through designing must be able to hold their own against aggressive personalities.

11. To be a good designer, one must have seen beautiful clothes worn with style, handled beautiful materials, and learned to enjoy the beauty of the past as it is displayed in museums.

12. A designer must have a place to work. This includes a workroom, money to buy the materials, a laboratory to produce the designs, a place to show the creations, and customers who will come to look and to buy. While gaining experience, the beginning designer may have to use an attic or her bedroom as the place where she designs and makes garments on a special-order basis.

In the United States, most designers are employed by the garment and pattern industries. These industries are highly specialized; not only will one factory make coats but in all probability it will produce only one price line of coats. The same is true of the other apparel articles. In Europe, a designer has usually operated as a small business, making complete wardrobes for a limited clientele. However, this is changing gradually to larger industries typical of the United States.

In order to become a designer in a factory, one may have to start as an apprentice. If the beginner is well trained in college and has ability in this field, her advancement will be fairly rapid as she learns the specific requirements of the industry.

Free-lance designers are those who design independently with the hope of selling their designs to small factories or exclusive shops. Although certain individuals have done very well "free-lancing," it is a very precarious way of making a living for a beginner. A reputation has to be established before one can depend on selling designs. There are also designers who have their own shops, where they design the articles and then hire workers to produce and sell them. These exclusive shops are found quite extensively in Europe and are not uncommon in the cities of this country.

PRODUCTION

Garment production is a colossal industry. Figures for 1966 indicated that the dress, suit, and coat industries for women alone were producing over 4 billion dollars worth of merchandise a year, and this is only one phase of the clothing and textile industry (17). The production field uses many types of employees (2), but perhaps the highest-paid worker in wholesale production is the *patternmaker.* The skill of the patternmaker determines her wages. She must be sufficiently skillful to make a salable garment from the design submitted, which is intricate and exacting work. The skill of the patternmaker determines the correctness of fit of the garment, as well as the ease of cutting and constructing the garment. Not all parts of a pattern can be drafted flat; some must be draped first on a form for best results; therefore a *draper* usually works with the patternmaker.

The patternmaker will have assistants who make various size ranges for each model. These *graders*, as they are called, may build the basic pattern into sizes from 10 to 20. Great care must be taken that the width of the shoulders, the depth of the armscye, the placing and depth of darts, the length of the waist, back, and sides, and the fall of the skirt are correct for each size. Next to patternmakers in order of importance in production come the *fabric buyers*. They must work very closely with the patternmakers, the business managers, and the stylists to ensure that the materials selected will be suitable for the patterns developed, the price range of the garments, and consumer appeal. They must know the market and be familiar with construction methods, colors, prices, and delivery.

The *cutter* in a clothing factory has much responsibility. A dressmaker cuts one garment at a time, but in a large factory which operates on a volume basis, a hundred garments may be cut at one time. The cutting room of a large factory has tables 40 to 50 inches wide and 8 to 20 yards long. The fabric is spread on this table in layers. To guide the cutter a "marker" or master pattern is made giving the arrangements of all the pieces for each size range. Great care in placing the pieces of the pattern on the cloth is taken to ensure the proper fall of the various pieces, the proper meeting of stripes and plaids, etc. (20).

The *training directors* or shop managers help develop skilled sewers and pressers so that the finished garments will be well constructed and have an appealing appearance. They must devise the correct procedures for sewing and finishing the garments, the details of pressing, aligning of buttonholes, and the addition of such items as buttons, fasteners, shoulder pads, and belts. They must work with the stylists to make sure that the correct trim appears on the dresses and that it is fashionable. Finally, they must see that the garments are inspected and ready for the buyer.

As the home economics student will realize, the clothing and textile industry is very complex, and there is much one must know before stepping into a responsible position in the field. The personal requirements for success in production are very similar to those for designing. Certainly a thorough knowledge of clothing construction and patternmaking is essential. The art and study of draping is of the first importance, for it teaches one how to work with materials, develop a rhythm of dress, and give an appreciation of the lines of the human body. In addition, production work in clothing requires a thorough knowledge of textiles and clothing economics as a background. An apprenticeship in the clothing industry is invaluable to a home economist who wishes to enter production.

Fig. 8-2 A home economist working in publicity and journalism has many challenges. She must have a thorough knowledge of her subject matter field in addition to her writing ability.

DISTRIBUTION

Distribution is divided into *retailing* and *promotion* (2, pp. 71–98; 8; 15, pp. 69–72). Before students can determine how much interest they have in careers in retailing, merchandising, or some phase of promotion, they must know what the fields have to offer.

Just what is retailing? The local grocer, baker, and yard-goods dealers are retailers. So are the chain stores, department stores, mail-order houses, and those that sell door to door. Retailing in clothing and textiles may be carried on through small stores, large department stores, specialty shops, or mail-order houses (5). A large department store employs several classes of workers. The *executive* may be the owner of the store, its president, or its manager. The store may have several departments, each of which may have a *merchandise manager,* a *buyer,* and *salespersons.* In addition there are *consultants* in such departments as the bridal shop, the interior decorating department, and the children's department whose function is to aid the consumers in making the correct choices. Many stores have a *college board.* These salespersons are especially qualified to help the young woman going away to college to select the correct wardrobe. Some stores have *fashion coordinators,* who are responsible for integrating the styles, colors, and materials in the various departments. Home economists may be found serving in all these capacities. Individuals trained in clothing and textiles usually do well as buyers, merchandise managers, personal shoppers, and consultants.

Retailing is a big field for ambitious women, and there are many advantages to the work (7). In the retail trade, women constitute nearly one-third of the managers and officials in apparel and accessories stores, and well over one-fifth in general merchandise and variety stores (9). Available information indicates that in department stores, the proportion of women executives is higher than in most other establishments of the general merchandising field. It is probably safe to assume, therefore, that somewhere between one-fourth and one-third are women (9). Retailing has many executive positions for those who have the determination and ability to move up (1, 13, 19). This is especially true in multiple-store operations, where women fill many of the executive positions. In fact, more than 46 percent of all retail executives are women. The retail store also offers wonderful opportunities for development and growth along a wide variety of lines because there are so many different divisions in the store. Furthermore, retailing is a field where individuals have an excellent chance to show what they can do and be recognized for it. To those who like to work with people or who enjoy seeing things move, retailing can be very rewarding and exciting. The retailer is always alerted to what is new and improved and is familiar with the details of the latest fashion trend. The privilege of seeing and handling the unusual is available. And for those who move to the top, retailing is very rewarding financially.

Retailing, however, has some disadvantages, as well. In many areas of the country, the beginning salaries in retailing are somewhat less than for comparable jobs in other businesses. This is partially offset for the well-trained person by the chance for more rapid advancement and by discounts on personal purchases. Some people object to the Saturday work and occasional nightwork of retailing; however, the work week does not exceed that in other occupations. Some college graduates feel that the beginning jobs in retailing do not carry sufficient prestige. Some retail organizations help this situation by having a formal training program where the title "trainee" is used. The beginner in any field of work where advancement is rapid must realize that a training period or apprenticeship is necessary before one can accept much responsibility.

What are the qualifications for entering the retailing field in clothing and textiles? Many of the factors or qualities that make for success in retailing are the same as for success in any field, but the following apply particularly to merchandising (2, pp. 71–98; 3; 14):

1. A genuine fondness for examining and working with the type of merchandise to be sold is important, for one cannot easily sell or promote something which does not interest her.

Fig. 8-3 Grace Richardson, Managing Editor of Publications in the Educational and Consumer Relations Department of the J. C. Penney Company, is conferring with an art director about the layout of one of the educational supplements. (Courtesy of the Educational and Consumer Relations Department of the J. C. Penney Company, Inc.)

2. A good personal appearance is an asset in all businesses, but especially so in the clothing field. It is difficult to encourage smartness in others if it is lacking in oneself. Good grooming includes neat and attractive hands and feet as well as attention to the hair, face, and dress.

3. Success in retailing requires physical stamina and the ability to work under pressure. All businesses and professions have periods of pressure, but this is especially true of executive positions in retailing.

4. Retailing requires the ability to make many pleasant and lasting contacts with people. It is very important to the store that the consumer return to buy again and again, and this will depend largely on the consumer's reaction to the store personnel.

5. Success in retailing requires initiative, ingenuity, aggressiveness, and decisiveness in the proper amount and at the right time. Being able to buy and sell requires almost "the sixth sense" of knowing when to insist and when to withdraw.

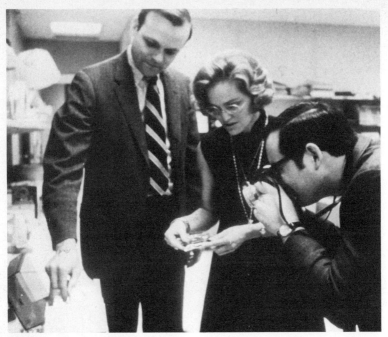

Fig. 8-4 Mrs. Carol Lindstrum, a home economist responsible for preparing educational materials in the Educational and Consumer Relations Department of the J. C. Penney Company, supervises the photography of electric hair curlers for one of the consumer buying guides. (Courtesy of the Educational and Consumer Relations Department of the J. C. Penney Company, Inc.)

6. An artistic sense is a wonderful asset in retailing. To be able to select or suggest just the right trim, hat, or dress which the customer's friends will admire builds confidence and sales.

7. The retailer should be able to sense and interpret in merchandise the needs of the customer.

8. Enthusiasm for one's work is important on any job. If the retailer can truly radiate zeal for the merchandise to the customer, sales are more easily made.

9. Last but not least, interest in retailing as a career is a must for advancement in the field. The person who plans to make a career in a field is ever alert to improve, to grow, and to develop.

Although few schools of home economics teach retailing, most home economics students can get basic preparation by entering the field. A good background in clothing selection and construction, textiles, and costume design is invaluable. Knowledge of economics, sociology, and psychology are necessary. Courses in distributive education (9, 16), advertising, salesmanship, and business organization are fine supplements to clothing and textile knowledge. Experience in retailing can be

Fig. 8-5 Linda Lucht, field home economist in the Educational and Consumer Relations Department of the J. C. Penney Company, is discussing artwork for a program to be presented to teachers in major cities throughout the United States. (Courtesy of the Educational and Consumer Relations Department of the J. C. Penney Company, Inc.)

obtained by all college students in the summer, at Christmas, or at other special times. With this background of knowledge and experience, the young person interested in retailing will find many challenging opportunities.

PROMOTION

Promotion work is very important in the clothing industry. It is the responsibility of the promotion department to bring the store or merchandise to the attention of the consumer. A large part of the promotion work falls to *advertising.* This may be done through the store, through newspapers and magazines, or by radio, TV, and various visual methods.

In a department store, the advertising department coordinates the various ready-to-wear departments for the consumer. The person who handles advertising must know how to collect the necessary information about the articles to be advertised, the buying habits of the people, and the policies of the store; she must, as well, be aware of special events which affect people's buying. In a large advertising or promotion department there are many different specialists (3; 5, pp. 623–674).

The *account executive* plans the broad pattern of the store's advertising program. *Copy writers* handle the actual wording of the advertisements. They are responsible for the catchy phrases and short, convincing descriptions found in advertising. The *art director* dictates the details of the layout and art work. The *photographers* or *artists* prepare the final art work. The *fashion reporter* writes articles for newspapers, women's magazines, fashion periodicals, trade publications, or pamphlets to alert the reader to the fashions to be found in the stores. The *space buyer* secures the required space in newspapers or magazines or the time on radio or TV. In a small store one person may perform all these duties.

The *fashion coordinators* see that the merchandise in the various departments can be assembled into a pleasing wardrobe. Furthermore, they see that the buying, advertising, and window and interior displays are in harmony. They are responsible for fashion shows and other consumer-education services.

Some of the really big positions in the promotion field of clothing and textiles are those of *fashion editors* for magazines or newspapers. The fashion editor must be an authority on fashion; this requires keeping in touch with leading designers here and abroad, knowing about new fabrics being produced, and being aware of garments and accessories new to the market. The fashion editor must understand the problems of merchandising and sense fashion trends in all parts of the country in which the magazine or newspaper is to be sold. This requires good organizational and executive sense, as well as the ability to work under pressure, for editorial work requires careful timing. Furthermore, the fashion editor must be able to write.

One field of work which appeals to many young women is that of *modeling*. Models usually display clothes in fashion shows, exclusive shops, manufacturers' showrooms, or for photographs. Anyone wishing to become a model must be willing to follow a strict regime, for modeling has rather rigid standards of health and appearance. A model must be striking in appearance, have poise and style, and be willing to retain these qualities.

Home economists are found in all areas of promotion in the clothing and textile field. Qualifications for the work are similar to those for distribution, as are the advantages and disadvantages. There is a place for a wide range of abilities in promotion, from the artist to the high-pressure business executive.

EDUCATION

Education in clothing and textiles is very important, for clothing has traditionally been one of man's primary needs. Throughout recorded history it has served as a means of protection and adornment. The outlay for clothing, accessories, and personal care in 1950 totaled 25 billion dollars; in 1969 this amount was over 69 billion dollars (18, p. 308). Although the expenditures for clothing, accessories, jewelry, and personal care were 13.7 percent of all personal consumer expenditures in 1951, it was only 12 percent in 1967 (18, p. 314).

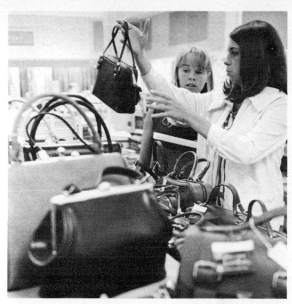

Fig. 8-6 Teaching students how to select clothing and accessories for quality and suitability is a function of the clothing teacher. (Courtesy of the Virginia Polytechnic Institute and State University)

Clothing and textile education should be keyed to the needs of our society (7). This responsibility falls to the educators at the college level, since they train the high school and adult education teachers, as well as many of the key people for industry.

Some of the oldest positions for well-trained home economists in the textile and clothing field will be found in education. These include teaching positions in colleges, universities, technical schools, and adult education programs such as extension and vocational home economics education. The dissemination of research findings and other information in clothing and textiles through pamphlets, bulletins, newspapers, and magazines, as well as through such media as radio and TV, has used the talents of many trained clothing and textiles persons.

All colleges that offer home economics have courses in clothing and textiles. In the larger colleges, many courses will be offered in these fields, culminating in a major in clothing and textiles and/or applied design (4).

In order to teach in a college, a master's degree with a major in clothing, textiles, or applied design—or a combination of these three—will be required, and more and more colleges and universities are requiring the doctor's degree. This means at least one to three years of college work beyond the bachelor's degree. Those who would select a career in teaching clothing and textiles must be thoroughly grounded in the field, including clothing selection, construction, and care, costume design, applied arts, textiles for clothing and the household, science applied to

Fig. 8-7 The business home economist must be able to handle many types of situations.

textiles, historic costume, clothing economics, sociology, and psychology. In addition they must know the general fundamentals of good teaching. The ability to build in the student a love for textiles and clothing, a feeling for good line and proportion in clothing, and the skill to execute ideas in fabrics are important for teachers. The teacher should keep in touch with newer findings in research and their application to the classroom. They should understand, for example, the characteristics and use of new fibers, or the effect of new treatments on old fibers. And they should be familiar enough with what is happening in industry to be able to orient students who wish to prepare for work in industry and make use of industrial procedures.

The college teacher of clothing and textiles, like other teachers, must have an intense interest in people. This includes an understanding of the way individuals of different backgrounds satisfy their clothing needs. The ability to express oneself well both in written and spoken English is also necessary. The teacher of clothing must be attractive in personal appearance and should have some knowledge of and experience in guidance. Creative talent and the ability to get along with others are essential for teachers.

Fig. 8-8 This business home economist is in the field of fashion designing. To be successful, she must have in addition to her designing ability a fashion sense, a thorough knowledge of clothing construction, and a feel for fabrics and how they handle as well as an understanding of the time and place for which she is designing.

Educators in the clothing and textile field must be concerned with the physical, social, and psychological aspects of clothing. This involves knowing the kinds and quantities of garments needed for various ages, incomes, vocations, and climates, and the ability to help people satisfy these needs on different income levels.

Technical schools employ many teachers in clothing and textiles. In order that their graduates can go directly into industry, these schools will be located in areas where there is a concentration of certain industries. For example, technical schools for design and fashion illustration will be found where there is a concentration of garment factories. Schools for training individuals in designing, weaving, or finishing textiles are in an area where the production of textiles is concentrated. In addition to these trade schools, however, there are a few professional schools where academic subject matter is combined with the trade-school preparation. Home economists in these schools teach many of the subjects they would teach in colleges, but everything is slanted to industry.

Some of the industries sponsor tours or workshops in the colleges for training home economists to teach in industry or for work with industry. Individuals who have college training in clothing and textiles can prepare for leadership in executive positions in industry through these special courses. Also, at many of the city colleges there are night classes which are designed to prepare students for industry (15). Enrolled in these night or special classes often are individuals who, having come up through the trade, hope to move into executive positions through additional schooling.

Adult education offers many opportunities for trained clothing and textiles personnel. In the field of home economics extension, clothing specialists are employed at the state and federal levels to help the county agents in developing adequate clothing programs for families. Requirements for clothing specialists are similar to those for college teaching. Usually a master's degree plus extension experience is needed, in addition to the general requirements for teaching. Clothing and textile specialists find employment in the adult education programs of home economics education and other special-interest groups, such as the YWCA.

REMUNERATION

What does the job pay? This is a question that concerns everyone who is thinking in terms of a career. In the clothing-and-textile business field, salaries and wages for the same position vary from one part of the country to another, as well as within an area for different sizes and types of establishments. Teachers of clothing and textiles will be paid the same as other teachers. In the designing and production fields salaries will range from $5,000 to $30,000. However, some executives will receive over $100,000. In promotion and communications, the salaries will range from $6,000 to approximately $30,000 per year.

INTEREST CHECKLIST FOR CLOTHING AND TEXTILES

Listed below are many types of jobs carried on by clothing and textile people. The jobs are listed under three divisions, namely, (1) designing and production, (2) distribution, and (3) education. On the right-hand side of the page are three columns headed "Much," "Average," and "Little." As you read each statement, decide how great your interest would be in this type of job, and place a check mark in the appropriate column. Directions for rating your interests are given at the end of the checklist. First check your degree of interest in all of the items, and then score them.

activities	degree of interest		
	much	average	little

I. Designing and production:
  1. Sketch costumes or make fashion plates. ____ ____ ____
  2. Plan materials and accessories for costumes. ____ ____ ____
  3. Select patterns for dresses, blouses, and skirts. ____ ____ ____
  4. Plan color schemes for wardrobes, including dresses, hats, coats, and accessories. ____ ____ ____
  5. Study fashion magazines. ____ ____ ____
  6. Study costumes of other peoples. ____ ____ ____
  7. Create interesting designs for fabrics. ____ ____ ____
  8. Design garments for different types of people. ____ ____ ____
  9. Plan and design costumes for a play. ____ ____ ____
  10. Select fabrics for different types of garments. ____ ____ ____
  11. Drape materials on dress forms. ____ ____ ____
  12. Plan and make dolls' clothes. ____ ____ ____
  13. Handle fabrics that are beautiful in design and texture. ____ ____ ____
  14. Study patterns to see the shape of pieces and how they go together. ____ ____ ____
  15. Sew for yourself or some member of your family. ____ ____ ____
  Score for Section I _____

II. Distribution:
  1. Visit stores to see the new merchandise being offered for sale. ____ ____ ____
  2. Study the procedures of salespersons in making sales. ____ ____ ____
  3. Talk to salespersons about the value and use of different fabrics or accessories. ____ ____ ____
  4. Help friends or family members select clothing articles. ____ ____ ____
  5. Organize class members to carry through a selling project. ____ ____ ____
  6. Arrange display windows. ____ ____ ____
  7. Plan and set up exhibits. ____ ____ ____
  8. Plan and conduct fashion shows. ____ ____ ____
  9. Model dresses, coats, and hats in a fashion show. ____ ____ ____
  10. Study different types of people to see what they like in clothing. ____ ____ ____
  11. Write newspaper articles about clothing and textiles. ____ ____ ____

activities	degree of interest		
	much	average	little
12. Work out more efficient ways of purchasing or caring for clothing.	_____	_____	_____
13. Make up ads suitable for selling textiles and clothing.	_____	_____	_____
14. Plan a wardrobe for a young girl going to college.	_____	_____	_____
Score for Section II	_____		
III. Education:			
1. Teach others how to sew or cut out a dress.	_____	_____	_____
2. Help friends plan their wardrobes.	_____	_____	_____
3. Give talks to clubs and other groups about clothes and fashions.	_____	_____	_____
4. Help children learn how to dress themselves.	_____	_____	_____
5. Read about historic costumes.	_____	_____	_____
6. Keep informed on current fashions and watch fashion trends.	_____	_____	_____
7. Experiment with new ways of using materials.	_____	_____	_____
8. Change patterns to make a garment more distinctive in appearance.	_____	_____	_____
9. Study ways to get people to improve their appearance.	_____	_____	_____
10. Explain how such things as buttonholes, darts, or tucks are made.	_____	_____	_____
11. Work out easier ways of making garments or parts of garments.	_____	_____	_____
12. Read all about new developments in textiles.	_____	_____	_____
13. Test materials to determine fiber content.	_____	_____	_____
14. Discover what is liked or disliked about certain fibers by homemakers.	_____	_____	_____
15. Read about how new fibers or new qualities for fibers are produced or how old fibers are given a new appearance.	_____	_____	_____
Score for Section III	_____		

To score, give yourself 2 points for each item scored "Much," 1 for each item scored "Average," and 0 for each item scored "Little." If your score is 70 to 90 for all items, you have considerable interest in the clothing and textile field. If your score is above 80, your interest in the clothing and textile field is very high. The division in which you have the largest proportion of "Much" scores suggests the type of work in which you are most interested. If you have a score of 20 to 30 in any single division, your interest is high in that field of work.

SUGGESTED ACTIVITIES

1. A study of fashion magazines and trade journals in clothing and textiles will give the student some idea of the ramifications of the field. Such trade journals as the *Women's Wear Daily* convey information for the retailers in the garment industry. There are trade journals for various types of merchandise.

2. A visit to a large advertising agency, a TV or radio station, or a newspaper office will help students understand the types of positions open in promotion work in the clothing and textile field for home economists. By talking with these workers, a better knowledge of the abilities required for success in the field can be obtained.

3. If there is a free-lance designer or a small specialty shop in the community, the persons responsible for the work may be willing to talk with the class. They could relate the type of training they had, how they became interested in the field, how they obtained their first job, and some of the advantages and disadvantages of their present positions.

4. Working in a department store, especially if the store has a training program, will help the student gain much insight into retailing. An enterprising student will be able to observe and participate in the work in many departments of the store.

5. Students can acquaint themselves with the opportunities in education by talking with the teachers of clothing and textiles in the college. Also, spending a day or so with the clothing specialist of the extension service in the state will give insight into the adult education phase. If the student lives in or near a city, a visit to a trade or technical school where workers are trained for designing, production, or distribution in clothing and textiles would be a profitable experience.

REFERENCES

1. Black, Bertram J., "The Consultant: A Developing Aspect of Professional Practice," *Journal of Home Economics,* vol. 49, pp. 17–19, January 1957.

2. Brenner, Barbara, *Careers and Opportunities in Fashion,* E. P. Dutton & Co., Inc., New York, 1964.

3. *Careers for Women in Retailing,* U.S. Department of Labor, Women's Bureau Bulletin 271, pp. 42–48, 1963.

4. Conference of College Teachers of Textiles and Clothing: Eastern Region, "Clothing and Textiles Move Forward," *Journal of Home Economics,* vol. 48, pp. 635–639, October 1956.

5. Davidson, William R., and Alton F. Doody, *Retailing Management,* 3d ed., The Ronald Press Company, New York.

6. Dickerson, Kitty G., "Textile Training for Retailers," *Journal of Home Economics,* vol. 58, p. 205, March 1966.

7. Duncan, Delbert J., and Charles F. Phillips, *Retailing Principles and Methods,* 7th edition, pp. 53–84, Richard D. Irwin, Inc., Homewood, Ill., 1967.

8. Gately, Olive P. (ed.), *A Distinctive Study of Your Future in the Fashion World,* pp. 23–60, Richard Rosen Press, Inc., New York, 1964.

9. Grossman, Shirley Bossherd, *Careers for Women in Retailing,* U.S. Department of Labor, Woman's Bureau Bulletin 271, 1963.

10. *Home Economics Has a Career for You in Textiles and Clothing,* American Home Economics Association, Washington, 1966.

11. Jarnew, Jeanette A., and Beatrice Judelle, *Inside the Fashion Business,* John Wiley & Sons, Inc., New York, 1966.

12. Lyle, Dorothy Siegert, "The Challenge of Textile Problems," *Journal of Home Economics,* vol. 43, pp. 85–88, February 1950.

13. Nager, Jean, "Retailing Opportunities in Textiles and Clothing," *Journal of Home Economics,* vol. 47, pp. 25–27, January 1955.

14. Richert, G. Henry, *Retailing, Principles and Practices,* 4th ed, pp. 163–219, McGraw-Hill Book Company, New York, 1962.

15. Settle, Alison, *Fashion as a Career,* Jarrold and Sons, Ltd, London, 1963.

16. *Textile Handbook, Revised Edition,* American Home Economics Association, Washington, 1963.

17. U.S. Bureau of the Census, *Apparel Survey, 1966,* Current Industrial Reports, Series MA(66)-1, pp. 3–4, 1968.

18. U.S. Bureau of the Census, *Statistical Abstracts of the United States, 1971 (92nd Ed.),* 1971. P. 308

19. Wingate, John W., *Retail Merchandising,* South Western Publishing Company, Cincinnatti, 1963.

20. Wright, Ellen, "Clothing and Textiles Internships in Texas," *Journal of Home Economics,* vol. 41, pp. 190–192, April 1949.

ADDITIONAL READINGS

Careers at the Simplicity Pattern Company, Simplicity Pattern Company, Inc., Educational Division, New York, 1964.

Compton, Norma H., "Characteristics of Clothing and Textile Students Compared with Those of Women in Fashion Careers," *Journal of Home Economics,* vol. 61, p. 183, March 1969.

Compton, Norma H., "The Language of Clothing," *Journal of Home Economics,* vol. 56, p. 686, November 1964.

"Creative Talents in Textiles and Clothing Are Encouraged by New Educational Instrument," *Journal of Home Economics,* vol. 58, pp. 266–272, April 1966.

Part I. Eileen Heagney and Dorothy Siegert Lyle

Part II. June Wilbur

The Evolution of a Simplicity Pattern, Simplicity Pattern Company, Inc., Educational Division, New York, 1964.

"Home Economics Sparks Unique Career," *What's New in Home Economics,* vol. 31, p. 18; October 1967; vol. 32, p. 32, February 1968.

"Home Economists in Action," *Forecast for Home Economics—Co-ed Section,* vol. 13, p. 82, May–June 1968; vol. 14, p. 67, September 1968; vol. 11, p. 18, April 1966; vol. 10, p. 38, April 1965.

Kaplan, Albert A., and Margaret De Mille, *Careers in Department Store Merchandising,* Henry Z. Walck, Inc., New York, 1962.

Kasnak, Mary Frances Drake, and Ruth W. Ayres, "Clothing Attitudes and Personality Characteristics of Fashion Innovaters," *Journal of Home Economics,* vol. 61, pp. 698–701, November 1969.

Wingate, John Williams, *Buying for Retail Stores,* 3d ed, Prentice-Hall, Inc., New York, 1960.

9 FOODS AND NUTRITION

The idea of a close connection between man and what he eats is not a discovery of the twentieth century. Nebuchadnezzar, the King of Babylon, in 607 B.C. conducted what was probably the first nutrition experiment. In Jerusalem, noble youths who were selected for training in the royal courts were ordered to have special diets consisting of the King's meat and wine. They were to be so nourished for three years "that at the end thereof, they might stand before the King" as specimens of good physical development. Daniel, one of the youths, objected to this and bargained for the privilege of some members of the group to continue on their original diet of "pulse [legumes and vegetables] to eat and water to drink." The request was granted, and at the end of a ten-day period, the youths adhering to the original diet "appeared fairer and fatter in flesh than all of the children which did eat the portion of the king's meat" (12). As a result, the King's portion of meat and wine was taken from all of the youths, and they were given "pulse."

Much research of recent years has highlighted the importance of foods and nutrition and made the public nutrition-conscious. As a result, the career opportunities in foods and nutrition for qualified home economists have greatly increased.

The usual careers in foods and nutrition are listed below under five headings. Within each major class of career opportunities, there are many positions (16, 38).

I. Hospitals and clinics
    A. Army, Air Force, and Navy hospitals
    B. City, county, and state supported hospitals (homes and institutions that care for the aged, infants, retarded, etc.)
    C. Private hospitals
    D. U.S. Public Health Service hospitals
    E. Veterans Administrations hospitals
    F. Medical clinics
II. Food service administration
    A. College and university (residence halls, student unions, and cafeterias)
    B. School programs
    C. Commercial (restaurants, hotels, department stores, and transportation lines)
    D. Hospitals and other institutions
    E. Industrial and catering
    F. Clubs
III. Community nutrition
    A. City, county, and state health departments
    B. Federal agencies in the United States and abroad (Peace Corps, World Health Organization, United Nations)

Fig. 9-1 Workers in the fields of food and nutrition must continuously study to keep up with the new advances. (Courtesy of the General Foods Kitchens)

    C. Private and voluntary agencies
    D. Food and product companies
    E. Gas and electric companies (research, instruction, and demonstration)
    F. Food service equipment companies
    G. Magazines and newspapers
    H. Radio and television stations (instruction and demonstration)
IV. Research
    A. Armed forces
    B. Business organizations
    C. Federal agencies (agriculture, education, health, and welfare)
    D. Universities
    E. Hospitals
V. Teaching
    A. Colleges and universities
    B. Commercial companies (food, products, and equipment)
    C. Health and welfare agencies
    D. Hospitals and clinics

    The exact number of career home economists in foods and nutrition is not known. In 1967, it was estimated that there were 30,000 employed dietitians in the United States. Of these, 20 percent were in hospitals and related institutions, including approximately 1,100 with the Veteran's Administration and the U.S. Public Health Service (31). There are over 17,000 members of the American Dietetic Association. Of these, 41 percent are hospital dietitians and 69 percent are nutritionists, namely, dietitians in schools, colleges, restaurants, and industry; college and university teachers; writers; research workers; and consultants; as well as full time homemakers who may return to professional activity at some time in the future. In addition, there are many graduates who majored in foods and nutrition or institution management, who are working in the field and who are not members of the American Dietetics Association. Each year there are from 1,000 to 1,200 professional vacancies to be filled in foods and nutrition.

Before discussing the various positions, we should determine whether there are qualities which apply to all who would have careers in foods and nutrition. Since career persons in these fields work with ordinary people, professional people, institution staffs, and food-service personnel, it is important that they like people and are interested in their health and welfare. They must have a flair for good food, including an appreciation of high standards of food preparation and service. They must enjoy sharing knowledge of what and why to eat and how to make foods "eatable" with others, including students, nurses, dietetic and medical interns, sick and well people, children and adults, general workers, and assistants. They must be able to counsel and advise. This requires patience and a sense of humor as well as technical and scientific knowledge (9). In preparation, they must acquire a basic understanding of the scientific principles applied to foods and nutrition. Much of the work deals with food nutrients and their use, the effect of food upon people, the composition of foods, food preparation, and ways of encouraging people to eat correctly. All of this requires a working knowledge of chemistry, physiology, bacteriology, psychology, and sociology, plus specialized training in foods and nutrition.

In addition to professional education and experience, the careerist in foods and nutrition must have good health and be able to practice good nutrition. Professional workers in any field must be able to live and look the part which they hope to project to others.

DIETETICS

Many people confuse *dietitians* and *nutritionists*. Although they have certain things in common, they differ in training and work. The work of the dietitian is to *feed* individuals and groups according to well-known principles of nutrition and physiology (14, 16, 41). Dietitians must know the foods essential for health, how to balance and select diets, and how to train workers to prepare foods that are palatable and nutritious. On the other hand, nutritionists are engaged in *interpreting* the principles and facts of nutrition to individuals and groups. Also, they carry on research to establish new principles and discover new facts about food and its use and need in the body (8, 10, 34, 40).

Dietitians are employed in all food-serving establishments of any size. In hospitals, where dietitians were first employed, the dietary department, the medical staff, and the nursing staff form the three major wings of a hospital. The hospital dietitians are found in three specializations.

In large hospitals, there is usually a *director of dietetics.* She administers, plans, and directs the activities of the department providing food services. She is responsible for the policies and procedures of the department, selects the professional staff, maintains a system of records for planning and control, coordinates the work in the food areas, and is responsible to the hospital administration for all food service.

Therapeutic dietitians are primarily concerned with the treatment of illness by means of specialized diets (29). Their responsibility is to plan the diet of the patients for whom the doctor has prescribed certain dietary requirements. They must instruct students in the relation of special or modified diets to normal diets and instruct the patients on the nature of the diet. They supervise or check the preparation of the special diets, and they may visit patients in hospitals or at home to instruct them and their families in proper dieting.

The food managers or *administrative dietitians* in a hospital have a more varied schedule than the therapeutic dietitians. It is their responsibility to feed the hospital staff and the patients on normal diets, as well as provide the supplies for the special diets. They are concerned with the hiring, training, and supervising of the dietary employees, buying and requisitioning of food and equipment, supervising quantity food production, and controlling the finances of the dietary department. In fact, they must see that the patients and staff in the hospital are fed nutritious and attractive meals on a specified budget (6).

The U.S. Army and the Air Force employ many dietitians. The armed services feel that they offer a unique opportunity for a dietitian to play three roles—to serve humanity, her country, and herself, either in the United States or in foreign lands. Army and Air Force dietitians are assigned for duty in all overseas theaters where troops are stationed, on hospital ships, to research units, in teaching positions in army hospitals in the United States, and in Veterans Administration hospitals (14, 41). An experienced dietitian who has met the educational and internship requirements is commissioned a rank commensurate with her age and experience. The grades from second lieutenant to colonel are held by dietitians now in service (17, 18).

Most of the companies dealing with people who travel employ dietitians to manage their food services. Some of the better-known ones are the airlines, railroad dining-car service, steamship companies, and hotel food services (8). These dietitians plan the food service and develop menus and methods of serving the food for the traveler, whether he goes by air, railway, or boat, or is spending his time at a hotel. When one realizes the hundreds of thousands of meals served weekly by these services, the need for trained dietitians can be appreciated.

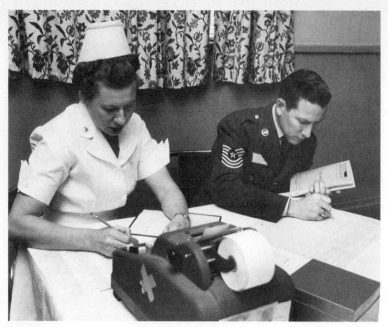

Fig. 9-2 Menu planning and preparation of the cook's work sheet are the responsibility of this Air Force dietitian. (Courtesy of the U.S. Air Force, Lackland Air Force Base)

Today, it is accepted that high standards of nutrition have a beneficial influence upon the mental and physical well-being of people, young and aged alike. Thus, homes for children, homes for the aged, and corrective institutions have great need for dietitians. The dietitian in this type of institution is expected to manage the food department and to provide menus that meet the nutritive needs of the group concerned (9, 20, 27). Usually the budget is limited, and special skill and imagination are required to do the job well. This type of work often requires an understanding of how to use food grown at the institution as well as how to buy and select. Since residents of the institutions often work in the food-service department, dietitians must be skillful in training workers and be very patient supervisors.

The minimum educational requirements for a dietitian is a bachelor's degree with a core of approved courses. The minimum academic requirements for membership or internship in the American Dietetics Association are as in chart on page 137.*

To qualify for professional recognition, the American Dietetics Association recommends the completion of a one-year internship program approved by the association or three years of approved experience (2). This training period affords the student an opportunity to put into practice what has been learned in college, to gain self-confidence, and to gain experience. Through classwork, projects, and practical experience, preparation is made for positions of responsibility in foods and nutrition.

MINIMUM ACADEMIC REQUIREMENTS FOR ADA MEMBERSHIP

The Core plus ONE Emphasis, plus ONE Concentration constitute the requirements for membership or internship, as designated for the specialties. Credit for a course may be used only once.

CORE SUBJECTS

22 semester hours* — Basic Minimum
All core subjects required

Natural Sciences—14 s. h.
human physiology } 6 s. h.
and bacteriology
chemistry—8 s. h.

Food—6 s. h.
selection, preparation, meal planning
Nutrition—2 s. h.

Plus one of the following:

EMPHASES

Choice of one Emphasis — 9 semester hours — Basic Minimum
Underlined subject areas required

I
FOOD SERVICE MANAGEMENT
organization and management
quantity food production and service
advanced food production management
equipment selection, maintenance, and layout
principles of accounting
purchasing

or

II
EDUCATION (Business and Industry, Clinic, College, Extension, School, and Public Health)
educational principles and techniques
educational psychology
anthropology
child psychology
sociology

or

III
FOODS—EXPERIMENTAL AND DEVELOPMENTAL
experimental foods
advanced bacteriology
consumer economics
cultural aspects of food
food styling
quantity food production and service
psychology of advertising
technology of food
theory and technique of communication

Plus one of the following:

CONCENTRATIONS

Choice of one Concentration — 15 semester hours — Basic Minimum
Underlined subject areas required

A
THERAPEUTIC AND ADMINISTRATIVE DIETETICS
advanced nutrition 2 s.h.
biochemistry**†
personnel management or industrial psychology
principles of learning or educational psychology
Remainder of credit:
diet therapy****
advanced food production management, equipment selection, maintenance, and layout***
foods: cultural, experimental or technological
principles of accounting***
purchasing***

or

B
BUSINESS ADMINISTRATION
advanced accounting
advanced food production management***
equipment selection, maintenance, and layout***
personnel management
purchasing***
Remainder of credit:
business law
communication
human relations
industrial psychology
labor economics

or

C
SCIENCE—FOODS AND NUTRITION
advanced nutrition 6 s.h.
biochemistry**
foods: cultural, experimental or technological
Remainder of credit:
child growth and nutrition
community nutrition
diet therapy****
principles of learning or educational psychology
statistics
food processing and preservation

1. Applicants for Internship and Membership
   a. Clinic Interns: Core + Emphasis I or II + Concentration A or C
   b. College, Business, or Industry Interns: Core + Emphasis I + Concentration A or B
   c. Hospital Interns: Core + Emphasis I + Concentration A or C

2. Experience applicants for membership:
   a: Bachelor's degree: Hospital: Core + Emphasis I + Concentration A or C.
      Food Service Administration: Core + Emphasis I + Concentration A or B.
   b. Master's degree: Core + Emphasis I, II, or III + Concentration A, B, or C.

LEGEND: *Social and behavioral sciences are considered to be essential and assumed to be included in college degree requirements.
**If not used in Core ***If not used in Emphasis I ****Required for hospital and clinic interns
†Food Chem. may be used by College or Industrial Interns

Adopted November 1, 1958   **Revised August 1967**

*Used with permission of The American Dietetics Association.

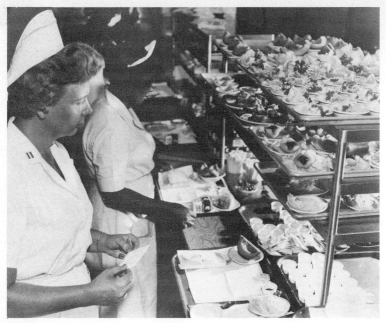

Fig. 9-3 The dietitian supervises the assembly of trays for service in the hospital. (Courtesy of the U.S Air Force, Andrews Air Force Base)

Also, at the end of this training, the student is eligible for membership in the American Dietetics Association. In September of 1969, there were approximately 900 dietetic internships available to qualified students (13).

NUTRITION

Nutritionists are engaged in discovering principles and facts about foods and nutrition and interpreting them to individuals and groups. They try to improve nutritional conditions through teaching and research. They may be employed in hospitals and health centers, by community health organizations, by the government, by public and private agencies, or by schools and other educational institutions.

The clinic and community health nutritionists are concerned with translating scientific information into simple, specific instructions which their coworkers and the public can understand and follow. Their duties may be summarized as follows (7):

1. Teaching nutrition in clinics, mothers' clubs, and public schools
2. Working with the medical staff and nurses in clinics

3. Serving allied health and welfare agencies, as well as hospitals, on a consultation basis

4. Planning and participating in nutrition surveys and studies

5. Preparing pamphlets and other informational materials, including exhibits and films, writing for bulletins, and preparing newspaper publicity

6. Giving talks before civic and professional groups and to radio and television audiences

Nutritionists in clinics or in community health work must know food and food values from the standpoint of cost, since they will be working with families with limited means. Furthermore, they must understand the food habits of regional and national groups.

Nutritionists engaged in city, county, state, or federal public health programs are called public health nutritionists. Their duties are similar to those of the clinic or community nutritionists, but they have a wider scope of activities (15, 25).

The nutritionists who are engaged in education usually will be found on the staffs of colleges and universities or the cooperative extension services of the several states. Also, they may be on the staffs of government agencies and such private agencies as the Red Cross. Departments and colleges of home economics will have one or more nutritionists to teach courses in foods and nutrition and institution management and to carry on research. These nutritionists are responsible for the basic training of the students who plan to enter careers in foods, dietetics, and nutrition, as well as the foods and nutrition training of other students in the college. In addition. they participate in training public health student nurses, and others going into health work (15).

The training of a college or university nutritionist at the undergraduate level is similar to that of a dietitian. In addition, graduate work leading to a master's degree is essential, and many of these nutritionists have a Ph.D., D.Sc., or M.D. degree, which are doctor's degrees.

Every state in the United States will have one or more nutritionists on the state extension staff. These nutritionists work with the county home demonstration agents in developing foods and nutrition programs for rural people. Through better utilization of food and improved eating habits, the extension nutritionist hopes to improve the health of the people: to do this, she must develop materials which interpret the facts of nutrition to uninformed people. In most states a master's degree in foods and nutrition, plus experience in extension, is required to become a foods and nutrition specialist with the extension service.

The American Red Cross, the American Dairy Council, and other private agencies employ many nutritionists who teach groups and voluntary instructors for these groups the basic essentials of nutrition. They work with the public schools, public health and social agencies, and social and professional groups to improve the health of the nation (4). One of their major responsibilities is to train workers for emergency feeding in times of disaster. The general educational requirement for a Red Cross nutritionist is a bachelor's degree in home economics with a major in foods and nutrition. In addition, two years of experience as a home economist in a social or health agency or in teaching or research are required.

In the large high schools the home economics work may be sufficiently departmentalized to have foods and nutrition teachers. To qualify, one must have a bachelor's degree in home economics with a major in foods and nutrition.

Foods and nutrition consultants work independently or are employed by food manufacturers, the government, or private agencies. They need to have a good background in foods and nutrition and have access to the most recent developments in scientific food research. The consultant may be responsible for seeing that the food that is offered for sale or that passes through the concern meets the required standards and that proper controls are employed in the processing, storing, and handling of food to protect its quality and usefulness. She will be in constant contact with specialists, which requires the ability to discuss technical and business matters with importers, advertising agencies, brokers, medical and legal practitioners, government officials, and many others in related professions (5, 37). The successful consultant usually has had years of experience in some phase of foods and nutrition where she has acquired expert knowledge in the field and established her reputation as a competent adviser.

FOOD SERVICE

One of the newer and very rapidly developing food-service programs is that of the *school lunch.* Although the school-lunch program developed later in the United States than in Europe, it has spread very rapidly throughout the country since its beginning. The purpose of the school-lunch program is threefold: it hopes to provide for the children attending school a well-balanced, nutritious lunch, to help them appreciate good food, and to encourage them to eat properly (21, 34, 37, 38).

The school lunchroom supervisor must be well grounded in foods, quantity cookery, food buying, equipment, personnel management, and education. The bachelor of science degree in home economics with special emphasis on foods and nutrition is considered a minimum for school-lunch management. School-lunch managers usually work as directly with the principals of the schools as do the teachers (34, 35). They are responsible for planning menus, buying all foods, standardizing recipes, training and supervising the workers in the school lunchroom, and serving the food in an attractive manner. In addition, they are expected to work with the teachers in carrying nutrition education into the classroom. Over the school lunchroom managers are supervisors of school lunchroom work: these women usually have a master's degree in foods and nutrition.

There is great demand for school lunchroom personnel. Young women who wish to combine foods and nutrition work with education will find school lunchroom management and supervision very challenging careers (21, 33).

INSTITUTION ADMINISTRATION

In *institution administration* there are many opportunities for home economists specializing in foods and nutrition. Mainly concerned with feeding groups of people, they are called *food-service managers,* and they find employment in educational, industrial, and commercial food services.

In a college or university, the manager of the college dining hall supervises the entire operation of the food service. Usually the manager is responsible for purchasing the kitchen equipment and for seeing that the equipment is kept in good and workable condition. Planning the meals and making them as attractive and nutritious as possible falls to the manager, as does the hiring of employees and the directing of their work. The manager orders the food and supervises its storage and preparation; he selects recipes for the cooks to follow and trains the personnel. One of the main responsibilities of the manager is to see that the cost of the food service is kept within the budget.

Industrial feeding is concerned mainly with the feeding of employees in industrial plants. The food-service managers in industrial plants must have the same general qualifications as managers of a college dining hall. Some industries have a cafeteria, a snack bar, or perhaps a mobile serving unit to take meals to employees who cannot come to a dining hall.

The commercial food services include restaurants, cafeterias, clubs, hotel dining and coffee shops, and tea rooms. The duties are similar in each but vary according to the organization (22, 35, 36).

In the commercial food centers, there are usually several persons who are responsible for the food service. They may be classified as follows:

1. General manager—has general supervision over the entire setup, including purchasing and preparation of foods, menus, dining-room service, and cost control. In fact, the final outcome of the business is in his or her hands.

2. Food production manager—has the responsibility of food ordering, menu planning, selecting equipment, and keeping records.

3. Purchasing agent—has the responsibility of buying food, equipment, and other supplies needed by the various divisions of the business. The best products for the least money must be purchased so that the business can show a profit.

4. Food cost-control supervisor—has predominantly office work. This person studies menus, estimates the cost per serving of foods, and determines the price for which food must sell. If a department does not make a profit, it is his responsibility to find where the trouble is.

5. Food supervisor—in each department of a food-service business there is a food supervisor. It is the food supervisor's responsibility to see that the menus in each division are strictly followed, that good-quality products are turned out, and that foods are ready for service when needed. Also, the supervision of the production workers in the unit falls to the supervisor.

Young people who wish to enter commercial food service should have a good background in quantity cookery, experimental cookery, cost accounting, institution equipment, purchasing, and personnel relationships, as well as a good knowledge of general foods and nutrition. After graduation from college, the general procedure is to take an internship with the American Restaurant Association, enter a special training program sponsored by the firm with which employment is sought, or start as an assistant to a restaurateur.

CREATIVE FOOD CAREERS

Creative food careers include many and varied money-making adventures by individuals trained in foods and nutrition. Many of these people work on a part-time basis, but some persons who have started on a part-time basis have come to head large industries (13, 19, 30).

A *cooked-food shop* in the home has proved successful for many women. To establish such a business requires little capital and equipment and no expensive advertising. Usually the plant grows as the business grows. If the food is good, the prices reasonable, and the surroundings clean and pleasant, word will spread quickly. If the operator knows how to buy wholesale and produce high-quality food, this can be a very well-paying home-production business.

Home catering is another type of creative work in foods. This might include serving attractive and novel sandwiches for teas, church groups, men's and women's clubs, or social groups. The preparing and serving of meals in homes for paying guests is another form of creative work. If one has a home suitable for guests, and especially if one lives in the country, a summer or year-round guest house can provide a very good income. The box-lunch business in college towns, factory areas, office buildings, newsstands, etc., has been a money-making activity for many.

A qualified dietitian who does not wish a full-time job may work with the community doctors in planning diets for invalids, convalescents, and others in the community who need special diets. In many communities this type of service is not available, and those in need of it are willing to pay for it. In addition, the dietitian may act as a consultant for the doctors and public health personnel in the community (5).

If persons trained in foods and nutrition have some capital, and the desire, they may establish small canning, preserving, or baking businesses. They must have enough capital to operate while the business is being built up. Often, this sort of firm is started on a special-order basis so that production and sales balance each other.

FOOD SPECIALISTS

The term *food specialist* is used to cover various careers which are open to men and women who experiment professionally with foods. Food specialists are employed by food manufacturers, public utility companies, advertising agencies, the Federal

a   *b*

Fig. 9-4 (*a*) and (*b*) One of the responsibilities of the school lunchroom supervisor is to serve good food and create an atmosphere which makes eating at school enjoyable to the children. (Courtesy of the Fairfax County, Va. school-lunch program)

Extension Service, grocery chains, and women's magazines. Persons who have a good knowledge of foods and nutrition and the ability to write and speak will find a variety of opportunities in promotion and publicity work in foods (7, 29).

Firms dealing in foods and household equipment, as well as electric and gas power companies, employ many home economists in their home-service departments to serve as a contact between the firm and the consumer. In their role as home economists, they give lectures and demonstrations on the use of the food product or the equipment in producing food, test new products and equipment, and develop recipes. They must know food preparation, meal planning, food buying, table service, equipment, and the intricacies of entertaining. They may make their contacts through employees of the firm, women's and men's clubs, church groups, schools, and scout groups.

In all the food-service careers, whether one is employed in a large or small concern or is self-employed, the purpose is to feed individuals and groups of people to promote the welfare of the business or employer.

a

b

Fig. 9-5 (a) and (b) These pictures were taken in the Creative Cookery Kitchen of a large foods industry. This is where the recipes for packages, recipe books, advertising, publicity, and special projects are prepared. (Courtesy of the General Foods Kitchens)

RESEARCH AND TESTING

The research worker in foods and nutrition puts science to work to discover new facts about foods and food needs for health and welfare. She may work with food technology, food testing, food analysis, food preparation, and nutritive requirements.

Food technology is the science of processing and manufacturing food. Problems associated with preserving food, maintaining its quality, putting it in a form acceptable to the consumer, and storing it until needed are parts of the food technologist's work. In addition, she develops new products or new uses for old products; this requires the ability to wonder, imagine, and be curious about foods in general. Anyone who visits a supermarket today is made aware of the many new types of foods and the many new forms in which familiar foods are presented to the consumer. The food technologist may work in a college or university, for a food manufacturer, or in a small laboratory of his own where foods are tested for business concerns (23).

Most large food manufacturers employ a staff of home economists in food research, food testing, and public relations (24). Positions with the food companies are of several types. Usually there is a home economics director whose responsibility is to investigate consumer needs, interpret them to the manufacturer, and provide the consumer with the information needed in understandable language. The director of the experimental kitchen will carry out the actual testing of the food products with the help of several testing and research associates and food consultants. They will also answer requests for food information from the general public. To fill such a position, the home economist needs a good background in foods and nutrition, management, handling of personnel, psychology, journalism, and public relations.

The field representatives for food industries are home economists who try to make the public conscious of the manufacturer's products. They visit schools, colleges, men's and women's clubs, and stores; and they attend conferences for the sole purpose of acquainting the public with the products which their business sells. Young home economists who like to travel, who do not object to spending their nights on a airplane or in a hotel, and who know foods and salesmanship will find these positions challenging.

Foods and equipment businesses and many advertising agencies have test kitchens. The chief purpose of these kitchens is to check constantly upon the salability of the product to be sold and create new ideas for influencing the public to buy the product. The workers in the test kitchens have varied jobs, depending upon the type of business, but the following activities are usually carried on:

1. Making food pictures for illustration in newspapers, magazines, and booklets
2. Creating new recipes for using the product to be sold

Fig. 9-6 Three students in the department of human nutrition and foods are evaluating the organoleptic values of turkey meat. (Courtesy of the Virginia Polytechnic Institute and State University)

3. Testing food flavors and food products and adapting them to the various markets
4. Writing newspaper food articles, and radio scripts and commercials

Anyone who wishes to work in a test kitchen should have a sound background in food preparation, chemistry, bacteriology, nutrition, household management, consumer education, and the social sciences. In addition, the ability to type and some knowledge of journalism and advertising are essential. Experience with grocery store operation and people's buying habits is invaluable.

The home economist engaged in foods and nutrition research in colleges and universities or in the government agencies does much the same work as the home economist in business. The chief difference is that the educational institutions and the government are primarily concerned with improving the health and welfare of the people, while the businesses are primarily concerned with the salability of their products. However, many business concerns finance research in the educational institutions, so the purposes of the two groups overlap. The famous home economics research laboratories of the Institute of Home Economics of the U.S. Department of Agriculture at Beltsville, Maryland, employ home economists working on research in foods and nutrition and related fields.

Home economists who wish to train for research in foods and nutrition must meet the general requirements for research workers, plus specialized training in foods and nutrition. They will need to have a good grounding in chemistry, physiology, biology, and mathematics, in addition to their specialty. They must have a desire to learn more about foods and nutrition and be willing to do the painstaking work which research requires.

COMMUNICATIONS

There are many opportunities in radio, TV, journalism, and advertising for home economists with foods and nutrition training. The women's and household magazines devote considerable space to articles on foods and nutrition, as well as food-preparation equipment. Food advertisers use home economists for food layouts, food photography, and food testing. The food demonstrator is not an uncommon figure on TV programs, and no doubt these opportunities will develop further. The preparation and presentation of the commercials for foods and equipment companies via TV, radio, and magazines and newspapers are good career opportunities for home economists. Many newspapers carry foods and nutrition columns, which offer challenging opportunities for home economists with experience in journalism.

WHAT DOES THE JOB PAY?

The salaries paid for the various types of work in foods and nutrition vary not only from one field to the other but from one section of the country to another. The ranges of salaries for dietitians employed in selected positions of the food and nutrition field are shown in Table 9–1. These have been based upon data received during the spring of 1970. Although it is impossible to give accurate data for salaries, since supply and demand, as well as qualifications and experience, are factors affecting salaries, these figures should give the student some idea of what to expect as remuneration in the field.

Table 9-1
Average salaries in foods, nutrition, and dietetics*

types of personnel	average annual salary range
Dietitians in hospitals	
Graduates of approved internships with	
no experience	$ 7,500–$8,500
Qualified dietitians with experience	7,800– 9,000
Chief dietitians	8,500–11,000
Dietitians in charge of very large departments	10,000–15,000
Veterans Administration	7,500–11,000
Army and Navy regular and reserve officers	8,000–15,000
Dietitians with business and industry	8,000–15,000
College food service	
Assistant	8,000–10,000
Director	10,000–12,000
School lunchroom supervisors	8,000–11,000
College and university teachers and research workers	7,800–16,000
Nutritionists	8,000–10,000

* These are unofficial figures, but they are representative of salaries reported to the American Dietetics Association by employers. Figures are for spring 1970.

INTEREST CHECKLIST FOR FOODS AND NUTRITION

Listed below are a number of activities associated with the foods and nutrition field. After reading each item listed at the left of the page, check your degree of interest in the type of work described in the appropriate column at the right. Directions for scoring are given at the end of the checklist.

activities	degree of interest		
	much	average	little
I. Dietetics:			
1. Plan food for sick members of the family.	———	———	———
2. Buy food in quantity for parties or dinners.	———	———	———
3. Read about diseases and diets prescribed for them.	———	———	———
4. Teach others how to prepare and serve food.	———	———	———
5. Study the qualities of kitchen equipment to see which is the best buy.	———	———	———
6. Plan menus for the family, clubs, and other groups.	———	———	———
7. Supervise the preparation of food for a large group.	———	———	———
8. Find new ways to prepare foods disliked by some family member.	———	———	———
9. Set up attractive trays for food service.	———	———	———
10. Work with nurses and doctors to help people get well through correct diets.	———	———	———
11. Prepare food for the family keeping in mind individual needs.	———	———	———
12. Make out shopping food lists, giving the type and amounts needed.	———	———	———
13. Carry trays to sick people in the home or in a hospital.	———	———	———
14. Plan interesting menus at different costs.	———	———	———
15. Talk with people about food likes and dislikes.	———	———	———
Score for Section I	———————————		
II. Nutrition:			
1. Go on trips with the health nurse to see what people eat.	———	———	———
2. Teach boys and girls the foods they should eat to be healthy.	———	———	———
3. Talk to people about improving their food habits.	———	———	———
4. Give demonstrations on how to prepare foods.	———	———	———
5. Write articles on foods or nutrition for the newspaper or school paper.	———	———	———
6. Prepare food exhibits or posters.	———	———	———

7. Study the vitamins, minerals, and other health substances in foods. _____ _____ _____
8. Experiment with different ways of preparing food. _____ _____ _____
9. Attend health clinics to see the needs of people. _____ _____ _____
10. Study experimental animals that are on good and poor diets. _____ _____ _____
11. Work with chemicals, test tubes, and other equipment. _____ _____ _____
12. Help people plan diets to gain or lose weight. _____ _____ _____
13. Observe a basal metabolism test. _____ _____ _____
14. Evaluate your own diet to see how many calories you are getting. _____ _____ _____
15. Listen to lectures about what effect different foods have on the body. _____ _____ _____
      Score for Section II _____

III. Food service:
1. Plan menus using different combinations of foods. _____ _____ _____
2. Set a table using different decorating ideas. _____ _____ _____
3. Study linen, silver, and china. _____ _____ _____
4. Supervise food projects for making money. _____ _____ _____
5. Talk to salesmen about the value and use of their products. _____ _____ _____
6. Plan teas, banquets, and other social events where food is served. _____ _____ _____
7. Develop recipes for new foods or for making old foods more interesting. _____ _____ _____
8. Compare the cost of different types of refreshments for a party. _____ _____ _____
9. Teach scouts or others how to bake or prepare foods. _____ _____ _____
10. Work on a schedule to see that foods are ready for service at a particular time. _____ _____ _____
11. Illustrate foods for a bake or foods sale. _____ _____ _____
12. Prepare dinners for 4-H or high school clubs or church groups. _____ _____ _____
13. Help in the school lunchroom in your school. _____ _____ _____
14. Supervise the cleaning of the stoves and other equipment in the kitchen. _____ _____ _____
15. Visit commercial kitchens to see how food is prepared on a large scale. _____ _____ _____
      Score for Section III _____

IV. Research:
1. Try out new equipment to see how it works. _____ _____ _____
2. Experiment with different ways of preparing a food. _____ _____ _____
3. Hear about how diet affects eyesight, health, etc. _____ _____ _____

activities	degree of interest		
	much	average	little
4. Feed experimental animals different types of diets and study results.	_____	_____	_____
5. Work in a chemistry laboratory to see what foods are composed of.	_____	_____	_____
6. Develop new recipes in a home or test kitchen.	_____	_____	_____
7. Read about the application of science to foods and health.	_____	_____	_____
8. Keep detailed records on projects.	_____	_____	_____
9. Ask people questions about what they eat.	_____	_____	_____
10. Work with systematic and methodical people.	_____	_____	_____
11. Write articles about new discoveries for magazines or papers.	_____	_____	_____
12. Study sciences and how the principles apply to food and health.	_____	_____	_____
13. Do work which requires one to wear a uniform.	_____	_____	_____
14. Do work which requires accuracy of the worker.	_____	_____	_____
15. Use arithmetic or work with figures.	_____	_____	_____
Score for Section IV	_____		
V. Communications:			
1. Attend food demonstrations.	_____	_____	_____
2. Visit radio or TV stations to see how programs originate.	_____	_____	_____
3. Study new cookbooks for ideas.	_____	_____	_____
4. Write recipes in a way that they are easier to use.	_____	_____	_____
5. Compile material for leaflets, cookbooks, recipe sets, etc.	_____	_____	_____
6. Watch food demonstrations on the TV.	_____	_____	_____
7. Appear on TV or the radio.	_____	_____	_____
8. Read the household hints and recipes in the magazines.	_____	_____	_____
9. Give demonstrations to members of your class or 4-H club.	_____	_____	_____
10. Make posters of food and equipment.	_____	_____	_____
11. Write articles for the school paper about parties, refreshments served, etc.	_____	_____	_____
12. Take pictures of food or equipment.	_____	_____	_____
13. Study color in food and prepare interesting combinations.	_____	_____	_____
14. Help with demonstrations by connecting appliances, assisting with equipment, etc.	_____	_____	_____
15. Direct a play which illustrates good eating habits.	_____	_____	_____
Score for Section V	_____		
Total score	_____		

In order to score each section, multiply the number of items checked "Much" by 2, and the number checked "Average" by 1. A score of 20–30 for any section indicates high interest in that area. A total score for the five sections of 100–150 indicates high interest in foods and nutrition as a field.

SUGGESTED ACTIVITIES

1. Read the life histories of outstanding men and women in the fields of foods and nutrition.
   a. What motivated them to work in these fields?
   b. What contributions did they make to mankind?
   c. What training did they have to prepare them for their jobs?
2. Visit a large cafeteria, tea room, or hotel dining room. Ask the manager to show you through the kitchens, dining rooms, etc.
   a. How many people are employed in the business?
   b. What different types of positions are open to home economics graduates who major in foods and nutrition?
   c. How much do the positions pay?
3. Invite the head of the dietary department of a hospital to your class.
   a. How many dietitians are employed by the hospital?
   b. What are the responsibilities of each dietitian?
   c. How much are the dietitians paid?
   d. How many meals are served daily in the hospital?
   e. What types of special diets are prepared in the hospital?
   f. How did the dietitian choose dietetics as a career?
4. Study the operation of a food production center, such as a cannery, bakery, meat processing plant, etc.
   a. What positions in the business are especially suited to the home economics graduate with foods and nutrition training?
   b. How much do these positions pay?
   c. How does one find employment in these business concerns?
5. Find out how many persons with foods and nutrition training are employed by the United States government.
   a. What are they doing?
   b. What salaries are they paid?
   c. What positions are open to students as they finish college? With advanced training?
6. How many foods and nutrition people are employed by the following agencies in your state?
   a. The Red Cross.
   b. Public health agencies.
   c. Public welfare agencies.
   d. Colleges and universities.
   e. High schools.
   f. Businesses.
   g. Cooperative extension service.
   h. Agricultural experiment station.
   (1). What are the educational requirements of each agency for a position in foods and nutrition?
   (2). What experience is required for a position with each agency?
   (3). How much do the positions pay?

7. Visit a college of home economics in your state where foods and nutrition research is being carried on.

 a. What questions are the research workers trying to answer?

 b. How will the research worker use the facts which she discovers?

 c. What was her training and experience before entering research?

 d. What special satisfaction does she receive?

8. Write to the Women's Medical Specialist Corps of the U.S. Army or Navy in your area and invite a representative to talk to your class about opportunities for foods and nutrition home economists with the United States armed services.

REFERENCES

1. "American Food Industry International," *What's New in Home Economics,* vol. 26, pp. 62–67, September 1962.

2. Ball, Margaret M., and Grace M. Gorgan, "A Profile of Dietitians in Colorado," *Journal of Home Economics,* vol. 60, p. 667, October 1958.

3. Beal, Mary Allen, and Marjorie E. Newton, "The Dietetic Intern," *Journal of Home Economics,* vol. 58, pp. 87–92, February 1966.

4. Brown, Janet S., "Training Program for Head Start Mothers," *Nutrition News,* vol. 31, p. 7, April 1968.

5. Brush, Miriam K., "A New Kind of Service," *Nutrition News,* vol. 28, p. 14, December 1965.

6. *Career Wise,* U.S. Army Medical Services, Woman's Army Specialist Corps, 1965.

7. "Careers as a Home Economist with Food Manufacturers," *What's New in Home Economics,* vol. 11, pp. 13, 80–82, November 1946.

8. *Careers for Women with Airlines,* The Institute for Research, Research No. 137, Chicago, 1966.

9. Cleveland, S. E., "Personality Characteristics of Dietitians and Nurses," *Journal of the American Dietetics Association* vol. 42, pp. 104–107, February 1963.

10. *College Teaching as a Career,* The Institute for Research, Research No. 164, Chicago, 1967.

11. Council, Buena, "Food Services for Senior Citizens," *Nutrition News,* vol. 30, p. 3, February 1967.

12. Daniel 1:7–16.

13. *Dietetic Internships Approved by the American Dietetic Association,* American Dietetic Association, Chicago, 1969.

14. *Dietetics,* The Institute for Research, Research No. 46, Chicago, 1965.

15. *Dietetics: A Career with a Challenge,* U.S. Army Medical Service, Woman's Army Specialist Corps, 1966.

16. *Dietitians in Demand,* American Dietetics Association, Chicago, 1969.

17. *The Dietitian in the Hospitals,* U.S. Public Health Service Bulletin 35, 1950.

18. *A Future for You in Dietetics,* Veteran's Administration Center, Los Angeles, Calif., n.d.

19. Gorman, Louis Burrough, Arline B. Zahalls, and Doris Johnson, "Weekend Dietitian," *Journal of the American Dietetic Association,* vol. 35, p. 709, July 1957.

20. Heaberlin, Ethel, "Nutrition Programs in State Institutions," *Journal of Home Economics,* vol. 47, pp. 669–672, January 1955.

21. Hill, Mary M., "Planning for Nutrition Education in Elementary Schools," *Journal of Home Economics,* vol. 52, pp. 259–262, 316, April 1960.

22. "Home Economics Sparks Unique Career," *What's New in Home Economics,* vol. 31, p. 12, November 1967.

23. "Home Economics Sparks Unique Career," *What's New in Home Economics,* Ibid, vol. 32, p. 32, February 1968.

24. "Home Economists in Action," *Forecast for Home Economics—Co-ed Section,* vol. 12, p. 6, January 1967.

25. *Home Economics Careers in Health and Welfare,* pp. 3–4, American Home Economics Association, Washington, 1965.

26. Johnson, Myrna, "Foods of the Future," *What's New in Home Economics,* vol. 26, pp. 76–79, March 1962.

27. Mason, Marion, "Nutrition Service in a Visiting Nurse Association," *Nutrition News,* vol. 25, p. 15, December 1962.

28. Medved, Eva, and Donna Schell, "Televised Food Demonstrations," *Journal of Home Economics,* vol. 59, pp. 357–360, May 1967.

29. Noland, M. S., "Activities of Therapeutic Dietitians—A Survey Report," *Journal of the American Dietetic Association,* vol. 46, pp. 477–481, June 1965.

30. O'Brien, Robert, "Walter Knott's Berry Farm and Ghost Town," *The American Mercury,* vol. 85, pp. 29–33, October 1957.

31. *Occupational Outlook Handbook,* U.S. Department of Labor, Bulletin No. 1550, pp. 80–86, 1968–1969.

32. Oser, Bernard L., "Role of the Independent Counseling Laboratory in the Service of the Food Industry," *Food Technology,* vol. 11, pp. 16–20, April 1957.

33. Paddick, Marian, and Geraldine Acke, "Help-by-Mail-Service for Homemakers," *Nutrition News,* vol. 31, p. 14, December 1968.

34. Patton, Mary Brown, and Others, "Working Together for a Better Understanding of the Nutrition of School Children," *Journal of Home Economics,* vol. 45, pp. 161–164, March 1953.

35. *Restaurant, Tea Room, and Cafeteria Operation Careers,* The Institute for Research, Research No. 69, Chicago, 1967.

36. Scheer, Wilbert E., "The Company Cafeteria," *Personnel Journal,* vol. 45, pp. 85–86, February 1964.

37. Sloan, Sara, "'Turn On' School Lunch Program," *Nutrition News,* vol. 32, p. 7, April 1969.

38. Spann, Virginia, *Dietitian,* Research Publishing Company, Inc., American Occupation No. 25, pp. 11–13, Boston, 1964.

39. Stone, Ruth H., "Food Experiences in an Elementary School," *Nutrition News,* vol. 22, p. 3, October 1959.

40. Wilson, Mary Margaret, and Mina W. Lamb, "Food Beliefs As Related to Ecological Factors in Women," *Journal of Home Economics,* vol. 60. pp. 115–118, February 1968.

41. *Your Bright Tomorrow,* U.S. Army Medical Services, Woman's Army Specialist Corps, 1966.

ADDITIONAL READINGS

Eck, Sarah, "Home Economics Paves the Way," *What's New in Home Economics,* vol. 31, pp. 71–72, March 1967.

"Food Service Director Wins International Fame," *What's New in Home Economics,* vol. 31, p. 12, November 1967.

"Hiring a Home Economist," *What's New in Home Economics,* vol. 28, p. 108, September 1964.

"Home Economics Sparks Unique Career," *What's New in Home Economics,* vol. 32, p. 32, February 1968.

"Home Economist in Action," *Forecast for Home Economics—Co-ed Section,* vol. 10, p. 38, April 1965.

Mathewson, Eleanor H., "Experience of a Lifetime—Serving as Dietitian on the S.S. Hope," *Journal of Home Economics,* vol. 60, pp. 285–286, April 1968.

Your Future as a Dietitian, American Dietetic Association, Richard Rosen Press, Inc., New York, 1964.

10 FAMILY ECONOMICS, HOME MANAGEMENT, HOUSING, FURNISHINGS, AND EQUIPMENT

Hundreds of decisions face the homemaker daily. Many of these have to do with the use of time, energy, money, and other family resources, including the house and its equipment. Here the trained home economist comes to assist the family in making wise decisions. As fields of employment, management and housing have lagged behind such areas as foods and nutrition as well as clothing and textiles in the number of home economists actually engaged in work. However, many home economists are employed in these fields, and opportunities are increasing. The conscientious home economics student will do well to consider the fields outlined below when selecting a career.

Careers in Family Economics, Home Management, Housing, Furnishings, and Equipment

I. College or university and high school teacher
    A. Consumer education
    B. Family economics
    C. Home or family management
    D. House planning
    E. Interior decoration
    F. Household equipment
    G. House furnishings
II. Adult educator
    A. Extension specialist in housing, house furnishings, consumer education
    B. Home service representative with utility companies, dairy councils, food and equipment manufacturers, etc.
    C. Adult education teachers in public school system
III. Consultant
    A. Consumer
    B. Home lighting
    C. Laundry
    D. Housing
    E. Public housing
    F. Family finance
IV. Administrator
    A. Manager
        1. College dormitories and residences
        2. Private or public housing projects
        3. Clubs or commercial housing
        4. Institution housing
    B. Department store manager or buyer
        1. House furnishings

2. Draperies
3. Equipment
  C. Interior decorator
  D. Home planning specialist
  E. Kitchen planner
  F. Home furnishing coordinator
V. Designer
  A. Products
  B. Interior decoration
  C. Household textiles
VI. Writer
VII. Researcher

MANAGEMENT AND FAMILY FINANCE

What is home management? It is a series of decisions made in relation to the use of family resources to reach family goals. In reality, it is "using what you have to get what you want" (5, 18). The trained home economist must assist homemakers to plan and organize family resources to ensure the best or most satisfactory living for the family.

Many of the home economists who have specialized in home management or family finance are in educational work. They will be found teaching in colleges and universities, working as specialists with the state and federal extension service, with banks, service agencies, and social welfare and health agencies, or in research.

The home-management educator must be thoroughly versed in the following types of subject matter, since these are the areas in which her educational efforts lie:

1. Understanding family goals and ways of meeting them
2. Work simplification
3. Time and energy management
4. Use of leisure time
5. Effective use of income
6. Feeding the family effectively on a given amount of money
7. Clothing the family satisfactorily on a given amount of money
8. Housing the family effectively, including financing, care, and upkeep
9. Providing financial security for the family
10. Special housing provision for the handicapped
11. Keeping the consumer informed
12. The why and how of decision making

In all the areas in which the home-management specialist teaches, she will be concerned with the development of appreciation, understanding, attitudes, judgments, and standards for the attainment of good living, i.e., the most satisfaction and security for the family with the least expenditure of time, energy and money (21).

In some colleges and universities, the teachers of home management and family finance may be the same, but in most large institutions the two areas employ different specialists. The rapid socioeconomic changes during the last few decades have altered patterns of family life and created many problems related to money. In the twenty years from 1950 to 1970 the population in the United States increased 33 percent and disposable personal income rose 231 percent while at the same time the consumer credit outstanding jumped 500 percent (18, 34). That there is some recognition of the growing need for the study of family finance is shown by the fact that there are fifteen colleges of home economics offering majors in family economics or finance (5): eight offer a bachelor's degree, ten offer a master's degree, and one offers a doctor's degree. Between 1940 and 1954, more than 150 colleges and universities introduced courses in personal and family finance (14).

Many welfare and public health agencies employ home management and family-finance specialists. For example, the Children's Bureau has twenty home economists serving in nineteen maternal- and infant-care, and children and youth projects in sixteen states (11). Nutritionists and dietitians have worked in these fields for years. Greater awareness of family problems in the areas of home management and family finance stimulated the nutrition staff of the Children's Bureau in 1965 to experiment with home economists as members of health teams. These experts have the responsibility for the preparation of the money-allowance schedules. They spend considerable time in consultation with the administrative staff, the supervisors, and the case workers concerning the philosophy and calculations required in the preparation of money allowances for families (2). In addition they set up standards for family food, clothing, and shelter, and they advise in other areas. Much work is being done today with the low-income and handicapped homemakers and in rehabilitation work. This was given considerable impetus by the passage of the 1968 amendment to the Vocational Rehabilitation Act (27, 31).

When one realizes that approximately 9 percent of the families in the United States earned less than $3,000 in 1970 (29), the need for help in finances and other areas of home management becomes evident. But it is not just the low-income families that need financial help; home economists believe that standards of living and well-being depend quite as much upon how incomes are used as upon their size (28).

The home economist who does educational work in home management and family finance will find it advantageous to take graduate training after finishing college—in most cases, at least a master's degree will be expected. In addition to a good background in home economics, including family clothing, foods, and nutrition, and family housing, leaders in home management and family finance must understand family life and the various ways by which families meet their needs. They must have a thorough knowledge of time, energy, and motion studies and their application to homemaking. In college course work they should include sociology, economics, finance, buying, insurance, budgeting, and the various types of family credit. They must know how to handle problems of family estates and investments. Some understanding of house planning and kitchen arrangement is essential, as are the ability to work with people and the capacity to win and hold confidences. Last, but not least, they must know how to teach.

ADMINISTRATION

College dormitories and residences, hotels, clubs, hospitals, and all institutions in which large groups of people live must have housekeeping managers to function well. These managers usually are called *institution* or *executive housekeepers*. Since there are over 7,000 hospitals and 22,000 hotels in the United States, many of which employ executive housekeepers, and 2,230 colleges and universities, the majority of which have residence halls, the employment opportunities of home economists trained in management are evident (9; 11; 29, p. 768).

In 1960, there were 122,000 executive housekeepers (29, p. 768). These executive or institution housekeepers keep house on a massive scale. It is their job to see that the establishment is clean, orderly, attractive, and safe and that guests' or patients' rooms are properly equipped and maintained twenty-four hours a day. They may have from one to many assistants to organize and supervise this task (9).

According to a former president of the National Executive Housekeeper Association, to be an executive housekeeper (32):

> . . . you have to be an expert on human relations, psychology, sociology, economics and many other subjects. Your housekeeper today makes out an annual budget in advance for all the things required in a hotel. She is a business woman of the first order. Upon her efficiency, resourcefulness and tact the manager has to depend.

The personal qualifications for such work are intelligence, poise, friendliness, dignity, flexibility, and a sense of humor. Managers must have the ability to meet and talk as equals to everyone around them, whether maid or houseman, doctor, nurse, manager, patient, or guest. Furthermore, executive or institution housekeepers must know management, for they not only manage their own work but that of subordinates. They must be good accountants and be able to keep records, prepare budgets and reports, and order and receive supplies systematically. They should also be shrewd buyers and loyal to the organization.

The home economist who would train for institution housekeeping should have, in addition to a good background in general home economics, training in institution management, textiles, psychology, chemistry of cleaning materials, interior decoration, business organization, household engineering, personnel management, purchasing, and accounting (1, 25).

CONSULTATION

The problem of how to get the most out of one's money, time, and possessions is of interest to more and more people. Since home economists can answer many questions on this point and make suggestions for better spending, they are employed by banks, insurance companies, department stores, and welfare agencies to assist clients with their budgeting problems.

Home economists employed by a bank, insurance company, investment house, or finance corporation are expected to promote a friendly, informal atmosphere so that families will come to them to discuss their personal financial problems, budget needs, or investment interests. Home economists prepare literature that will encourage savings and investments and take an active part in thrift education programs. Also, they make contacts for the company through talks before various women's organizations, civic clubs, social service organizations, public schools, or on radio and TV. One finance corporation with a large consumer education service, in the foreword to bulletins on money management prepared by its home-service department, states (20):

> Each year well over a million families come to Household for help on money problems. . . . Because we lend money to these families we are interested in their efficiency as "going concerns." Our success as a business is measured by the effectiveness of our service in helping customers solve their financial problems.

If the organization has an education program, a home economist probably will be in charge of it. This may involve writing and distributing booklets, planning and producing educational films, and handling correspondence from persons asking for help.

A few experienced home economists have taken up selling life insurance. In life insurance, unlike many industries, the sales opportunities for women are equal to those of men. Several large agencies in metropolitan areas have established women's departments: such units are staffed by women underwriters, and sometimes even the unit manager is a woman (4). Since insurance is so closely allied to home problems, the home economist's ability to assist with wise expenditures and help find ways of saving money with which to buy the insurance has been of genuine help in building sales.

Many department stores maintain personal advisory services, family information services, and budget advisory services for customers. Although their chief purpose is financial advice, people come to them for many kinds of help. In these services, homemakers are assisted in choosing their own and their children's clothing, furnishings, and toilet articles, all of which are selected for their appropriateness to the customer's buying power and needs. Since women buy about 70 percent of these consumer goods, and since husbands and wives shopping together buy 22 percent, the confidence and good will of the homemaker are important to any concern dealing in consumer goods (3, 6, 13, 26).

Often the home economics advisers may prepare booklets for the store to distribute to its customers, but they bring in new business to the store through many other channels: working with public schools, cooperating in home economics class projects, setting up practical and efficient kitchens for display in the store, etc.

In some large cities, women's organizations, in cooperation with business firms, maintain consultation centers and employ home economists to answer questions on family problems, to lecture, and to give demonstrations to women's clubs, schools, and college groups.

An enterprising home economist may go into business for herself (7, 19). For example, she may as a bridal consultant be a liaison worker between the bride and the merchants, in which capacity she advises and helps the bride in all of her purchases, from towels to water heaters. She may work out a budget for the bride's trousseau and house furnishings and assist her in her selection problems. Occasionally, a counselor will maintain a model apartment or house where changing displays are set up by cooperating merchants. Some real estate firms employ home economists to help clients work out plans which will enable them to meet payments on homes they have or intend to buy.

The chief disadvantage of working as a home-management or finance specialist with business and finance institutions is that the worker must be able to prove her efforts are of financial value to the company.

The educational requirements for the management specialist in business are similar to those for education; however, advanced degrees are not as important as an understanding of business. In addition to her education training, she must have the ability to understand, contact, and communicate with people on all income levels. She will find that tactfulness is especially important for one who wishes to serve the public. She must also understand thoroughly the aims, methods, and objectives of the concern for which she is working.

HOUSING AND EQUIPMENT

Ever since home economics began, housing has been recognized as one of its educational responsibilities. In colleges and universities, home economists are found teaching or giving help in house planning, house architecture, household physics, and home equipment. In addition, they write bulletins and prepare materials on housing for families. Home economists try to help homemakers and families answer such questions as the following: size of house needed, family composition in relation to size and design, the needs of families that are increasing or decreasing in number, leases, cost, remodeling, activities for which families need to provide and their special space needs, requirements for comfort, convenience, and health, and house maintenance and care of possessions (15).

Certain building industries employ home economists to interpret the builder's point of view to the family and the family's to the builder—they are the firm's chief contact with the family. These women need to be conversant with the subjects of building materials and costs, art, architecture, decorating, heating, new materials, and new methods of construction. They must be able to speak the language of the builder, the subcontractor, the architect, the interior decorator, and the prospective owner. On the whole, these jobs have been created by the women holding them, and the remuneration is high for the successful home economist. Home economists are rendering a very valuable service in public housing, housing for special groups as the aged and handicapped. In this connection, they may be employed by the government or private industry (15, 22, 30).

INTERIOR DECORATION

An interior decorator is technically defined as one who "plans, designs and executes building interiors and furnishings, to create attractive surroundings in good taste and suited to the needs and desires of the occupants" (17). Where do the interior decorators work? Many are in business for themselves. Others work in retail and department stores, where they serve as the heads of such departments as furniture, floor covering, draperies, or gifts and accessories. They are employed by real estate and housing construction firms, hotels, branches of the government, steamship lines, and other organizations which hire their own decorators on a salary basis. And they are employed by firms which design wallpaper, rugs, furniture, kitchen equipment, and household textiles.

An interior decorator is a combination of artist, businesswoman, psychologist, and salesperson. To be a success, she must possess taste, artistic sense, creative talent, and imagination. She must know the decorative arts, be able to present her ideas well, and be willing to accept trends. She must know families, their needs, and how they meet them, and she must understand family finance. She must be able to handle people with tact and patience, to inspire confidence, and to analyze the desires and needs of the client.

The home economist who is looking forward to a career as an interior decorator should add to her basic training such courses as building construction, advanced work in color and form, history of art, materials of decoration, mechanical drawing, house planning, psychology of selling, and business fundamentals. In addition, she should get some experience with a commercial decorator.

A career in interior decorating can prove fascinating to those who are suited to it and willing to accept that it is not entirely a matter of handling beautiful materials and furnishings. There are many details to handle, such as writing orders and canceling them, figuring estimates, measuring floors and windows, checking yardage, replacing samples, and securing competent assistants (17).

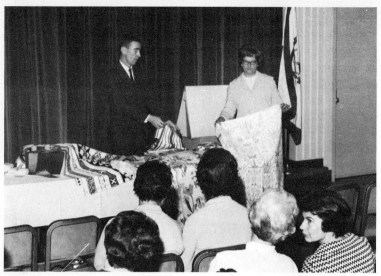

Fig. 10-1 Home economists are involved in the whole range of home living. For example, interior decorating can be a speciality. Here, a home economist helps demonstrate fabrics to a group of housewives. (Courtesy of the Appalachian Power Company)

The American Institute of Decorating, founded in 1931, is working toward making interior decorating a profession which will require the licensing and registering of interior decorators (17).

HOUSEHOLD EQUIPMENT

Manufacturers and distributors of household equipment, as well as the power companies, employ many home economists. Their responsibility is to acquaint the consumer with, and to create a desire for, the new types of equipment available to them. The home economist has the dual role of serving both the consumer and the producer, i.e., she teaches the consumer to use the equipment efficiently, and she helps the producer or retailer by ensuring customer satisfaction. These home economists are usually known as home-service directors, field representatives, or simply home economists.

The duties of a home-service director are many and varied. She may supervise the home service in one city only or in a large area, and she may have a few or many home economists working under her. In any case, she will have the responsibility for organizing the work and obtaining the home economists to do it. In fact, she operates as a minor business executive.

The work of a home economist with a manufacturer or retailer of equipment is fourfold: (1) to acquaint the public with the products and services of the company, (2)

Fig. 10-2 Helping housewives choose the proper size and design appliances is a duty of home economists. (Courtesy of the Appalachian Power Company)

to develop good will for the company and consumer confidence in the company's service and products, (3) to promote the sales of the products by dispensing interesting and reliable information about the products, and (4) to cooperate with other departments of the company, other agencies, and the schools in acquainting the public with the company.

Home economists who work for utilities must know all types of equipment—ranges, refrigerators, water heaters, laundry machines, washers and dryers, ironers, irons, electric pads, lamps, toasters, and other equipment produced by various manufacturers. They must know something of its construction, control, and efficiency of operation. Their purpose is not to sell any one manufacturer's equipment but to sell the services of the utility which they represent by promoting greater use of the equipment.

The following statement gives some idea of what one company expects of its home economists (33):

> Columbia's 90 graduate home economists form an important liaison between the system and the public. They give cooking demonstrations and classes in schools, company kitchens and appliance stores. They prepare radio and television scripts, recipe and menu books and sheets, and

distribute promotional material which is helpful to the homemaker. They answer homemakers' questions by phone, mail, and personal talks, and they help to plan new and remodeled kitchens. Attractive company kitchens are used for cooking classes, demonstrations and research.

The graduate home economists . . . keep up with the latest food and equipment research. Generally they participate in their local commercial business and professional organizations. They may be assigned to field work, lectures, and demonstrations or research.

Those who would train for positions as home economists with utilities and household-equipment and appliance companies will find that a bachelor's degree with a major in household equipment is the minimum. During college, their training should include physics related to the household, food preparation, nutrition, quantity cookery, experimental cookery, interior decoration, house planning, demonstration methods, family finance, kitchen designing and arrangement, public speaking, group leadership, and family relationships. The business side of their education should include a basic knowledge of advertising, salesmanship, business organization, and labor problems.

How many home economists are employed by utilities and household equipment and appliance businesses is not known. In 1962, there were 186 different utilities represented in the membership of the Home Economics Business Department of the American Home Economics Association. Individual utilities in the group employ fifty or more home economists. If to these are added all the producers and retailers of household equipment and appliances who employ home economists, the number becomes sizable.

WHAT THE POSITION PAYS

In many areas of the fields which have just been discussed, it is difficult to get reliable salary figures. In most businesses, the person commands a wage in keeping with her

Table 10-1
Careers in home management, family finance, housing, and equipment

field	average annual salaries*
Education	
College teaching or extension	$7,500–$20,000
Business and industry	7,500– 25,000
Adminstration	
College dormitories and residences	6,000– 10,000
Institution housing, including hotels	5,500– 15,000
Consultation	5,500– 25,000

* These figures are estimates based upon information received by author in spring of 1970.

ability to produce. Those who stay with the business over a period of time usually are able to move up into the better income brackets. The figures given in Table 10-1 concern not only beginners but also those who have been successful in the field and are averages for several different parts of the country.

INTEREST CHECKLIST

Below are listed a number of activities in which home economists engaged in management, housing, and household equipment are participating. As you read each statement, check on the right-hand side the degree to which you would enjoy this activity.

activities	degree of interest		
	much	average	little
I. Home management and family finance			
1. Find easier ways of performing household tasks.	_____	_____	_____
2. Organize activities so that they can be performed in less time.	_____	_____	_____
3. Plan work activities for yourself and others.	_____	_____	_____
4. Plan and organize outings for your group, deciding what needs to be done and who should do it.	_____	_____	_____
5. Try out new types of cleaners or supplies to see if they are better than the ones being used.	_____	_____	_____
6. Read articles telling about the merits of different types of equipment.	_____	_____	_____
7. Plan menus for the family for a given amount of money.	_____	_____	_____
8. Take over the duties of the home periodically to see how well and efficiently the house can be run.	_____	_____	_____
9. Compare prices in different stores for the same articles to see which is the best bargain.	_____	_____	_____
10. Advise your friends on how to earn money or how to buy efficiently.	_____	_____	_____
11. Supervise others doing a job, helping them to perform better.	_____	_____	_____
12. Visit a hospital or hotel to learn how the housekeeping is done, how many employees are used, and how their work is organized.	_____	_____	_____
13. Work with people of various income groups to see their needs and how they can be met.	_____	_____	_____
14. Keep records of expenditures for a club, write out orders, and balance the books.	_____	_____	_____
15. Check in supplies in the department recording those received, those missing.	_____	_____	_____
Score for Section I	_____	_____	_____

activities	degree of interest		
	much	average	little
II. Housing and household equipment:			
1. Study house plans and try to improve the arrangement of rooms, etc.	_____	_____	_____
2. Plan color schemes for your room, your home, or the department.	_____	_____	_____
3. Visit furniture and furnishing departments in stores to see what is being shown for homes.	_____	_____	_____
4. Study ways to rearrange the family kitchen or living room to make it more efficient or attractive.	_____	_____	_____
5. Create designs suitable for wallpaper, draperies, etc., and picture how they would look.	_____	_____	_____
6. Try out new equipment to see if it operates as the directions suggest.	_____	_____	_____
7. Demonstrate the use of new equipment to your friends or class.	_____	_____	_____
8. Give talks on uses of equipment, new products, care of equipment, etc.	_____	_____	_____
9. Talk with friends concerning their wants in clothing, house furnishings, etc., and then visit stores to see where they can be obtained.	_____	_____	_____
10. Watch houses being constructed and learn what the various parts are called by the builders.	_____	_____	_____
11. Compare the ease with which two pieces of equipment perform a task, trying to understand why one does a better job than the other.	_____	_____	_____
12. Work in an interior decoration firm, helping people to select their draperies, lamps, etc.	_____	_____	_____
13. Help your teacher put on a food demonstration for your class or others.	_____	_____	_____
14. Watch demonstrations of equipment or foods on TV, criticizing the techniques the demonstrator uses to put over her ideas.	_____	_____	_____
15. Study the homes of your friends to see how they could be made more attractive.	_____	_____	_____
Score for Section II	_____		
Total score	_____		

In scoring your answers use the following procedure. For each activity which you check in the "Much" column, give a score of 2. To each activity which you check in the "Average" column, give a score of 1. If the total score for a section is between 20 and 30, you have indicated considerable interest for this particular type of work. If the combined score of the two sections is between 40 and 60, you have indicated considerable interest for this field of work.

SUGGESTED ACTIVITIES

1. Find out how many home economists are employed in your state in home management, family finance, housing, and equipment. By writing to the utilities in your state, you can find out how many home economists they employ. Your state home economics association can give you some help in this venture.

2. Invite the housing and home-management specialists of your home economics college and your extension service to speak to your class. Talk with them concerning the types of work they are doing and the requests which they receive from homemakers.

3. Visit a household-equipment store in your town or nearby city. Ask the dealer to explain some of the new types of equipment being offered for sale, the merits of the equipment, etc.

4. Talk with homemakers about the problems they have in getting everything done in the time available. What activities do they like best and which ones do they dislike? Try to work out some plans that will make it easier for these homemakers to perform their tasks in the time available.

5. Keep a time schedule for yourself for a week, indicating the amount of time you spend on the various activities each day. At the end of the week evaluate the way in which you have spent your time. Were you allowing sufficient time for all the activities necessary? Were you wasting time? Were you giving too much time to certain activities to the neglect of others? You may wish to talk with the home-management teacher concerning a better use of your time.

6. Ask to accompany a home economist who works for a utility or equipment company for a day to get a better understanding of her field of work. Many questions will arise on which you will wish to seek information. She will be able to tell you some of the training needs for home economics students who wish to go into this type of work.

7. It would be worthwhile to talk with a home economist who is doing research in management or housing and equipment. Let her explain how they find out the information which appears in the published pamphlets and bulletins. She can discuss with you the training necessary for a research career and the rewards from doing it.

REFERENCES

1. Bradley, Lewis Allen, "The Selection, Care, and Laundering of Institutional Textiles," *Cornell Hotel and Restaurant Administration Quarterly of the School of Hotel Administration,* Cornell University Press, Ithaca, N.Y., 1963.

2. Bricker, A. June, and Ruth B. Hayes, "Home Management Orientation for the Social Worker," *Journal of Home Economics,* vol. 45, pp. 101–104, February 1953.

3. Bymers, Gwen J., "Consumer Education and the Home Economist," *Journal of Home Economics*, vol. 55, pp. 327–330, May 1963.

4. *Careers in Life Insurance*, The Institute of Research, Research No. 40, Chicago, 1953.

5. *Colleges and Universities with Undergraduate Majors in Home Economics*, American Home Economics Association, Washington, June 1967.

6. Converse, Paul D., and Harvey W. Huegy, *The Elements of Marketing*, p. 27, Prentice-Hall, Inc., Englewood Cliffs, N.J., 1941.

7. Dendel, Esther S., "My Career as Home-Economist–Artist–Manufacturer," *Journal of Home Economics*, vol. 45, pp. 257–258, April 1953.

8. *Directory—Home Economics in Business, 1962*, American Home Economics Association, Wellington Printing Co., St. Louis, n.d.

9. *Executive Housekeeping as a Career*, The Institute for Research, Research No. 181, Chicago, 1958.

10. Freeman, Ruth Crawford, and Jean M. Due, "Influence of Goals on Family Financial Management," *Journal of Home Economics*, vol. 53, pp. 448–452, June 1961.

11. Green, Geraldine W., "The Potential for Home Economics in the Rehabilitation Service," *Journal of Home Economics*, vol. 61, pp. 418–420, June 1969.

12. Gross, Irma H., and E. W. Crandell, *Management for Modern Families*, pp. 98–99, Appleton-Century-Crofts, Inc., New York, 1963.

13. Hallburt, Helen and others, "Business Speaks to the Consumer through Home Economics," *Journal of Home Economics*, vol. 55, pp. 420–422, June 1963.

14. Hanson, Arthur W., and Jerome B. Cohen, *Personal Finance*, Richard D. Irwin, Inc., Homewood, Ill., 1954.

15. Hodge, Madeline C., "Serving the Needs of Families in Public Housing Development," *Journal of Home Economics*, vol. 55, pp. 127–128, October 1963.

16. *Hotel Management as a Career*, The Institute of Research, Research No. 34, Chicago, 1955.

17. *Interior Decorating as a Career*, The Institute of Research, Research No. 5, Chicago, 1967.

18. Margolius, Sidney K., *The Innocent Consumer vs the Exploiters*, p. 6, Trident Press, New York, 1967.

19. Mills, Nancy, *Home Economists in Action*, pp. 107–117, Scholastic Book Service, New York, 1968.

20. *Money Management: Your Shopping Dollar*, Household Finance Corporation, Consumer Education Department, Chicago, 1952.

21. Moore, Alverda M., and Richard Morse, "Consumer Demand for Homemaker Services," *Journal of Home Economics*, vol. 58, pp. 262–265, April 1966.

22. Muse, Marianne, "Homes for Old Age," *Journal of Home Economics*, vol. 57, pp. 183–187, March 1965.

23. Nicpon, Janet, and Eileen E. Quigley, "The Challenge, the Need, the Opportunity in Home Economics through Graduate Study," *Journal of Home Economics,* vol. 58, pp. 736–739, November 1966.

24. Olmstead, Agnes Reasor, "The Home Economists' Responsibilities to the Family in the Consumer Age," *Journal of Home Economics,* vol. 53, pp. 537–542, September 1961.

25. Riker, Harold C., *College Students Live Here: A Study of College Housing,* Educational Facilities Laboratories, New York, 1961.

26. Rogers, Willie Mae and others, "Organizations Speak to Consumers through Home Economics," *Journal of Home Economics,* vol. 53, pp. 331–334, May 1963.

27. Thal, Helen M., and Lois J. Gutherie, "Consumer Education—Dynamics of Teaching," *Journal of Home Economics,* vol. 61, pp. 762–767, December 1969.

28. Trotter, Virginia, "Dimensions of Home Economics in Rehabilitation," *Journal of Home Economics,* vol. 61, pp. 405–407, June 1969.

29. U.S. Bureau of the Census, *Statistical Abstracts of the United States, 1971,* 92d ed. p. 316.

30. Weeks, Shirley S., "Home Economics Education in a Low-income Housing Development," *Journal of Home Economics,* vol. 57, pp. 437–441, June 1965.

31. Whitten, E. B., "Rehabilitation Philosophy of Today and the 1970's," *Journal of Home Economics,* vol. 61, pp. 412–414, June 1969.

32. Winchester, Maude, Address Delivered before the 47th Annual Convention of the American Hotel Association, Philadelphia, as reported in *The Roanoke Times,* Sept. 25, 1958.

33. *Your Career with the Columbia Gas Company,* The Columbia Gas Company, New York, n.d.

34. *Statistical Abstracts of the United States: 1971,* 92nd, pp. 310, 443, U.S. Department of Commerce, 1971.

ADDITIONAL READINGS

Beaver, Irene, "Contributions Home Economists Can Make to Low Income Families," *Journal of Home Economics,* vol. 57, pp. 107–111, February 1965.

Donnelly, Jean, "Home Economics Sparks Unique Career," *What's New in Home Economics,* vol. 31, p. 20, September 1967.

Eck, Sarah, "Home Economics Paves the Way," *What's New in Home Economics,* vol. 31, pp. 7, 103, February 1967.

"Home Economics Sparks Unique Career," *What's New in Home Economics,* vol. 32, p. 8, November 1968.

Humpheries, Theresa R., *Future for Home Economists,* pp. 127–164, Prentice-Hall, Inc., Englewood Cliffs, N.J., 1963.

Phillips, Velma, *Home Economics Careers for You*, pp. 105–115, 122–127, Harper & Row, New York, 1962.

Preston, Nathalie, "Home Economists Have Much to Contribute to Home-maker-services Programs," *Journal of Home Economics*, vol. 57, pp. 105–106, February 1965.

Rushing, Ann, "Home Economists in Action," *Forecast for Home Economics—Co-ed Section*, vol. 13, p. 37, January 1968.

11 BUSINESS AND COMMUNICATIONS

Business may need home economists for any or all of six reasons: (1) to make a profit, (2) to increase sales, (3) to meet competition, (4) to handle consumer matters, (5) to achieve more efficiency at lower cost, and (6) to repeat previous success experienced with other home economists (29). Business and industry are becoming quite conscious of the fact that women buy more consumer goods than do men (23). Thus it is very important that business be able to supply the type of products women want in a way that is acceptable to them. The home economist in business performs a dual role: she has the responsibility of interpreting the needs and wishes of the woman consumer to the manufacturer and retailer while bringing the products and services of business and industry to the attention of the consumer and making them appealing to her (6).

Women are found in increasing numbers at all levels of business organization in all kinds of business, and the trend is toward an even greater variety of jobs and responsibility. Although it is common knowledge that the number of positions in business for women has increased materially, the great increase at the executive level may be surprising. There are approximately $5^1/_2$ million women in positions of responsibility in every part of business today, as managers, officials, proprietors, technical workers, and in professions—a 51 percent increase since 1950 (31). It has been estimated that 69 percent of the executives in business are retired each year, with an available male replacement rate of only 45 percent (2). The other 24 percent will have to be filled by women, and many industries are especially suited to the activities of the trained home economist.

Women do all types of work in business. Research and analysis work in such organizations as banks, insurance companies, investment firms, and large industries and manufacturing companies usually require as an entering wedge at least a basic knowledge of accounting and statistics. Promotions depend upon experience as much as training. Merchandising, public relations, advertising, the women's magazine field, and food, textile, and similar industries make great use of home economists. These presuppose some creative talent and special training, which in combination with training in business administration can lead to very highly paid and responsible positions in comparatively short time. The competition is keen, and job security is dependent on individual performance.

Home economics careers in business are classified in the *Directory of the Department of Home Economics in Business* of the American Home Economics Association under eighteen headings (10, p. 7):

Advertising	Hotels
Advertising promotion	Journalism
Consultant	Journalism on magazines
Detergents	Journalism on newspapers
Equipment	Public relations
Finance	Radio
Foods	Restaurant and tea rooms
General business	Textiles
Home service	Television

The Home Economics in Business Department of the American Home Economics Association was officially formed in 1923, with a membership of 62. In 1962, it had 2,468 members (24). Of course, there are many more home economists employed by businesses than this number would indicate, for the requirements for membership in the HEIB are rather high. An applicant for membership must (10, p. 7):

1. Be a member of the American Home Economics Association
2. Hold a degree in home economics or a degree with a major in home economics from an accredited college as described in Article 2 of the bylaws of the HEIB constitution
3. Be connected in a home economics capacity with a business run for profit or with an association supported by business run for profit (This does not include cafeterias or tea rooms financed by educational institutions, government agencies, social agencies, or welfare organizations.)
4. Be employed for four consecutive months with her present employer in a home economics capacity before application is made
5. Be engaged in home economics work, such as:
    a. Sales promotion through educational work
    b. Educational publicity
    c. Management of own business in the home economics field
    d. Research applied to problems in home economics in business
    e. Free-lance or consultant service to which over 50 percent of average working year is given
    f. Any application of home economics training in the business field which may develop, and which, in the minds of the membership committee, is included in the term "home economics in business"

The HEIB membership in 1962 represented 362 agencies, associations, manufacturers, and miscellaneous organizations; 86 publications, radio and TV stations; and 186 public utilities (10, pp. 81–87). Many of these concerns have offices or plants in several sections of the country. This raises the total number of businesses that have home economists with membership in the American Home Economics Association to approximately 2,000. In a 1966 survey of the HEIB membership, it was found that 40 percent of these home economists were employed as home service representatives by utility companies; 20 percent worked for food processing or appliance companies; 8 percent were employed in journalism or in writing; 6 percent were in some form of public relations; 6 percent were employed by dairy councils; 5 percent were free-lance consultants; and 15 percent were in a wide variety of other occupations (16).

In the discussion which follows, the fields of clothing and house furnishings are omitted, since business opportunities in these fields were discussed in Chapters 8 and 10.

ADVERTISING

The advertising business is one of the great new industries created by the high-speed, high-pressure, and high-production world in which we all live and work today. It is also an occupation whose ancestry goes back beyond the earliest historical records. The town criers of medieval Europe were among the early advertising men: it was their job to shout news about wines, spices, or tapestries that ships brought in from foreign ports (8).

Advertising today is a tremendous business. America spends approximately 18 billion dollars annually for advertising (31). Although there are only about 65,000 people directly employed in advertising agencies, advertising is an important part of many businesses that employ thousands of nonadvertising workers. It has been estimated that 25,000 new items are introduced on the American market every year through advertising (4).

Advertising jobs may be divided into three main groups: those connected with (1) advertising agencies, (2) the firms which have goods and services to sell, and (3) the media. "Media" refers to the instruments actually used to carry advertising to the public, such as magazines, radio stations, TV, signs, and direct mail.

Advertising uses people of very different talents and training (9). The art department of an advertising agency has the responsibility for creating the art work and layouts. The artists draw, paint, sketch, and design for the advertising, and they retouch and copy photographs. For these positions, art ability and ideas are essential.

The writing of the advertising is done in the copy department. An employee in this department needs to be good at writing slogans, headlines, and short, telling sentences and paragraphs pointing up the trade-mark or the products of the company.

People in many different types of positions are involved in producing advertising. Some employees advise the clients and buy the types of service needed. Others select the radio or TV time and stations, engage the talent to put on the program, and rehearse it, in addition to creating the program and advertising messages. Still others must produce and time new releases for the newspapers and periodicals.

Fig. 11-1 A home economist in business is conducting a cook-in for appliance saleswomen. (Courtesy of Corning Glass Works)

The home economist will find almost limitless opportunity in the advertising field if she is prepared for the demands that will be made upon her. Anyone considering advertising as a career should ask herself the following questions: Do I like to work with all sorts of people? Do I work well under pressure? Do I like to explore the ever-new problems of analyzing and selling products? Do I have creative ability?

The home economist going into advertising must know home economics subject matter and skills. She will not have time to learn them after she is on the job. Since most advertising agencies handle many types of products and services, wide information in many fields is valuable. She must know the fundamentals of food preparation, the elements of nutrition, household equipment and its uses or possible uses to homemakers, and textile and textile products and their appeal to the consumer. She must know fashion trends in clothing, textiles, foods, equipment, and furnishings, to mention only a few. A knowledge of merchandising and sales problems, and an understanding of the buying habits of the public are musts in advertising. In addition, the advertiser must know how to write in simple, understandable terms, have a wide, usable vocabulary, and know the language usage of the

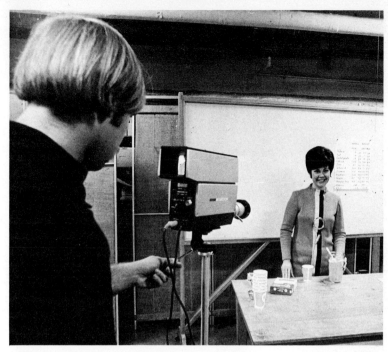

Fig. 11-2   The home economist in business engages in many types of publicity work. This home economist is preparing for a television demonstration. (Courtesy of the College of Education, University of Kentucky)

group whom she wishes to attract. Some knowledge of photography and drawing are essential. Last but not least, the would-be advertiser must learn how to organize her thinking quickly under pressure and develop good work habits, for in advertising *deadlines must be met.*

HOME SERVICE AND EQUIPMENT

The manufacture and sales of home appliances have risen consistently since 1960 providing a wide variety of opportunities for home economists in home service and equipment (20). For example, the manufacturers of such equipment as ranges, laundry equipment, electric houseware, kitchen utensils, and cabinets have home economics staffs. The requirements for these positions differ; certain types of equipment jobs call for women with a highly developed promotional sense, while others demand almost the research worker's approach. However, all businesses that employ home economists expect them to interpret the company's products to prospective buyers in terms that they can understand and that will induce them to buy (13). Any ambitious graduate in home economics will find excellent opportunities

Fig. 11-3 Home economists cooperate with appliance dealers in demonstrations during open-house or appliance shows in the store. (Courtesy of the Appalachian Power Company)

for advancement in home service, because a great variety of activities are included in a home-service program. These include (14, 15):

1. Advising and assisting customers with all homemaking problems with which the company is concerned
2. Demonstrating or discussing food, equipment, home lighting, kitchen or laundry planning with groups of women or teenagers
3. Giving instructions on proper care and reconditioning of appliances
4. Talking to club groups or schools on subjects relating to food and equipment
5. Handling complaint calls on use of equipment, cost, etc.
6. Testing recipes and developing new uses for equipment
7. Writing homemaking articles for newspapers
8. Preparing food for photographs
9. Appearing on radio and TV shows
10. Providing information by telephone and printed literature
11. Training company and appliance-dealer salesmen through classes and demonstrations
12. Assisting customers with laundry problems as new fabrics and equipment come on the market
13. Building good will toward the company

Fig. 11-4 Cooperation with the Girl Scouts in conducting cooking classes for young members of the organization is one of the many activities in which home economists engage. (Courtesy of the Appalachian Power Company)

Equipment and home-service companies offer a chance for the practical application of many things learned in home economics. In addition, many companies give additional, on-the-job training to new employees, as well as an initial training course. Such training is provided the beginners as follows (5):

1. By working with experienced home economists
2. By supervisors
3. Through training meetings
4. By sending them to educational meetings held by distributors and manufacturers
5. Through use of films, meetings, etc.
6. By studying magazines, literature, periodicals, etc.

Positions are open to home economics graduates as they leave college if they have majored in household equipment or a related field. There also are many opportunities for home economists with experience in related fields such as teaching or dietetics.

In training for equipment or home-service work, one should have, in addition to her general education and her knowledge of general home economics subject

Fig. 11-5 Home economists are sought for radio and television broadcasts because of their expert advice, demonstrated here in this live performance in an appliance dealer's store. (Courtesy of the Appalachian Power Company)

matter, courses in household equipment and physics, experimental and quantity cookery, demonstration methods, journalism, public speaking, radio and TV presentation, and advertising and sales promotion.

PERSONNEL AND PUBLIC RELATIONS

Most businesses and industries today have departments of personnel and public relations, for example, in manufacturing plants, department stores, life insurance companies, hotels, banks, and advertising agencies. Personnel and public relations departments began to be considered necessary when business recognized that there is an interrelationship between the emotional adjustment of individuals and their performance on the job and also that a feeling of good will for the business by the employees and the public in general is an important asset to any business. This growing need for personnel workers is shown by the fact that while there were 3,000 employed service counselors in 1965, the Office of Economic Opportunity estimated that there would be need for 7,742 workers in 1970, and 8,292 in 1975 (30).

Webster's Dictionary defines public relations as "the activities of a corporation, union, government, or other organization in building and maintaining sound and productive relations with special publics such as customers, employees, or stockholders, and with the public at large, so as to adapt itself to its environment and interpret itself to society." Personnel officers advise and assist at all levels in matters relating to the people in the organization. The personnel department has many duties, including maintaining good relations among employees and between employees and the business, selecting the right employees for the job, starting and training new employees, and developing their potential abilities. Also, this department must develop a source of qualified applicants. The personnel department must also analyze duties and write job specifications, interpret the policies of the business to the employees, and develop and maintain a high level of morale among workers. Finally, it must look after the welfare of the workers generally; this includes protecting their health and physical conditions and helping them with their personal and job-adjustment problems (26).

Home economists who have the special training and aptitude for personnel or public relations work are finding many opportunities open to them. Personnel work is regarded as a natural field for women, and it is even more so for home economists because of their special training for, and interest in, working with individuals and families. Home economists will find that their opportunities are especially good with those companies where home economics subject-matter information is important, such as concerns that have to deal with consumer interests and problems, food, clothing, household equipment and furnishings, and industries which deal with or employ large groups of women. Where women constitute a major part of the working force, there seems to be more chance of a woman becoming head of personnel than in companies where men predominate. New fields and new companies where employees are few and "everyone gets a chance to do everything" seem promising to women's advancement (4).

The home economist who wishes to go into personnel and public relations work needs to have a good understanding of people and families. Her degree in home economics will furnish the wedge for entering the field if she has the other qualifications. Additional requirements include the ability to write, speak, and handle meetings and interviews. The ability to work with and help people, a friendly personality and the ability to generate confidence, and an understanding and sympathetic approach to people are musts, as is a genuine interest in people. Personnel and public relations workers must have a basic curiosity and at the same time be able to maintain a high degree of objectivity and a high ethical level in these contacts (1). Furthermore, they must be able to work under pressure.

If they are to do counseling, they must understand its fundamentals. This requires a good background in psychology, including developmental psychology, personal dynamics and motivation, learning principles, plus some knowledge of clinical and abnormal psychology. A working knowledge of health and medicine, sociology, marriage and family life, child guidance, and family economics are essential to success.

The home economist who wishes to go to the top in personnel and public relations must accept that the stepping stones to success are the years of hard work in which one learns and unlearns, observes and tests, plans and re-plans, and gradually grows more efficient in the selection and use of the tools and techniques of public relations and counseling.

BUSINESS FOOD POSITIONS

Food positions in business are found in two different types of industries. The first includes the manufacturers, the processors and distributors of food products, and the trade associations (19). The other is made up of the commercial feeding establishments, such as restaurants, hotels, tea rooms, camps, cafeterias, and clubs (11).

There are about 350,000 commercial eating establishments whose main business is the serving of food and beverages. Over 2 million people work in them and an additional million are employed in establishments which serve meals in connection with some other activity such as hotels, drug and department stores, private clubs, schools, and industrial plants. According to government statistics, more than 800 million meals are served in public eating places each week.

Most large food processors and manufacturers employ a staff of home economists as directors of the home economics program and as workers in food research, food testing, and public relations. These home economists have a wide range of responsibility, including investigating the needs of consumers and interpreting them to the manufacturer. Their research on the development and use of new products, as well as on consumer acceptance of these products, goes on continuously. The home economics staff also answers all food information requests from the general public and brings the products of the business to the attention of the consumer. This entails writing leaflets, recipe sheets, and directions for use which go on the packages, as well as preparing food for photography to be used in advertising. Supplying material and checking radio and TV scripts, acting as technical directors or participating in radio and TV programs, giving demonstrations in churches, stores, schools, and club groups all are a part of the duties of some of the home economists.

The distributors of food products and the trade associations have home economists employed to do similar work. Their jobs are primarily concerned with the education of the consumer to use the products which they are distributing or sponsoring. The activities of these home economists also include radio and TV programs, writing recipe leaflets, giving demonstrations of how to use the products and why they should be used as demonstrated, and answering many requests of consumers.

The food-service industry is an outstanding field for home economists. Not only does the field pay well for the qualified worker but it furnishes opportunities to help realize the home economist's high ideals and high standards in the selection of well-balanced menus and in the cooking and serving of nutritious foods. High standards in food service can have a far-reaching effect in the home and the community. As more and more people eat away from home, the restaurant industry has an even greater service to render in the future (11, 13). When one realizes that over 25 percent of all the food consumed in the United States today is eaten in commercial outlets such as restaurants, hotels, and tea rooms, the increasing need for trained people to staff these establishments can be appreciated.

Food-service industries have a contrasting variety of operations to be performed and therefore have many types of positions—some requiring great executive ability and others calling for various degrees of education and responsibility. The food-service industries list many advantages for employment with them. These may be grouped as follows (10):

1. Restaurants provide excellent opportunities for well-trained young men and women.

2. Employment in restaurants operating year-round is steady. There are no dull seasons and no layoffs.

3. The work of an executive in a restaurant involves the study of such a wide variety of subjects that keeping up to date is a continuous education—a veritable graduate course.

4. Knowledge gained in school can be applied both directly and indirectly.

5. Opportunities for advancement in the industry reach all the way to the top: there is priority for the able.

6. Provision of such essential service in a community brings recognition and satisfaction to the executive.

7. Knowledge of good restaurant operation and service is valuable in any food position or in the home.

8. Salaries are regular—in booms or depressions, during war or in peacetime.

9. Hospitalization plans, health and accident insurance, group life insurance, old-age pensions, bonuses, incentive plans, and other benefits are furnished by many restaurants to bring additional security to those employed.

10. Vacations with pay are regularly granted.

11. Opportunities are now available for training on and for the job.

Training for the business field of foods should include, in addition to a general background in home economics, a good understanding of food selection and preparation, meal planning and service, and experimental cookery. A knowledge of nutrition and dietetics is as essential as in institution management. The institution-management courses should include quantity cookery, organization and management, and institution accounting. As background work, chemistry, human physiology, bacteriology, and psychology are required, as are courses in personnel management, economics, and some methods of teaching. If one is to be responsible for food testing, some experience and training in research methods and statistics would be helpful.

From a personal standpoint, anyone going into foods as a business should have genuine interest and skill in their handling. She must look well, develop a professional attitude toward food, and be able to believe in the products she is promoting. As in all business positions, alertness, loyalty, ability to work with others, and willingness to start at the bottom and work up are requirements for success.

COMMUNICATIONS

"Communications" refers to that process through which information, ideas, and attitudes are shared by people, firms, or agencies. Communication is a process so basic to everyday life that we tend to take it for granted. It is only when it breaks down or one gets into trouble because of its misuse that one becomes aware of its importance, which is as true of person-to-person contacts as of mass communications. The mass communicators usually are considered to be the newspapers, magazines, and other printed media, and the radio and TV networks (22). The home economics subjects given the most attention as materials for mass communication, arranged in order of greatest importance, are as follows:

1. Foods
2. Home management
3. Clothing
4. Home demonstration
5. Housing
6. Family life
7. Child care

Journalism is becoming a very important field for home economists (23). Journalists present the news in many ways: in writing for newspapers and magazines; in writing and presenting radio and television programs; in factual and interpretive reporting; in special and dramatic presentations; and in many other ways (17).

There are over fifty women's magazines on the newsstands today, and at least that many more have editorial sections on home economics. These magazines buy well-written, accurate articles on subjects about the home—and who is better qualified to write them than home economists? Home economists who wish to write should remember that writing is not so much a matter of inspiration as of information plus hard work.

The journalist, first of all, must like and be able to write rapidly, factually, and well. She must have an intense desire to learn what is happening, and to communicate the information to others. She must have an alert, inquiring mind which never takes anything for granted. She must be able to get along with people and have initiative. She must, of course, be able to type her stories rapidly and meet deadlines (17). The home economist who wishes to follow journalism as a career must be able to translate trustworthy technical information into language that is easily read and understood by the homemakers who read the paper or magazine in which the work appears. This requires knowledge of readers and their interests, needs, and problems. The home economist must know the services in the communities from which their readers come, and if she is writing about merchandise, she must know the markets.

Many abilities in addition to that of being able to write are necessary for home economics journalists. They must have sufficient knowledge of testing and research to try out new ideas in the laboratory before writing about them. This includes knowledge of clothing and textiles, developing or testing recipes, trying out new appliances, following through on shopping hints, figuring out budget problems, interviewing individuals and families, and keeping up to date on housing and furnishings. The ability to draw and sketch or photograph is of untold use to the journalist, and shorthand and typing are excellent tools. In addition, the journalist must understand the preparation of materials for printing and what constitutes good writing, acceptable English, and publishable form. The home economist must be able to write creatively, pick out the errors in her own writing, present an interesting message with a limited number of words. A good journalist must be a good storyteller, whether the story is told in an advertising slogan, a picture, or an article.

RADIO AND TV

Radio and TV, unlike most of the other business areas open to home economists, are limited in their opportunities, and radio, though the older of the two, offers even fewer openings than does TV. These outlets are growing, however, and do have good career possibilities for home economists who succeed (6).

Home economists may play any number of roles in radio or TV and may be sponsored by business or an educational institution. They may have a feature program in which they are the principal performers, which requires dramatic talent and the ability to speak so as to give a pleasing, convincing presentation. On the other hand, they may be responsible for writing and "putting over" the commercials. This requires a good knowledge of the products advertised and their use, as well as the ability to produce "catchy" slogans and phrases and present them interestingly. In some cases, home economists may have the task of demonstrating the use of the product or equipment manufactured by the sponsor. Again, they may be found writing the script, developing the stage scenes or interiors, and preparing the products for the show. At times they may have the responsibility of directing the broadcast or the show.

Home economists may use any number of methods in presenting their story to the public, which is usually the homemaker or family (7, 12, 15, 21). Demonstration is a popular method for dealing with many home economics subjects; however, the interview, the roundtable discussion, the quiz program, and the symposium are useful procedures. Pantomime, puppets, "chalk talks," "flannel-board talks," films and slides, and any other means which give good results as teaching tools may be used to carry the home economist's message.

Personal qualifications for radio and TV work are similar to those of other business fields; however, greater emphasis is placed upon the use of dramatic devices which appeal through the eye and ear. The home economist who aspires to a career in the visual and sound media should, in addition to having a thorough understanding of home economics, study play production, voice and diction, journalism, and motivation dynamics. College experience in radio and TV production is a great asset. The student should try to be ready to fill all the positions in the radio and TV studio, from script writer or editor to producer. Any experience in working with the public, presenting ideas to it, or selling to it are invaluable for the one who would choose radio and television as a career.

Irrespective of the field of business the home economist enters, certain personal qualities will help her make a success of the job. One home economist expresses them in the following words (27):

> Our first responsibility to our company is integrity.... Integrity of purpose, of standards, and of work. It means loyalty and honesty in what we think and say and do. And if the company we work for does not inspire that kind of integrity in us—we'd better get ourselves another job.
>
> Second, we owe the company an ability to recognize the need for occasional compromise—and the ability to select the degree and method of compromise.... [We must] be reasonably flexible.... We have a responsibility to develop, an ability to separate personal opinion from research....
>
> We owe our company a desire and an ability to grow and develop as the needs of the job indicate. There's no such thing as standing still—we either go forward or backward....
>
> We owe the company maturity ... acting our professional age....
>
> Home economics is a wonderful profession. It gives all of us an opportunity to do a woman's work in a man's world, work which only women can do.

The qualifications for a career in business are summed up in the following statement, prepared by the American Home Economics Association (5).

> The best training for business is a good, general course in home economics, with special courses in the major areas that most interest you. Typing, public speaking, journalism, consumer economics, and business practice are all helpful. Extracurricular activities develop poise and personality.
>
> Business demands much of its home economists. Requirements include a good appearance, physical endurance, poise and ability to work well under

pressure, a sense of responsibility, and of course, a sound knowledge of your subject based on well-rounded home economics fundamentals. No matter what career you choose you will find that enthusiasm, willingness to learn, accuracy and attention to detail, initiative, ingenuity, and the ability to get along with others and to take criticism are important. You'll find place, too, for a sense of humor and an awareness of what is going on in the world.

WHAT THE POSITIONS PAY

It is almost impossible to give a salary figure for positions in business. The ability of the individual home economists to produce or render services which the business concern needs constitutes their bargaining power, and their remuneration will be based upon the felt need of the businesses for their services. The competition in business is keen, and those who go to the top command handsome salaries. In most of these business fields, the salaries for a college graduate beginning in the field is around $5,000 to $6,000, while the experienced and successful worker's salary will be in the $10,000 to $25,000 bracket.

INTEREST CHECKLIST FOR CAREERS

Below are listed a number of activities in which home economists in business engage. As you read the statement on the left-hand side of the page, check the column on the right-hand side which describes the extent to which you would be interested in each activity. When you have checked all of the items, score your interests as described at the end of the test.

activities	degree of interest		
	much	average	little
1. Sell or demonstrate products or equipment to consumers.	_____	_____	_____
2. Prepare slogans for advertising.	_____	_____	_____
3. Try out new equipment for preparing foods or carrying on household activities.	_____	_____	_____
4. Test new products to see if they meet requirements for performance.	_____	_____	_____
5. Develop educational materials which promote the use of a product or service of business.	_____	_____	_____
6. Do research to develop new products or new uses for old products for a manufacturer.	_____	_____	_____
7. Act as a special consultant for business or industry.	_____	_____	_____
8. Write articles on foods, clothing, design, or family relationships for magazines.	_____	_____	_____

activities	degree of interest		
	much	average	little
9. Maintain a regular newspaper column in one or more home economics subject-matter fields.	————	————	————
10. Work with men in promoting sales or advertising.	————	————	————
11. Provide information by telephone or in printed literature for consumers.	————	————	————
12. Prepare window and floor sales displays.	————	————	————
13. Attend meetings with other business employees to discuss promotion of company's products.	————	————	————
14. Train employees to perform specific jobs in business.	————	————	————
15. Prepare food, clothing, equipment, or furnishings for photographing.	————	————	————
16. Appear on radio and TV shows.	————	————	————
17. Develop radio and TV programs, including selecting and training performers.	————	————	————
18. Handle complaint calls on use of equipment, cost, etc.	————	————	————
19. Talk to club groups or schools on subjects relating to foods, equipment, furnishings, and other household interests.	————	————	————
20. Represent the business firm at conferences, promotion meetings, and other public affairs.	————	————	————
21. Interview applicants for positions, and judge their qualifications.	————	————	————
22. Counsel with workers concerning their job or personal problems.	————	————	————
23. Analyze and write specifications for various jobs in business or industry.	————	————	————
24. Develop sales-promotion programs for a business or industry.	————	————	————
25. Manage a commercial feeding establishment or a large department in a store or industry.	————	————	————
Total score	————————————————		

To score your interest responses give a value of 2 to each one marked "Much," and a value of 1 to each one marked "Average." If your total score is between 35 and 50, your interest in the activities associated with business is high.

SUGGESTED ACTIVITIES

1. The names of the home economists in business in the state can be obtained from the state home economics association. By writing to or talking with some of these home economists, the following information can be secured:

a. What different types of work are these home economists doing?

b. What were their training and experience before going on to the jobs they now have?

c. Why did they choose business instead of some of the other fields of home economics?

d. What do they think are the advantages and disadvantages of work in business?

e. What advice do they have for the home economics students who are considering a career in business?

2. Invite a nearby home economist in business to speak to the class. Ask her to discuss the following:

a. What is a typical day like for a business home economist?

b. How does she use her home economics training in her work?

c. How does she help her company or firm through her knowledge of home economics?

d. How can she serve her company and at the same time help families and homemakers?

3. Visit a large department store to learn the types of consumer services which home economists are especially qualified to perform.

a. What consumer services are provided by the store?

b. How many of these services fall into the subject-matter fields of home economics?

c. How does rendering these services aid the store in sales promotion?

d. What additional services could be provided by the store if it had well-qualified home economists on its staff?

4. Make a study of the magazines found in the homes of the community.

a. How many and what types of articles are carried by the magazines specifically for homemakers?

b. Who are the authors of these articles? What training have they had?

c. In what ways could the magazines be of greater service to the homemakers and their families by carrying better-written or different types of articles?

5. Study the advertising in the women's magazines.

a. What special abilities would the designing of this advertising require?

b. Is the advertising informative or misleading? How could it be improved by a home economist?

6. Visit the sales department of a business that deals in household equipment, home furnishings, clothing, or some other type of consumer goods.

a. What procedures are used to catch the attention of the homemakers?

b. Are home economists employed in the advertising and selling aspects of the business? Why?

c. What are the requirements for good sales-promotion people as seen by these business executives?

d. Does the business have a home economics service?

7. Cover the radio and TV programs for a given period of time.

a. How many home economists appeared on these programs?

b. How representative were they of what home economics stands for?

c. Consult the advertising concerns on these programs to ascertain how many are employing home economists? What do the home economists do?

d. How could these programs be improved by trained home economists?

REFERENCES

1. Auchord, Denny, "What Every Profession Should Know about Today's Guidance Counselor," *What's New in Home Economics,* vol. 30, pp. 18–23, November-December 1966.

2. Bates, Mercedes, "The Home Economist as a Leader in Business," *Forecast for Home Economics,* vol. 13, pp. 42–43, March 1968.

3. Bensman, Joseph, *Dollars and Sense,* p. 9, The Macmillan Company, New York, 1967.

4. Bogart, Lee, *Strategy in Advertising,* p. 18, Harcourt, Brace & World, Inc., New York, 1967.

5. *Career Opportunities in Home Economics in Business,* American Home Economics Association, Washington, 1954.

6. *A Career with a Future,* American Home Economics Association, Washington, 1968.

7. Chapitis, Gladys, "Making a Television Series," *Journal of Home Economics,* vol. 56, pp. 99–101, February 1964.

8. Davis, Edwin W., *Advertising as an Occupation,* Occupational Monograph 9, PR 5, 10, Science Research Associates, Inc., Chicago, 1969.

9. Dichert, Ernest, "How Word-of-mouth Advertising Works," *Harvard Business Review,* vol. 44, pp. 147–166, November-December 1966.

10. *Directory of Home Economists in Business,* American Home Economics Association, Washington, 1963.

11. Erdman, Herbert, "Home Economists: Director of Cafeterias," *Journal of Home Economics,* vol. 53, pp. 79–82, February 1961.

12. Griffith, Barton L., "Some Uses of Television by Home Economies," *Journal of Home Economics,* vol. 56, pp. 95–98, February 1964.

13. Gurvich, Bernice, "A Guide to Judging Women Job Candidates," *Personnel Journal,* vol. 47, pp. 259–261, 270, April 1968.

14. Home Service Committee, *Home Service Opportunities Unlimited,* American National Gas Association, New York, 1953.

15. Howe, Edna, "Summary of the Results and Conclusions of a Study of the Use of Television in Home Economics Extension Programs," *Journal of Home Economics,* vol. 56, pp. 102–104, February 1964.

16. Johnson, Jack T., "Can Home Economics Meet the Challenge of Change," *Forecast for Home Economics,* vol. 12, p. F-24, January 1968.

17. *Journalism as a Career,* The Institute for Research, Research No. 19, Chicago, 1954.

18. Kay, M. June, "What Do Women in Personnel Do," *Personnel Journal,* vol. 48, pp. 810–812, October 1969.

19. Lodge, George C., "Food Processing—Key to Economics Development," *Harvard Business Review,* vol. 44, pp. 6–16, September–October 1966.

20. Mayer, Lawrence A., "Home Goods: But What Will They Think of Next," *Fortune,* vol. 76, pp. 114–118, 139–140, August 1967.

21. Meacham, Esther, "Television in the Clothing Classroom," *Journal of Home Economics,* vol. 56, pp. 89–94, February 1964.

22. Mills, Nancy, *Home Economists in Action,* pp. 86–106, Scholastic Book Services, New York, 1968.

23. National Project in Agricultural Communication, *Agrisearch,* The Michigan State University Press, East Lansing, December 1956.

24. "1967–68 Report of AHEA Activities; From Professional Sections," *Journal of Home Economics,* vol. 60, pp. 546–547, September 1968.

25. *Restaurant Management: Ownership and Careers in Restaurant Work,* Institute for Research, Research No. 69, Chicago, 1967, p. 3.

26. *Restaurant, Tea-rooms, and Cafeteria Operation—Careers,* The Institute for Research, Research No. 69, Chicago, 1967.

27. Rogers, Willie Mae, "A Home Economist Looks at Her Job," *What's New in Home Economics,* vol. 16, p. 200, September 1951.

28. Saltonstall, Robert, "Who's Who in Personnel Administration," *Harvard Business Review,* vol. 33, pp. 75–83, July–August 1955.

29. Strain, Robert W., "Business Values the Home Economist," *Journal of Home Economics,* vol. 62, pp. 49–53, January 1970.

30. Torpey, William G., "Shortage of Counseling Personnel Handicaps Scientific and Technical Development," *Personnel Journal,* vol. 45, pp. 489–493, September 1966.

31. U.S. Bureau of the Census, *Statistical Abstracts of the United States: 1969,* 90th ed.

ADDITIONAL READINGS

Baird, Gladys A., "College Preparation for Home Economists in Business," *What's New in Home Economics,* vol. 29, pp. F8–F11, F17, November–December 1965.

Britt, Helen, "Home Economists Have Interest in What Consumers Like," *What's New in Home Economics,* vol. 26, pp. 38–39, May–June 1962.

Ech, Sarah, "Home Economics Paves the Way," *What's New in Home Economics,* vol. 31, pp. 28–48, January 1967.

Ech, Sarah, "Home Economics Paves the Way," *What's New in Home Economics,* vol. 31, pp. 7, 103, February 1967.

"A Home Economics Career in Business," *What's New in Home Economics,* vol. 28, pp. 105–107, September 1964.

"Home Economics Sparks Unique Career," *What's New in Home Economics,* vol. 31, p. 18, October 1967.

"Home Economics Sparks Unique Career," *What's New in Home Economics,* vol. 31, p. 7, December 1967.

"Home Economics Sparks Unique Career," What's New in Home Economics, vol. 32, p. 42, September 1968.

"Home Economists in Action," *Forecast for Home Economics—Co-ed Section,* vol. 10, p. 38, April 1965.

"Industry Contributes Funds for Home Economics Education," *What's New in Home Economics,* vol. 31, p. 100, September 1963.

Johnson, Mryna, "Foods of the Future," *What's New in Home Economics,* vol. 26, pp. 76–79, March 1962.

"New In-business Courses Spur Interest in Careers," *What's New in Home Economics,* vol. 27, pp. 12–13, January 1963.

Price, Gladys B., "Careers in Home Economics," *What's New in Home Economics,* vol. 25, p. 43, February 1961.

12
HOME ECONOMICS RESEARCH

Looking for alert young career people with inquiring minds! Are these young people interested in searching out new facts or testing accepted viewpoints? If they are motivated toward helping individuals and families live more abundant and creative lives, their career choice should be home economics research.

The purpose of all research is to provide new knowledge. Home economics research aims to discover new truths, principles, or products which will improve homes and the well-being of families and their members (7).

Home economists in research discover basic facts on food, fibers, shelter, child development, family relations, and economics (10). In addition to searching out these new facts and principles, home economics research assumes the responsibility for ascertaining family and individual needs and preferences in clothing, housing, food, equipment, etc., and interpreting these needs and preferences to the manufacturers, producers, government officials, and agencies who serve the family.

The influence of home economics research has been widespread (13). According to the Public Relations and Communications Committee of the American Home Economics Association (10):

> *In the past fifty years* home economics research has: influenced the design of all major household appliances; played a key role in developing easy-to-prepare foods; provided recommended cooking methods for new food products and equipment; provided basic facts on clothing construction, garment and pattern sizing, cleaning techniques, and fiber and fabric quality; provided basic information on lighting, design, and scientific use of space for household activities; contributed vital information on the health-giving ingredients of foods; taken important steps to develop clothing for the physically disabled.

Careers in Home Economics Research

I. Areas in which research is carried on
   a. Foods and food science
   b. Nutrition
   c. Textiles and clothing
   d. Consumer education and marketing
   e. Family housing, equipment, and household processes
   f. Consumption and household economics

g. Institution management
h. Family relations and child development
i. Home economics education
II. Agencies supporting home economics research
a. Colleges and universities
b. Business and industry
c. Private agencies and public foundations
d. Government agencies

FIELDS OF RESEARCH

Although there are research opportunities in many fields for qualified home economists, most home economics research concerns itself with finding answers to questions
in the above-mentioned fields (15, 22). Let us look at a few of the fields in more detail.

Foods and Nutrition Research

More research has been done in foods and nutrition by home economists than
in any other area (12). The major interest of home economists is to help families have
a wholesome food supply that provides the nutrients for growth and body maintenance for health and physical well-being (20). This has led home economists to study
human requirements for various nutrients and the utilization of nutrients from usual
food sources. Many studies have been made of food preparation and preservation as
they affect quality, cost, and the time expenditures by both families and institutions.
Studies have been made of the use of food by individuals to satisfy their nutrient and
personal needs. Studies of quality and types of food available to different segments
of the population have been made. This information has been transmitted to food
producers and the food industry and has affected the kind and quality of products
available to the consumer. Furthermore, this knowledge has been used to guide
consumers in making decisions concerning food choices. Because of the many new
foods on the market, research designed to determine the nutritional value or
acceptability of foods continues (3, 14).

Another large area of food research has been directed toward studying the
eating patterns of people. Much more information is needed about why people eat as
they do and how people can be influenced to choose the best foods for nutrition.
According to a report of the Community-Family-Consumer Research Committee, the
following questions related to food need to be answered (2):

1. What factors operate in consumer choices of food?
2. How are food habits formed?
3. What are common misconceptions about food and nutritional needs? What
is their effect on dietary habits?
4. What are desirable food habits and attitudes? How can they be established
and undesirable ones modified?

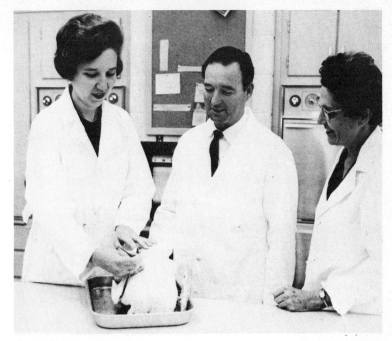

Fig. 12-1 Home economists are inserting thermocouples in a turkey to determine the end-point temperature of roasting. (Courtesy of the Virginia Polytechnic Institute and State University)

5. What meaning does food have in the American culture? How does social significance of food vary among segments of the population?

To answer these questions, food and nutrition research workers must be better educated in the social sciences or must team up with social scientists in conducting research. Research workers presently in food and nutrition have come predominately from a biochemistry background.

Textiles and Clothing Research

Textiles and clothing research is fundamentally concerned with the need of, the desire for, and the satisfaction to be achieved by consumers with respect to clothing and other textile products (6, 15). Research positions in clothing and textiles range from studies of clothing construction and performance to development of fibers and laundry research. The tremendous textile industry, with its emphasis on research, offers the home economist many avenues for professional growth (6, 13). The home economist doing research in clothing and textiles may be studying such problems as the following:

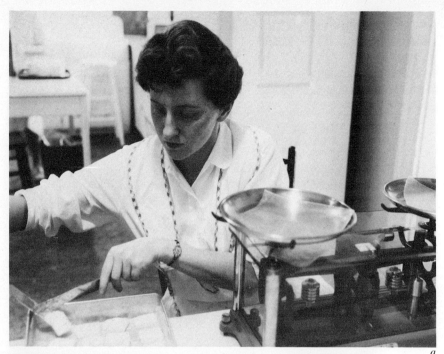

a

b

Fig. 12-2 (*a*) and (*b*) Exact measurements and weights are very important in nutrition research. In (*a*), the nutritionist is studying weight loss of baked products. In (*b*), three preadolescent girls are participating in a nutrition balance study. They lick their plates to make sure that all food placed on their plates is taken into the body. (Courtesy of the Virginia Polytechnic Institute and State University)

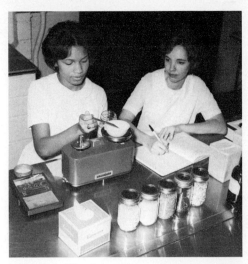

Fig. 12-3 The home economics students are studying the effects of cooking methods on foods. (Courtesy of the College of Education, University of Kentucky)

1. The properties and characteristics of new fibers, finishes, and materials, such as
   a. The use, serviceability, and acceptability of new fibers
   b. Stabilizing fibers against shrinkage and stretch; color fastness
   c. The characteristics of new finishes as they affect the materials, including spot- and soil-resistant treatment, wrinkle resistance, heat and mildew resistance, and fire retardants
   d. Fiber blending as it affects wearing quality and comfort
2. The practices followed by consumers in the purchase of clothing and household textiles
3. Factors related to efficiency in the selection and buying of clothing and textiles
4. Expenditures for clothing and household textiles
5. The preferences of consumers for different types of textile products for different uses
6. The relation between consumers' choices of textile products and satisfaction received
7. The effects of laundrying and dry-cleaning procedures, light, and heat on textiles and textile products
8. The designing of textiles and clothing for different uses, different family types, and different geographical locations
9. The special needs of groups such as the elderly, the handicapped, and the economically and socially deprived

Housing and Equipment Research

When one realizes that housing encompasses all of the physical environment in which people live, and that the quality of living is in part determined by the influence of the physical surroundings on actions and attitudes, housing research becomes of great importance. Most of the housing research is directed toward two groups (2, 19): (1) the housing industry, to encourage them to influence builders to construct houses that meet the needs of families that are going to live in them, and (2) consumers, to

Fig. 12-4 This is a "research chair." By taking hundreds of measurements, the dimensions of chairs necessary to provide comfortable seating for persons of various sizes are determined. (Courtesy of the Home Economics Department, University of Arkansas)

educate them to demand better housing and choose more intelligently among the houses available.

Home economists engaging in housing research are interested in securing the facts to get good housing for families. They recognize that good housing is much more than adequate housing space and equipment and furnishings. It is housing that, in size and design, equipment and furnishings, flexibility, location, and cost to its occupants, encourages and sustains a rich and secure family life (19). The home economists in housing research have concerned themselves primarily with:

1. Space requirements for household and family activities and storage
2. Preferences of homemakers and families in housing
3. Housing conditions of families of various sizes, incomes, and locations
4. Functional requirements for houses as a basis for improved living
5. The effect of families living in multi-unit dwellings, in special neighborhoods, and in housing segregated on the basis of age, income, or color

Household equipment research is primarily concerned with the functional aspects of equipment as it effects the home and family living. Research in household equipment determines to what extent appliances save household labor and provide the means for performing the majority of the household operations better, more easily, more quickly, and more cheaply and satisfactorily than can be done by hand. Home economists educate the homemaker to judge the relationship between price and quality of selected equipment and standards for good equipment.

Consumer Education, Consumption and Household Economics, and Marketing Research

Consumer education is a study of the needs, problems, and activities of consumers in the market place. It attempts to acquaint consumers with the influence of their demands and practices on retail prices and policies. Also, it seeks to acquaint consumers with pricing concepts and policies, advertising methods, sales promotion and selling techniques, advantages and disadvantages of various types of consumer credit, and consumer-protection policies of the government and industry (2, 21).

Consumer research deals with the decisions of families and individuals in the using of their resources to obtain goods, services, and experiences (2, 21). In marketing research, the emphasis is on learning what qualities are desired in products, how choices are made in the marketplace, and how these choices are influenced.

In addition, home economists want to know the adequacy of labeling and the use homemakers make of it, the pricing and marketing practices and policies of business and industry and their effect upon the products that consumers must buy, the effect of marketing procedures upon the quality and acceptability of a product, and the cost of products from which the consumer must choose. Much of the research in these areas to date has been conducted on food products, and has been oriented toward the interests of industry (22). To improve consumption patterns, knowledge of the factors that influence consumer choices and the effect of these choices upon goods and services available to families must be known (2).

Consumption and household economics research has grown greatly in recent years. The household economist directs her efforts toward seeking information on the following: income, expenditures, and savings of families and their adjustment to changing economic conditions, family cycles, and periods of crisis; the living levels of families and the needs associated with them; family goals, values, attitudes, and standards and their influence on family spending patterns; decision-making and managerial processes in the home, and consumer practices and their effect on the economic well-being of families.

Family Relations and Child Development

Home economists recognize that no unit in society is as significant as the family, for it is paramount in determining the behavior, basic beliefs, values, aspirations of people, and in setting the pattern for the development of youth. Middle-class values and goals have been dominant in society's expectations for others. However, American families exemplify widely different patterns of living and

Fig. 12-5 Studying and teaching child development is one function of child development or family-life specialists. The progress of skeletal development can be ascertained by the bone structure in the hands. (Courtesy of the Merrill-Palmer Institute)

various socioeconomic levels. Home economics research has been concerned with such matters as these (2):

  1. Human growth and development, and the physical and social processes whereby individuals move through life's stages
  2. Aspirations of youth as affected by socioeconomic conditions
  3. Courtship and marriage
  4. The problems, needs, and interests of homemakers and associated factors
  5. The characteristics of homemakers in the United States, including health, personal adjustment, training, earning capacity, activities in the community, work load, and problems (15)
  6. Understanding how activities, such as those associated with child care, feeding and housing the family, and caring for the house and its equipment, are carried on in families
  7. The effect on families of the growing up of children
  8. The growth and personality patterns of children as they are affected by the family and the home
  9. The effect of changing socioeconomic conditions upon family stability

Fig. 12-6 People are the subjects for study by the research worker in family life. In this picture, a home economist is studying the food preferences of children. (Courtesy of the Merrill-Palmer Institute)

10. The services available to families through private and public agencies and the uses made of these services by families

11. The expectations of disadvantaged families and the effect of these on the young people

12. The effect that increased technology, mobility, leisure time, working wives, and early retirement have upon the well-being of families

Home Economics Education Research

Research in home economics education is designed to improve the teaching of home economics and to aid in the preparation of young people for jobs (8, 11). This research usually is concerned with student and adult learning processes, teaching methods, teaching materials, administrative procedures and outcomes, student guidance, and cost of instruction. Such topics as the following would fall under home economics education research:

1. Evaluation of home economics teaching in developing attitudes, knowledge, and skills that are fundamental to home and family living

2. Uses made by homemakers of the educational skills, attitudes, and knowledge received in homemaking classes

3. Cost of homemaking education in relation to size of class and methods of teaching

4. Relation of illustrative materials, visual aids, field trips, and other aids to students' progress in homemaking

5. Students' attitudes toward homemaking classes in relation to performance

6. Subject matter and experiences suitable for homemaking for classes of boys or girls, or both, at different age levels, socioeconomic groups, and locations

7. Developmental levels in clothing construction and other skill areas for elementary and high school students as a basis for program planning

8. Curriculum needs and program building for preparing teachers of homemaking

9. The special needs of students from low-income families and deprived neighborhoods.

Any attempt to cite all topics suitable for research by home economists would be a never-ending undertaking, for home economists are concerned about all factors which impinge upon the family. These brief listings are purely suggestive and are not intended to be inclusive; however, they should give some idea of types of problems studied by home economists in research.

Research in home economics was never needed more than it is today. The complexity of our society and the rapid changes taking place bring about ever-increasing problems for families. The more problems the families have to face, and the more decisions they have to make, the greater is the need to apply science in the laboratory or in the field to the solution of these problems. When one realizes that there are over 25 million homemakers in the United States with families to care for and homes to manage, the multiplicity of problems needing solution by home economists becomes evident.

TRAINING FOR RESEARCH

Those who would do research in home economics must meet certain educational requirements. In the first place, they must have at least a bachelor's degree from an accredited college or university offering a major in home economics with specialization in one of the home economics subject-matter areas. A well-rounded background in home economics is a decided advantage, irrespective of the field in which research is to be done, for the home economist must see the overall picture of the family and the interrelatedness of its problems. Research workers in all fields of home economics must know the tools of research, which include mathematics, statistics, research methods, laboratory procedures, record keeping, and report writing.

The specific requirements for research in specialized fields vary. The person who is training for research in foods and nutrition must be thoroughly grounded in the related sciences, as well as in foods and nutrition, and so must acquire a working knowledge of chemistry, biology, bacteriology, physiology, anatomy, and psychology. Sociology, economics, and education give necessary additional background information. Since the nutritionist must also work with families, she needs to know how they meet their food and nutrition needs.

Research in textiles and clothing also draws on many related fields for methods of attack. Training for research in clothing and textiles places strong emphasis on art, chemistry, physics, biology, history, psychology, economics, and sociology, in addition to a thorough understanding of clothing selection, construction and care, clothing economics, human growth and development, and textile products.

The researcher in family life will place more emphasis in her training upon the social and biological sciences. She must be thoroughly grounded in child development, psychology, physiology, economics, family relations, marriage, sociology, and all aspects of interpersonal relationships. In addition, a knowledge of family law, anthropology, and bacteriology would aid her in her work.

Research in housing and household equipment requires an understanding of art, physics, psychology, economics, home management, work simplification, energy expenditure, textiles, household equipment, housing materials, and elementary housing design. Some experience in drafting and some knowledge of bacteriology are important.

Consumer education and marketing research involve a study of economics, marketing, psychology, sociology, business organization and practices, prices, and family economics, as well as family relationships and family buying practices.

The person who wishes to do research in home economics education must know the subject matter of education, including tests and measurements, learning processes, and learning motivation. In addition to a good background in home economics, an understanding of sociology, human growth and development, and counseling are necessary.

PERSONAL QUALIFICATIONS

Good training for research is necessary, but equally important are the personal qualities of the individual. Keen intellectual inquisitiveness is perhaps the first prerequisite of a scientist, followed by ingenuity in designing experiments, patience, accuracy, precision, and meticulous care in the way one works (7). The would-be researcher in home economics must be alert to everyday problems and have an interest in helping others. Complete objectivity is a difficult trait to develop, but in research there is no place for preconceived ideas or personal preferences: results must be interpreted objectively and without bias.

Dependability is a must for research, as is the ability to organize and carry through an experiment. Researchers must not be afraid of hard work, and neither must they be easily discouraged. Also, anyone doing research must be able to take a long-range view of problems. A research worker must also be able to share ideas and findings with others, for one successful piece of research becomes the steppingstone to the next. As a part of this, the ability to cooperate with others is essential, for rarely are scientific discoveries made by lone workers.

After the research is completed, the research worker must be able to present her findings in a form which others can understand. This usually requires the ability to write for scientific journals as well as popular publications.

EMPLOYMENT OPPORTUNITIES

There are many levels of positions in the research field which require various degrees of responsibility and training. The person with a bachelor's degree usually finds a job at the technical level or as an assistant to an established worker; if the established researcher is in a university, the assistant may be permitted to take graduate work. After several years of experience, or with a master's degree, the capable person usually can have more freedom in planning and carrying out a research project. To do independent research, one must have a doctor's degree or have exhibited outstanding ability through years of experience.

Those who are engaged in research may work in a university, in government service, in industry, or for a foundation. The research work may be supported by a private foundation or private business, by federal and/or state funds through the university experiment station, by business and industry through cooperation with the university, or in business or industry itself. The worker may be giving her full time to research activities or she may be combining teaching and research, extension and research—in some cases she may do all three.

In the universities, there are different types of research positions, but the educational requirements for these positions will be those of the university staff generally. Many people enjoy living in a community or city where there is a university, for they gain much from the advantages which the university offers.

The U.S. Department of Agriculture has a rather extensive home economics research program (11, 12, 14, 15). The home economics research laboratories at Beltsville, Maryland, and the offices in Washington have over 140 home economists working on research. Most of their findings are made available to the public through government bulletins or pamphlets. The U.S. Department of Agriculture distributes millions of home economics bulletins yearly.

To enter any phase of government work, one must pass a federal service entrance examination. Information on these examinations is obtainable at most post offices or can be secured by writing to the U.S. Civil Service Commission, Washington, D.C.

Industrial organizations have special research laboratories in which research is constantly going on. Textile research laboratories are working on color fastness, developing new fibers and fiber blends, and improving the durability and acceptability of fibers. Clothing manufacturers are doing research in sizing, acceptability of types and styles of garments, wearing qualities, etc.

Food companies have large research kitchens where recipe testing is done, where foods are analyzed, and where new and attractive food combinations and ways of serving them are developed. Household equipment and furnishings manufacturers have research laboratories where experimentation is carried on to improve equipment, develop new equipment and designs, or find new uses for equipment. Home economists will find employment in all these laboratories. Directors, research assistants, and technicians needed in these laboratories are trained college people.

ADVANTAGES AND DISADVANTAGES

There are many advantages to research as a profession. A qualified person usually finds great satisfaction in being able to experiment with materials and try out new ideas. Seldom is the pressure on a research worker as great as that found in many other fields. Although the researcher may spend long hours, they result from her interest in following an idea or process through to completion. Research is respected by one's associates and has a position of status.

The scientific investigator seldom masses great wealth and infrequently achieves widespread fame and recognition. Yet, research brings its rewards, and its salaries are usually similar to those of other professional people who have comparable training. The researcher often is an authority in her field of specialization and thus commands the respect of her fellows. She has the opportunity to be adventurous and share with other scientists the thrills of new discoveries; this gives a feeling of belonging not always found in other professions.

Salaries for research personnel are comparable to those of other professional workers. The research technicians command salaries from $5,000 to $7,500 per year. The research assistants and independent researchers' salaries range from $7,500 to $25,000, depending upon the type of research and the place of employment.

INTEREST CHECKLIST FOR RESEARCH

Below are ten statements which describe interests or activities of research workers. As you read each item listed on the left, check the column on the right which expresses your interest in the activity.

activities	degree of interest		
	much	average	little
1. Work in a chemistry, nutrition, or textiles laboratory.	————	————	————
2. Test efficiency of different pieces of household equipment.	————	————	————
3. Feed experimental animals and keep records on them.	————	————	————

activities	degree of interest		
	much	average	little
4. Test textile materials to determine the type of fibers in the material.	———	———	———
5. Work out mathematics problems.	———	———	———
6. Design experiments to study the effect of methods of cooking upon the appearance and palatability of vegetables.	———	———	———
7. Write bulletins and reports on the findings of a study, explaining what was discovered.	———	———	———
8. Interview people, finding out their ideas or practices concerning selected subjects.	———	———	———
9. Study children's behavior under different types of discipline or control.	———	———	———
10. Plan for the systematic carrying out of a project.	———	———	———
Total score			

To score your answers, give each item to which you answered "Much" a score of 2 and to each item marked "Average" a score of 1. If your total score ranges from 10 to 20, you indicate considerable interest in research.

SUGGESTED ACTIVITIES

1. In order to learn more about research generally, invite the director of the research division in your university to speak to your class about research. He will be able to tell you something about the various research programs which the state and federal governments are sponsoring. Also, he can discuss with you what he expects of a research worker, how one initiates a research project, and many of the advantages of research careers.

2. Plan to make a visit to the land-grant university or any other educational institution in your state where home economics research is carried on. The research home economists will be able to tell you about their research and explain their research laboratories to you. You may wish to discuss with them such questions as why they selected research as a career, the training they have had, and what they enjoy most about research.

3. If you have industries in your communities where home economists are engaged in research, a visit to the laboratories to discuss the research going on will help you see opportunities in these fields.

4. By writing the Cooperative State Experiment Station in your state, or the U.S. Department of Agriculture, students may secure copies of research bulletins prepared by home economists. A study of these should help students gain some idea of what research means and how the findings are handled. A discussion of the application of the findings in each bulletin to a better

understanding of home economics practices should be carried on by the students.

REFERENCES

1. Adams, Georgian, "Fifty Years of Home Economics Research," *Journal of Home Economics*, vol. 51, pp. 12–18, January 1959.

2. "Community-Family-Consumer Research," *Agricultural Science Review*, vol. 2, p. 8, February 1969.

3. Davis, Elizabeth Y., "Research in Changing Tomorrow's Nutrition," *What's New in Home Economics*, vol. 31, pp. 61–62, October 1967.

4. Elvehyen, C. A., "From the Minds of Men to the Lives of People," *Journal of Home Economics*, vol. 49, pp. 503–507, September 1957.

5. Fitzgerald, Elizabeth, "Home Economics Research in the U.S.D.A." *Journal of Home Economics*, vol. 55, pp. 362, May 1963.

6. "A Future in Textile Research," *Journal of Home Economics*, vol. 49, pp. 220–225, March 1957.

7. Harrison, Dorothy L., "A Career for the Curious," *Journal of Home Economics*, vol. 47, p. 200, March 1956.

8. Hatcher, Hazel M., "What Research Offers to the Homemaking Teacher," *Journal of Home Economics*, vol. 35, pp. 151–153, March 1943.

9. Hoffman, Doretta S., "Interdisciplinary Approach to Research in Home Economics," *Journal of Home Economics*, vol. 61, pp. 159–163, March 1969.

10. *Home Economists in Research*, Home Economics Career Profile, American Home Economics Association, Washington, January 1963.

11. Hurt, Mary Lee, "Expanded Research Programs under Vocational Education," *Journal of Home Economics*, vol. 57, pp. 173–175, March 1965.

12. *Joint Task Force Reports*, Prepared by the U.S. Department of Agriculture, the State Department of Agriculture, and the State Universities and Land-Grant Colleges, 1967 and 1968. (See 16, 17, and 18 below.)

13. Leverton, Ruth M., "Speeding the Application of Research Findings through International Cooperation in Home Economics," *Journal of Home Economics*, vol. 61, pp. 247–251, April 1969.

14. Lodge, George C., "Food Processing—Key to Economic Development," *Harvard Business Review*, vol. 44, p. 6–16, September–October 1966.

15. Minden, Mary Beth, *A Forward Look: Home Management Research*, Presented before the National Conference on the Family, Pennsylvania State University, University Park, July 1, 1969.

16. *A National Program of Research for Food and Nutrition*, Prepared by the U.S. Department of Agriculture, the State Department of Agriculture, and the State Universities and Land-Grant Colleges, December 1967.

17. *A National Program of Research for Food Safety*, Prepared by the U.S.

Department of Agriculture, the State Department of Agriculture, and the State Universities and Land-Grant Colleges, November 1968.

18. *A National Program of Research for Rural Development and Family Living,* Prepared by the U.S. Department of Agriculture, the State Department of Agriculture, and the State Universities and Land-Grant Colleges, November 1968.

19. *Progress Report of Home Economics Steering Committee on Research in Housing,* Division of Home Economics, Association of Land-Grant Colleges and Universities, Housing Sub-committee, Kansas City, Mo., October 1949.

20. Personius, Catherine, "Home Economics in the National Scientific Effort," *Proceedings: National Seminar and Workshop for Home Economics Research Administrators,* Cooperative State Research Service, U.S.D.A., Washington, 1967.

21. Reid, Margaret, "Expanding Research in Family Consumption," *Journal of Home Economics,* vol. 35, pp. 151–153, March 1943.

22. Russel, Ruthanna, "Priorities Needed for Home Economics Research," *Journal of Home Economics,* vol. 61, p. 158, March 1969.

23. Swanson, Pearl, "New Resources for Research," *Journal of Home Economics,* vol. 53, pp. 161–172, March 1961.

ADDITIONAL READINGS

Coon, Beulah I., "Co-operative Research in Home Economics Education," *Journal of Home Economics,* vol. 54, pp. 191–194, March 1962.

De Alley, Margaret, "Home Economics Based upon Scientific Principles Is Concerned with Better Living," *What's New in Home Economics,* vol. 26, pp. 42–45, February 1962.

Johnson, Myrna, "Foods of the Future," *What's New in Home Economics,* vol. 26, pp. 76–79, March 1962.

Lehman, Ruth T., "The Next Fifty Years in Home Economics Research," *Journal of Home Economics,* vol. 52, pp. 23–26, January 1960.

Leverton, Ruth M., "The Future of Home Economics Research," *Journal of Home Economics,* vol. 57, pp. 169–172, March 1965.

Lindsay, Dale, "Home Economics Research: Interest of National Institutes of Health," *Journal of Home Economics,* vol. 54, pp. 26–31, January 1962.

Lippeatt, Selma, "The Research Dimension in Teaching," *What's New in Home Economics,* vol. 27, pp. 76–77, September 1963.

Personius, Catherine J., "Objectives and Philosophy of Home Economics Research," *Journal of Home Economics,* vol. 51, pp. 94–96, January 1969.

Southword, G. B., "New Fabrics Saving Lives in Vietnam," *Daily News Record,* vol. 126, Np. 23147, p. 2, June 27, 1969.

13 INTERNATIONAL SERVICE

To those interested in seeing the world as they work and give service, home economics positions offer splendid opportunities. Home economists go overseas for several reasons: to study, lecture, teach, do research, give service, or observe and consult. Since home economics is recognized as a medium for improving the many aspects of family living, its people are sought after in those countries where programs are being designed to improve the life and living standards of the people.

The work for home economists in foreign service is endless (7); however, the number of positions available at any one time is limited. Most of the people of the world want improved diets, housing, clothing, health, education, child welfare, and personal and community relationships, and these are the fields of primary concern to home economists. In many countries there is a very rapidly growing population, a low standard of living for the majority of the families, and an inferior status for women.

The world population increased at the rate of 61 million per year between 1960 and 1967 (12). It is estimated that within the lifetime of the present generation, the number of people to be fed, housed, and cared for will be doubled (10, p. 23). The majority of these people—two-thirds of the world's population—are rural, and rural people on the whole are inadequately housed, fed, and clothed. The homemakers among these people are in great need of help and leadership, for not only do women have the responsibility of caring for families the world over but they constitute the largest percentage of the world's illiterate population. In some countries, illiteracy among women still ranks as high as 80 percent.

Home economists who are well trained, have zest for helping people to improve their living, appreciate the worth of people of all cultures and levels of living, recognize the many and varied ways used by different people for achieving suitable goals, and are dedicated to service will find many challenging opportunities in foreign service.

The chief agencies or programs employing or sponsoring home economists for overseas work or study may be grouped as in Table 13-1.

PROGRAMS OF THE DEPARTMENT OF STATE

The Congress of the United States, through educational and technical assistance programs in foreign lands, is attempting to strengthen cooperative international relations by promoting a better understanding of the United States in other countries and by furthering mutual understanding between the peoples of other countries.

Table 13-1
International service for home economists

organization or agency	service rendered	source of information
U.S. Bureau of Educational and Cultural Affairs		
Fulbright-Hays Act		
1. Agency for International Development	Assists in development of teacher-training centers, provides college and university teachers of subject matter areas, develops extension and community educational programs, and carries on research	Agency for International Development Washington, D.C. 20402
2. The Peace Corps	Provides foreign countries with manpower leadership for education, public works, rural and urban community action, health services, and agricultural extension.	Director of the Peace Corps Washington, D.C. 20402
3. Department of Defense Dependent Schools	Supplies teachers for over 300 schools set up by the Department of Defense for American school children abroad	Department of Defense Washington, D.C. 20402
The United Nations		
1. The United Nations Educational Scientific, and Cultural Organization (UNESCO)	Is concerned with the education of the children of the world in order to advance peace and the common welfare of mankind	Public Liaison Division New York Office of UNESCO United Nations New York, N.Y.
2. The United Nations International Children's Fund (UNICEF)	Is concerned with the improvement of health and welfare of children and mothers	UNICEF United Nations Headquarters New York, N.Y.
3. Food and Agriculture Organization (FAO)	Is concerned with the development of practical programs in nutrition and home economics to raise the standard of living in cooperating countries	FAO—North American Office United States Department of Agriculture Washington, D.C. 20402
4. World Health Organization (WHO)	Directs and coordinates international health work, including sanitation, maternal and child health, and com-	World Health Organization United Nations Headquarters New York, N.Y.

Table 13-1 *(cont.)*

organization or agency	service rendered	source of information
	municable disease in cooperating countries	
5. International Voluntary Services, Inc. (IVS)	Specializes in services to rural people in emerging countries to enable them to advance culturally and economically	International Voluntary Services, Inc. 3636 Sixteenth St., N.W. Washington, D.C. 20010
6. International Farm Youth Exchange (IFYE)	Sends students to foreign countries to live with foreign families and carry on the activities of their counterpart, and bring students to United States from foreign countries	National 4-H Foundation 7100 Connecticut Ave. Washington, D.C.
Private Foundations and Organizations		
Ford Foundation	Is concerned with rural village development, public administration, social and economic research. Offers teaching and research grants	Ford Foundation 471 Madison Ave. New York, N.Y. 10022
Rockefeller Foundation	Is concerned with the welfare of mankind and peace through helping nations to improve economically and socially	The Rockefeller Foundation 49 W. 49th St. New York, N.Y. 10017
Near East Foundation	Is concerned with home economics extension programs throughout the Near East	Near East Foundation 54 E. 64th St. New York, N.Y. 10021
African-American Institute	Is concerned primarily with the placement of teachers in secondary schools	African-American Institute 345 E. 46th St. New York, N.Y. 10017
Business—Private Enterprise (List is not inclusive)		
Frigidaire	Is concerned with product development and utilization, food service operation, and preparation of materials for foreign consumption	Frigidaire Division General Motors Corporation Dayton, Ohio
General Electric Company	Is concerned with product development and utilization, food service operation, and preparation of materials for foreign consumption	General Electric Company Bridgeport, Conn.

Table 13-1 *(cont.)*

organization or agency	service rendered	source of information
General Foods Corporation	Is concerned with product development and utilization, food service operation, and preparation of materials for foreign consumption	General Foods Corporation 250 North St. White Plains, N.Y. 10602
Kraft Foods	Is concerned with product development and utilization, food service operation, and preparation of materials for foreign consumption	Kraft Food Company Chicago, Ill.
Nestle Company	Is concerned with product development and utilization, food service operation, and preparation of materials for foreign consumption	Nestle Company White Plains, N.Y.
Sunbeam Corporation	Is concerned with product development and utilization, food service operation, and preparation of materials for foreign consumption	Sunbeam Corporation Chicago, Ill.
American Can Company	Is concerned with product development and utilization, food service operation, and preparation of materials for foreign consumption	
United Fruit Company	Is concerned with product development and utilization, food service operation, and preparation of materials for foreign consumption	
Church-related Organizations		
The American Board of Commissions for Foreign Missions (Congregational Christian Church)	Is concerned with teaching appointments in schools, colleges, and universities sponsored by the church, child feeding operations, family life work	The American Board for Commissioners for Foreign Missions 14 Beacon St. Boston, Mass.
American Friends of the Middle East	Offers teacher and professional placement service and	American Friends of the Middle East

Table 13-1 (*cont.*)

organization or agency	service rendered	source of information
	provides information about openings in governmental and private educational institutions in the Middle East	1607 New Hampshire Ave., N.W. Washington, D.C. 20009
American Friends Service Committee (AFSC)	Assigns volunteers to work through AFSC in newly emerging countries	American Friends Service Committee 160 N. 15th St. Philadelphia, Pa. 19102
Mennonite Central Committee	Home economists actively participate in planned programs	Mennonite Central Committee Menno Travel Service Adren, Pa.
World Council of Churches, composed of various denominations, two of which follow		
Board of Missions of the United Methodist Church Woman's Division of Christian Service	Is concerned with the placing of home economics teachers in schools, colleges, and universitites sponsored by church	Board of Missions of the United Methodist Church Office of Missionary Personnel 475 Riverside Dr. New York, N.Y. 10027
The United Church Board for World Ministries	Is concerned with the placing of home economics teachers in schools, colleges, and universitites sponsored by church	The United Church Board of World Ministries Commission on Ecumenical Mission and Relations The United Presbyterian Church, U.S. 475 Riverside Dr. New York, N.Y. 10027

The Fulbright-Hays Act

The Fulbright program has been the core of the United States educational and cultural exchange program. The program had its beginning in 1946 when Senator J. W. Fulbright, himself once a Rhodes Scholar, in an amendment to the Property Act of 1944, proposed that foreign currency, resulting from the sales of United States surplus war property overseas, be used to finance the study of American students abroad and the travel cost of foreign students to the United States. The innocuous-sounding amendment which would make Fulbright's surname a common noun was passed without a flurry. The Fulbright Act was extended and enlarged through the passage of the Smith-Mundt Act of 1962. Since 1948, over 25,000 Americans and

Fig. 13-1 This home economist is working with the extension teachers in a costume study at the University of Baroda in India. (Courtesy of Howard University)

31,500 foreign students have been supported by these acts. At the present time, there are approximately 2,500 United States citizens and 6,000 foreign nationals from more than 130 countries and territories studying each year as a result of the benefits of the Fulbright-Hays Act. A number of different types of grants are offered under this program. Those for United States citizens enable them to pursue the following programs (3, 4):

1. Study at the graduate level for a year at a university or other institution of higher learning
2. Teach for a year in an elementary or secondary school, or attend a summer seminar for teachers of foreign languages or history
3. Lecture, preferably for a year but at least for a semester, in a college or university
4. Conduct advanced research, preferably for a year but at least for a semester, at a college, university, or other institution of higher learning
5. Serve as a consultant in a special field or lecture before general audiences on topics of current interest for a period of three to six months
6. Participate in summer seminars abroad in such areas as foreign languages, social studies, or education

The Americans who are chosen for these grants are selected on the basis of their ability to promote the objectives of the program by carrying out the activities for which they receive grants. There are certain personal qualifications which a grantee must have. In the first place, he must be emotionally mature and he must really be interested in other cultures and people. He must be able to adapt himself easily to different, and sometimes difficult, living conditions. He must show professional or scholastic competence. Finally, he must propose a plan of activity in keeping with his qualifications or be willing to undertake an assignment proposed by the Department of State and the Foreign Service hosts in the country or countries to which he will go. Most grants are awarded on the basis of widely publicized competitions.

The procedure to be followed in applying for a grant depends upon the grant desired (3). If one wishes to do graduate work abroad, he may apply for a grant under the Fulbright-Hays Act. A grantee must be a United States citizen, hold a bachelor's degree or its equivalent before the beginning date of the grant, and present an acceptable plan of study. He must have a knowledge of the language of the host country sufficient enough to carry on the proposed study. Candidates should be in good health and usually should be under 35 years of age. A student currently enrolled in an American college or university and who wishes to apply for a grant should get in touch with the Fulbright program adviser on his campus. If he is not enrolled in an American college or university, application should be made to the Institute of International Education, 809 United Nations Plaza, New York, N.Y. 10017, or one of its regional offices.

If one wishes to teach in an elementary or secondary school abroad, application should be made to the *Teacher Exchange Section,* International Exchange and Training Branch, Division of Educational Personnel Training, Office of Education, Washington, D.C., 20202. To be eligible for one of these exchanges, a bachelor's degree and at least three years of successful teaching experience are required.

For those wishing to lecture or teach in a foreign university, the Fulbright-Hays Act provides opportunities (3; 11, p. 561). The money value of these grants varies, depending upon the country to which the grantee is going. In addition to the grant, transportation and necessary expenses in the foreign country usually are included. Applications for university lecturing or teaching should be addressed to the Conference Board of Associated Research Councils, 2101 Constitution Avenue, N.W., Washington, D.C. 20418.

The Agency for International Development handles the foreign aid and technical assistance program of the United States (10). This agency, known as AID, has a strong involvement in education, particularly in the educational development projects, and the "exchange of persons" movement. Its technical assistance programs bring foreign nationals to the United States and send American technicians to other countries on a consultation or supervisory basis. These programs are handled primarily by agencies of the United States government, but also by contract with American universities.

Each year the International Training Division of AID brings about 5,000 "participants" to the United States for training and sends about 2,000 "participants" to other countries for training and education, and it sends about 5,000 technical

Fig. 13-2 Here a home economist is supervising a class in clothing construction in a school in India. (Courtesy of the College of Home Economics, University of Tennessee)

advisors overseas (9). In addition, about 300 persons are sent abroad as educational advisors (8).

The home economists under these programs work with technical cooperation and certain special programs. The technical programs are designed to share our knowledge, experience, techniques, and skills with the people of the less well-developed areas of the world for the purpose of helping them to further their economic development and raise their standard of living. The home economists in extension, foods and nutrition, child development and family life, housing, and sanitation are especially suited for these programs.

The work done abroad by the home economists under these programs includes working with ministers of agriculture, education, and health; serving as specialists in health, nutrition, and home crafts; doing research; teaching and training teachers; assisting with the development of community projects; helping to establish home economics programs in elementary and secondary schools and colleges; setting up home economics extension programs; and helping to establish school-lunch programs (8).

An award usually follows competition, is granted for one year, and is made to coincide with the academic year of the country that is designated. Applicants for a visiting lectureship will be expected to have a doctor's degree and at least one year of college or university teaching experience (3). If applying for a research award, they must have, at the time of the application, a doctor's degree from a recognized institution of higher learning or recognized standing as a mature and well-established scholar or professional worker.

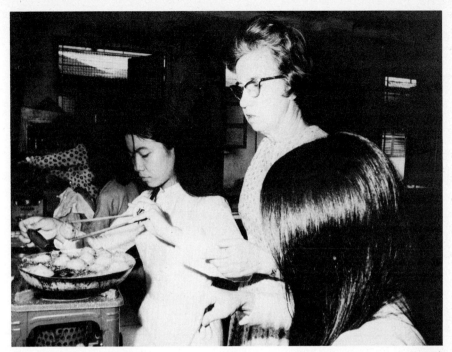

Fig. 13-3 A young Vietnamese district worker practices her cooking at a two-week demonstration training seminar in Saigon, conducted by a home economist. (Courtesy of the U.S. Department of Agriculture, Federal Extension Service)

A few foreign teaching posts are available for home economists in defense service dependent schools. In the high schools for American children, teachers must be prepared to teach in more than one subject field, since schools are small. The greatest number of vacancies, moreover, are in the elementary schools. A teacher at the time of appointment agrees to serve one school year overseas, and on this basis government transportation is furnished.

Among the qualifications for teaching in these dependent schools are U.S. citizenship, a bachelor's degree, eighteen semester hours in education courses, at least two years of recent public school teaching, and a valid teaching certificate.

In addition to teachers, the defense services need dietitians and recreation directors. The contracts for these jobs usually are on a two-year basis and are awarded under the competitive civil service system. The Defense Career Development Program rotates its employees through interesting and career-building assignments so as to give value and attractiveness to lifetime careers with the service.

The Peace Corps

The Peace Corps was established in 1961 with a threefold purpose: (1) providing qualified men and women to help foreign countries to meet their needs for

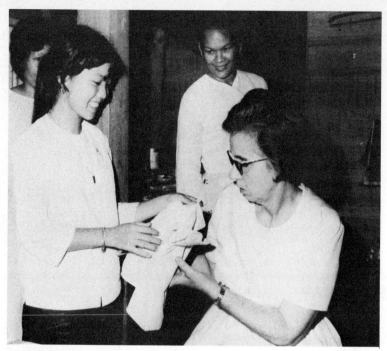

Fig. 13-4 Viewing the latest sewing project of home improvement club members by a home economist in international service. (Courtesy of the U.S. Department of Agriculture, Federal Extension Service)

manpower; (2) promoting a better understanding of the American people on the part of the people served; and (3) promoting a better understanding of other people on the part of the American people. In response to specific requests from host country governments, the Peace Corps sends carefully selected and well-trained volunteers overseas for a term of service which is normally twenty-four to twenty-seven months. They serve within the frame work of the local institutions and live at a level comparable to that of their host-counry coworker. Peace corps volunteers may also be utilized to support existing programs of the United States, the United Nations, or other international organizations (4, pp. 28–34).

The principal field of activity at the present time is education. In 1968, the Peace Corps volunteers were divided as follows:

area	no. of volunteers
Africa	2,935
East Asia – Pacific	2,442
Latin America	3,985
North Africa, Near East, and South Asia	1,870
Total	11,232

Fig. 13-5 Teaching food preparation in a foreign land may be very different from that in the United States. This picture shows a food-preparation class for women in Greece. (Courtesy of Montana State University)

The impact of the Peace Corps workers was ably stated by Mr. Sargent Shriver in 1965 at the end of his four years of Peace Corps work (2):

> These volunteers have racked up enough accomplishments, in the usual sense of the term to fill a fat volume. In that time, they taught literally millions of hours of classes. They fed hundreds of thousands of children in school lunch programs in thousands of remote villages. They organized programs in the slums of most of the major cities of Latin America. They reformed agricultural practices, built schools, helped modernize hospitals, organized country clinics. They conducted surveys and geological expeditions, codified laws, organized cooperatives, and found markets for the works of craftsmen where none existed before. They even assisted countries at the birth of nationwide educational television systems.

PROGRAMS OF THE UNITED NATIONS

The major programs of the United Nations which employ the services of home economists are the World Health Organization (WHO) and the Food and Agriculture Organization (FAO). These programs are all concerned with helping people raise their level of living through helping themselves (11, pp. 52–53). Home economists trained in such specialities as foods, nutrition, child development, public health, home management, and education have contributions to make to these programs. They deal with a people's most pressing problems in the areas of their specialities, problems which usually relate to health, food, clothing, shelter, and the improvement

Fig. 13-6 A home economist is working with a Vietnamese farm family, helping them to learn to take care of their new field of high-yielding "miracle" rice. (Courtesy of the U.S. Department of Agriculture, Federal Extension Service)

of family and community relations—the special domain of the home economist.

The World Health Organization came into being in 1948, for it was recognized that health was a major concern to the United Nations. The major undertaking of WHO includes assistance to countries in strengthening their public health service, including various activities such as environmental sanitation, maternal and child health, and communicable-disease control. WHO offers fellowships for individual study as well as group training programs, lasting from six to twelve months, to approximately 1,500 persons a year. In addition, it sends professors to other countries (11, pp. 54, 589; 4, pp. 28–34).

The Food and Agricultural Organization (FAO) came into being in 1954. Its purpose is to raise the level of nutrition and standards of living of the people in the cooperating countries through improvement in the efficiency of the production and distribution of agricultural products, to better the conditions of rural populations, and thus to contribute toward an expanded world economy (11, pp. 52–53; 4, pp. 28–34).

NONGOVERNMENT AGENCIES

Nongovernment agencies have many appealing employment opportunities abroad for teachers and health workers. These positions fall into three major groups: those in schools supported by mission boards, those in programs supported by private foundations, and those in installations of large commercial companies.

Fig. 13-7 A Peace Corps volunteer is acting as home science coordinator in a school operated by the All-India Women's Federation for tribal Adivasi and untouchable caste girls. (Courtesy of Dr. Mary Frances Reed, Northern Illinois University)

Foreign mission boards have schools around the world, and in many of these teachers of home economics are wanted (7). Teaching in mission schools abroad may be carried on in English, in the language of the country, or through an interpreter. Not everyone is suited for missionary work, but if one is religious and altruistic, missionary work can take one to the far corners of the earth.

To work in a foreign land in a church-sponsored program requires a strong Christian faith. In addition, one must possess a high standard of physical fitness and a college degree. The terms of appointment vary with the different mission boards, but most provide for pensions, medical care, and the education of the children of the missionaries. Short-term appointments are for three years or less, while full-time or career appointments may be for a longer period. Salaries usually are small when compared with United States levels, but they are generally adequate. In many places there are positions for a husband-and-wife team. Anyone interested in missionary service should write to the foreign mission board of his own denomination or to the University Christian Movement, 475 Riverside Drive, New York, N.Y., or to The National Council of Churches of Christ In The U.S.A., 475 Riverside Drive, New York, N.Y. 10027.

Many private foundations are supporting work abroad designed to demonstrate new patterns and procedures which can be adopted by the nations and peoples concerned and to train the leaders and technicians necessary for effective dissemination of these new methods and ideas. There are about 15,000 foundations in the United States with assets of over 14.5 billion dollars making grants of over 800 million dollars each year (1).

The Ford Foundation's Foreign Area Fellowship Program has enabled several foreign institutions to engage American home economists to develop and conduct home economics programs in their countries (10, pp. 58–59). Its program is concerned with rural village development, education and vocational training, public administration, and social and economics research.

In 1963, the Rockefeller Foundation completed a half-century of activity which had been directed toward the "well-being of man-kind"—as its charter defines its purpose. The Carnegie Foundation has given substantial support to the development of area study centers, supporting universities abroad, and furthering peace.

A number of private agencies have fellowships available to American students for study abroad at the graduate level. Some that may be of interest to home economists are as follows:

1. American Association of University Women
   2401 Virginia Avenue, N.W.
   Washington, D.C. 20037
2. The Rotary Foundation of Rotary International
   1600 Ridge Avenue
   Evanston, Illinois 60201
3. The American-Scandinavian Foundation
   127 East 73 Street
   New York, New York 10021
4. Institute of International Education
   809 United Nations Plaza
   New York, New York 10017

The Institute of International Education offers approximately 300 scholarships to United States students for academic study in any field. Candidates must have bachelor's degrees and usually are required to have demonstrated their ability and capacity for independent study (11, pp. 52–53).

The *International Farm Youth Exchange* program, better known as IFYE, seeks to promote international understanding by arranging for young men and women, twenty to thirty years of age, from farms in this country to live and work with farm families in other countries for four to six months and for rural youths from other countries to come to the United States for a similar experience. The program is sponsored by the National 4-H Club Foundation in cooperation with the Federal Extension Service of the U.S. Department of Agriculture and the land-grant colleges. For additional information on the IFYE program write to the National 4-H Club Foundation, 7100 Connecticut Avenue, Washington, D.C. 20015.

A few home economists are employed abroad by such business firms as the United Fruit Company, Canada Packers, Ltd., and the American Can Company. Many of these are dietitians, who work in the company's hospitals. An organization or business firm in another country may occasionally seek a United States home economist for a special project, but these opportunities are limited.

Stewardess work with airlines opens doors to foreign travel for thousands of young women. Although the requirements of the different airlines are various, the general requirements for overseas flying are that a stewardess be a United States citizen, twenty to twenty-eight years of age, and in good physical condition; and that she have good appearance and poise, at least two years of college or the equivalent, and the ability to use the language of the countries in which travel takes place.

Any student interested in foreign scholarships, work camps, youth camps, UNESCO projects, educational exchanges, and study or vocation opportunities overseas will do well to consult the publication *Study Abroad* which is published by the Columbia University Press in New York.

QUALIFICATIONS FOR FOREIGN SERVICE

Although each foreign program has certain specific requirements to be met by those selected for service, are there not certain qualifications necessary for anyone who is representing a private or public agency of the United States in a foreign land?

If those going abroad are to be of service to the people of a foreign land, they must know the culture of that country. Home economics cannot be taught in a foreign land as it is taught in the United States: patterns of family and community life, customs, status of men and women, ways of earning a living, and ways of meeting personal and family needs vary greatly from one country to another, and in some countries there are great variations among the sections or classes within the country. To understand the culture of another country requires a knowledge of its patterns and habits of family living, the history of its people, its art and traditions, its social and economic conditions, its religious beliefs and customs, and the values and meaning associated with the various cultural phenomena and ways of life. To be aware of the treasures as well as the shortcomings of other cultures is a must for foreign service.

In addition to knowing the culture, one must obtain as much information as possible about the resources of the people, the products available to them, and the means they have for procuring these products. For example, if one wishes to teach clothing in a foreign land, one must realize that some countries do not have basic patterns, that they do not have mass-produced cloth, that they may be satisfied with the way they dress, and that they may not have the equipment considered essential by American standards for making clothing. Likewise, modern laundry and dry-cleaning facilities may be very scarce and expensive. Similar illustrations could be used for foods and nutrition, housing and management, and family life.

In most countries there are vast differences between students coming from rich and poor families, differences that are more pronounced in those countries where there is a very small middle class. In the rich homes, most things are done by servants, and thus the students may have few skills of homemaking and little interest in developing them. The simple living and few resources of the poor homes may have denied students coming from that class the opportunities to learn better ways of homemaking. For both groups of students, it may take great effort and finesse to stimulate respect for efficient methods of work, better standards of living, and desire for improved homes and families for everyone.

Foreign service requires the ability and willingness to start with the felt needs of the people with whom one is working, which necessitate insight, patience, gentleness, ability to compromise, and appreciation and consideration of other ways and values. The home economist abroad must know how to make use of the skills and facts known and accepted by the people as a step toward the new and the unknown. In other words, other peoples may not move so fast or want to move so fast as citizens of the United States are prone to do.

The professional home economist in foreign service must also be willing and able to cooperate effectively with workers in other professions and groups, for home economics is in its infancy in many nations of the world, and its success as a force for improved family living will depend upon the foundation of service and good will which the home economist in foreign service lays.

The home economist who wishes to serve in foreign lands must be dedicated to the job of improving the home and family living of the people with whom she will work within the framework of their own culture. This will require a great deal of maturity and knowledge on her part, but the personal satisfactions and rewards for a job well done will be great, and the job itself is of international importance.

SUGGESTED ACTIVITIES

1. On most campuses there are a number of foreign students. One who is studying home economics or a related field may be invited to talk with the class members.

a. In how many colleges or universities in the country of the foreign student is home economics offered? What special fields are emphasized?

b. What contributions can home economics make in a foreign country toward helping families and homemakers?

c. How does the foreign student plan to use her home economics training when she returns to her native land?

d. What type of education is offered to most of the women in the foreign country? How many of them enter the colleges and universities?

2. In most states there are home economists who have worked or taught in foreign countries. They are in a position to discuss with students the following ideas:

a. Why is home economics needed in the country in which the home economist worked?

b. What are the difficulties in developing a program of home economics there?

c. What should be the qualifications of home economists going into foreign service?

d. How should one prepare herself for foreign service?

3. In most states there are former IFYE (International Farm Youth Exchange) students. Their names can be obtained by writing to the state 4-H club department of the land-grant college. These students are in a position to discuss foreign service experiences with the class.

a. Ask them to describe the experiences they had in the foreign country.

b. What did they learn through the IFYE experience which would contribute to international understanding?

c. What advice do they have to give to other students who may wish to go abroad on a similar program?

4. By writing to the Institute of International Education, 809 United Nations Plaza, New York, New York 10017, information on foreign students programs can be obtained. These probrams may be discussed in class from the following aspects:

a. What different types of student programs are available for home economics students?

b. What are the requirements for participating in the various programs?

c. What are the procedures for applying for appointments in these foreign student programs?

REFERENCES

1. Andrews, F. Anderson, (ed.), *Foundations, 20 View Points,* p. 6, Russell Sage Foundation, 1965.

2. Erickson, Aaron J., *The Peace Corps: A Pictorial History,* Hill and Wang, Inc., New York, 1965.

3. *Educational and Cultural Exchange Opportunities,* U.S. Department of State, pp. 1–31, Bureau of Educational and Cultural Affairs, Publication 7543, International and Cultural Series 83, 1967.

4. *A Guide to United States Government Agencies Involved in International Educational and Cultural Activities,* U.S. Department of State, pp. 1–21, Bureau of Educational and Cultural Affairs, September 1968.

5. Hockin, Margaret L., "The Home Economist and Changing Patterns of Living around the World," *New Dimensions in International Programs of Home Economics,* pp. 33–45, American Home Economics Association, Washington, 1954.

6. Johnson, Walter, and Francis J. Colligan, *The Fulbright Program, a History,* The University of Chicago Press, Chicago, 1965.

7. Reuter, Richard W., "Home Economics: American Export," *Journal of Home Economics*, vol. 53, pp. 753–755, November 1961.

8. *Some Opportunities Abroad for Teachers, 1970–71*, p. 5, U.S. Office of Education, 1969.

9. *Some United States Agencies Involved in International Activities*, United States Department of State, Bureau of Educational and Cultural Affairs, 1963.

10. Speakman, Cummins E., Jr., *International Exchange in Education*, The Center for Applied Research in Education, Inc., New York, 1966.

11. United Nations Educational, Scientific and Cultural Organizations, *Study Abroad*, XVIII, Paris, 1969.

12. U.S. Bureau of the Census, *Statistical Abstracts of the United States: 1969*, 90th ed., p. 827.

13. Walton, Peggy, "Be a Home Economist and See the World," *What's New in Home Economics*, vol. 28, pp. 66–68, February 1964.

14. Zimmerman, Oswald T., and Irwin Lavine, *College Placement Directory*, 2d ed., pp. 373, 432–436, Industrial Research Service, Inc., Dover, N.H., 1965.

ADDITIONAL READINGS

Abrams, Irwin, *Study Abroad*, U.S. Department of Health, Education, and Welfare, Office of Education, New Dimensions in Higher Education, Number 6, n.d.

Beckett, Lois M., and Mildred Horton, "The U.S.A. Speaks to the International Consumer through Home Economics," *Journal of Home Economics*, vol. 53, pp. 251–254, April 1963.

Career Employment in the U.S. Foreign Service, The Institute for Research, Research No. 18, Chicago, 1968.

"Home Economics Sparks Unique Career," *What's New in Home Economics*, vol. 32, p. 32, February 1968.

"Home Economists in Action," *Forecast for Home Economics—CoEd Section*, vol. 11, p. 38, November 1965.

Hoope, Roy, *The Peace Corps Experience*, Clarkson N. Potter, Inc., New York, 1968.

Mallory, Bernice, "International Cooperation through Home Economics Education," *Journal of Home Economics*, vol. 61, pp. 239–246, April 1969.

Parker, Ida G., and Hazel Hatcher, "International Opportunities for Home Economists," *Journal of Home Economics*, vol. 56, pp. 257–260, April 1964.

Schumm, Ruth, "Peace Corps Home Economists," *What's New in Home Economics*, vol. 28, pp. 64–65, February 1964.

14 HOMEMAKING

Homemaking must be the most appealing occupation of all, to judge by the numbers who enter it. In the United States more than 90 percent of the people marry, and most of them establish homes, thus becoming homemakers. Furthermore, homemaking probably is the oldest occupation for both men and women. In so far as history tells the story of mankind, wherever there have been families there have been homemakers nurturing and ministering to the members' needs, providing a place for them to live, and protecting them from the ravages of weather and disease. Although the term "homemaker" usually refers to the woman in the family, who is chiefly responsible for managing and running the home, homemaking is a cooperative venture among all members of the family. This joint enterprise is directed toward the goal of satisfying, happy, and growth-providing family living experiences. The family is a partnership in that when a man and woman choose each other for marriage, together they enter a partnership for family living. As children enter the family, the number of partners increases, but the essential relationship of "all for one and one for all" remains.

As is true of all partnerships, there must be a division of labor in the family. At one time in the United States, and still in many parts of the world, it was assumed that this division should be on the basis of the man's earning money or providing the economic necessities of life and the woman's managing the resources within the home and providing care for the family members. Students of economics know that this dichotomy was at no time completely true of the United States, and certainly it is misrepresentative of the facts today. Of the approximately 63 million households in this country in 1970, women head 24 percent of all homes. In 1970, 38 percent of the employed workers in the United States were women, and 43 percent of all women over 16 years of age were working for wages (12).

Many homemakers in complete and intact families share wage-earning activities with their husbands. Over one-half of the women now working are married to men who are the chief bread winners in the family (13). Three-fourths of the married women without small children are working, as well as 30 percent of the young women whose children are not yet of school age (12). Because of their responsibilities at home, many of the women with young children hold part-time jobs or work part of the year and are likely to leave and enter the labor force several times in a relatively short period. As soon as the children reach school age, the proportion of mothers who go to work outside the home rises sharply. About one-half of the women with children between the ages of six and seventeen with a husband present are in the labor force (15).

Increasingly in the United States, women marry early (half of them before they reach twenty-one), work until the coming of their first child, and return to work as soon as the children are of school age. It is generally accepted that this trend for women to combine homemaking and wage earning will increase steadily. As women have taken on more wage-earning responsibilities, men have assumed somewhat more responsibility for homemaking tasks (10). The wage-earning role of married women, as well as the increasing demand for their services in community activities, has greatly increased the need for efficiency in home management and housekeeping.

The homemaker is many things, and to adequately prepare for homemaking she must take note of the great diversity in her jobs. Her activities or jobs fall into many occupational categories, from common labor work to professional and scientific tasks. Not all homemakers are equipped to perform well in all of these occupations, but good homemaking demands relative efficiency and a satisfactory level of performance in all.

HOME ECONOMISTS AS HOMEMAKERS

The majority of home economists, that is, those who have graduated from college with a major in home economics or a related field, are homemakers either on a full- or part-time basis. They are called "home economists in homemaking" and have several types of household arrangements. The home economist may be a full-time homemaker, devoting all her professional knowledge and skill to providing for the comfort and welfare of family members and seeing that the home operates as an efficient economic unit and a base for sound character building. She may also be a part-time homemaker, combining homemaking with paid employment or volunteer services outside the home. The members of the home which she manages and cares for may be her husband and children only, or there may be, in addition, related or unrelated adults and children; or her home may be made up solely of related or unrelated adults and/or children.

As stated earlier, there are as many grades of homemakers as of workers in business and industry, ranging from the unskilled to the professional and scientific. The home economist in homemaking should be able to enter the occupation at the upper levels—as a professional who can apply the principles of the arts and sciences to the decisions to be made and the processes to be carried out in the home.

Homemaking at the professional and scientific level challenges the ability and knowledge of the best-educated home economist. The possibilities for applying a knowledge of the arts and sciences to homemaking are boundless; there is scarcely a branch of knowledge or a new discovery that does not affect the home in one way or another.* The management and productive processes in industry tend to parallel

---

* The housekeeping phase of homemaking has become a highly technical occupation that demands skill, training in the use of equipment, and up-to-date information. The managerial and personnel phases demand expert knowledge and ability in weighing values, making sound decisions, and providing a growth-stimulating environment for family members.

those in the home, with one notable exception: the homemaker usually is both the manager who makes the plans and the worker who carries them out. Thus, her education and training must be adequate for efficient performance at both levels.

At what point in homemaking is the know-how of a home economist needed for efficient and satisfactory homemaking? The answer is at all points. A brief glance at the functions carried on in the home will support this conclusion (Table 14-1).

Management

The home economist in homemaking is in a position to apply scientific principles to the management of the home (5, 17). The scientific homemaker scrutinizes her own practices and those of other family members, analyzes each step of the job to see where time, energy, or money may be saved, and then devises and puts into operation plans for more efficient operation. Efficiency in home management is of major importance to the economy of our country. As long ago as 1914, an efficiency expert said to a group of industrial workers (1):

> Half your power to think and to work is made and established or delayed and destroyed in your home. The effect of your home habits, people,

Table 14-1
Occupational categories of homemaking activities

occupational category	homemaking activity	occupational category	homemaking activity
Professional	Teacher Dietitian Nurse Social worker	Craftsman	Dressmaker Drapery maker

Semiprofessional	Interior
	  decorator
	Stylist
	Recreational
	  director
		Operative	Laundress
			Repairman
			Presser
			Gardener
			Caterer

Managerial	Purchasing agent Planner Organizer Supervisor of work Personnel officer	Domestic service	Family cook Housekeeper
		Personal service	Baby sitter Family chauffeur Hostess
Clerical	Budget maker Record keeper Letter writer Bill payer	Protective service	Watchman First-aid service
		Building service	House cleaner Purchaser of equipment

Sales	Shopper
	Taker of
	  inventories
		Laborer	Odd jobs
			Unpaid family
			  work

SOURCE: Walter J. Greenleaf, *Occupations and Careers,* p. 55, McGraw-Hill Book Company, Inc., New York, 1955. Modified and expanded by the author.

surroundings, associations and incentives . . . will do more than any other one factor in life to push you on and up, or down and out. The housewives of America, if they would learn their profession, could save their families at least $500,000,000 a year, now being wasted in hospitals, asylums, sanitariums and drug stores.

This statement was made over forty years ago, and how much more true it is today!

The decisions which the homemaker must make are limitless and continuous (2). To be sound, these decisions must be based upon facts analyzed in the light of the needs of the family. The number and range of these decisions demand wide knowledge and ability on the part of the homemaker. A homemaker, not trained in home management and operating on a trial-and-error basis, cannot help but be wasteful of family resources. It is well known that the productive energies of homemakers have been wasted in useless drudgery in all ages and all countries.

The home economist, as she successfully manages the home, is practicing conservation in much the same way as the soil or forest conservationist. Saving an hour of energy for each member of a group means the conservation of many days and years of effort. Extending the lifetime and efficiency of a piece of household equipment through correct use and care means the conservation of material resources and additional money for raising the standard and level of living. Protecting health and providing conditions for optimal growth and work for family members through good nutrition, suitable and comfortable living conditions, and a secure home, conserves untold hours of human energy, as well as public and private funds for the care of those who are socially maladjusted and mentally and physically incapacitated.

Sheltering the Family

Providing the suitable space and arrangements for living, working, and playing in the home requires both knowledge and leadership. It has often been said that families are forced to take on the shape of the house because houses are not made to fit the family. The home economist is in a position to shape the house to fit family needs. In her college course work she will have studied the effects of housing upon individuals, the requirements of adequate and effective space in the home, equipment, house furnishings, lighting, color, safety measures, and ways to provide flexibility in the home.

It is very important in this age of increased pressure that the home be a place to reduce tension and fatigue (6). Eye fatigue can be overcome by proper lighting; ear fatigue with careful planning can be greatly diminished in spite of TV, radio, record players, and noisy children; body fatigue can be reduced by providing good working tools, good planning of work, and proper conditions for work; and psychological fatigue can be lessened through improved family relationships. The homemaker is in a position to provide the setting for the reduction of these fatigues, but it takes a very ingenious and well-informed homemaker to be able to do it.

Feeding the Family

The feeding of a family should not be left in uninformed hands (7, 18). A person's health is to a large extent dependent upon the adequacy of his diet. Also, the family food pattern influences the individual throughout his life. As a child he eats what the homemaker provides, and as an adult he usually continues to eat according to habits established in his home.

For the average family, expenditures for food account for approximately 25 to 30 percent of the total income. Any item that consumes so great a part of the family budget must be carefully handled as a part of ensuring good use of the family income. To do this requires more than dedication on the part of the homemaker. Sifting out the information and misinformation concerning food which comes to the home via radio, TV, newspapers, and the back fence; keeping up with the new findings on the adequacy of foods; adjusting nutrition requirements to family likes and dislikes—all require the know-how and skill of the specialist.

Food activities as a class, including the purchasing, storage, preparation and serving of food, clearing away after meals, and dishwashing consume more of the homemaker's time than does any other group of activities. If good family nutrition and satisfaction with food do not result from the eighteen to twenty-four hours of time expended every week on food activities, the homemaker is reaping little reward for her efforts.

Clothing the Family

Family goals for clothing include the provision within the limits of the budget for clothes that are becoming and suitable for all members of the family to the various occasions which arise from their activities. This is difficult in the clothing and textiles field because of the continued lack of a science of clothing in the United States. The homemaker does not have information on the amount of heat-providing qualities to expect from different types of garments or their suitability for varying conditions of work or activity. In view of this, she must make her selections on the basis of her own knowledge of textiles, fiber qualities, and construction and wearing principles.

To meet the social and psychological needs of all family members in clothing on a limited income takes wise planning and purchasing, as well as care. Clothing is available in a much wider range of prices than is food; this makes decision making somewhat more difficult. Since clothing expenditures consume from 10 to 15 percent of the family income, unwise selection and improper care of clothing cause great economic waste for the families of the nation.

Knowledge furnishes the greatest defense against bad choices in any form. The more one knows, the greater one's capability of selecting the best for the money available and, even more important, using the selections in such a way as to increase their value in comfort and appearance.

Providing a Suitable Environment

No doubt, the happiness and effectiveness of an individual today depend more upon his skill in human relationships than was true a generation ago, and much of this skill and understanding is acquired in the home. The family sets the pattern of attitudes, beliefs, and general behavior of the individual, as well as his life's goals. Good homes and families must increasingly offer relief from tension resulting from mass production and high competition, crowding, and general insecurity. Keen sensitivity and unlimited effort on the part of the homemaker are necessary to provide a satisfactory environment for the family under varying conditions. Dr. E. Neige Todhunter indicated this need for well-educated homemakers in the following statement (11):

> Homemaking is something very different from housekeeping. Homemaking is not accomplished by instinct, at least not in our modern complex civilization. No instinct guides us in what to eat; . . . No instinct tells how to make a cake or cook a meal; to run a household (literally a miniature factory or production center); to raise children, settle children's conflicts and disputes; to budget and manage the family income; to handle modern gadgets and electrical equipment; to select clothing and furnishings and make an artistic and beautiful setting for the family; to bandage cuts and nurse mumps and measles and other ailments (to be a nurse and household physician); to know the quality of goods and how to buy them; and with it all to have a charming disposition, an unruffled countenance, time to read and know what is going on in the world in order to be a good conversationalist, a charming companion, and a good citizen who knows how to vote and to be a community leader. This is what homemaking requires, and there is no instinct for all of that. It requires a background of sciences; chemistry, physics, biology, physiology, and bacteriology and their application to food preparation, nutrition, clothing and equipment. It requires a knowledge of psychology and sociology and their applications to child development and family relations. It requires training in management, economics, and finance.

Community Life and Self-expression

The home economist finds use for her education in many community services, and she is always ready for a call for help from others in the community. One home economics–trained homemaker who was living in a small college community, for one week in which she kept records, had twenty-two requests for information and help with family and household questions from other homemakers. Studies of home economics graduates indicate that they have a gratifying interest in community activities (8), for the educated homemaker realizes that the world is her field. At no other time in history have families been on the move as they are today or as influenced by happenings outside their local area, state, or country. Furthermore, the educated homemaker is fully aware of the fact that learning democracy begins at home.

The home is one of the few opportunities remaining for relatively individual expression. To be both the worker and manager, the "doer" and the planner, the designer and the craftsman is a privilege that was lost to industry with the passing of the handicraft stage of production and the coming of specialization. It is still the opportunity of the homemaker who is educated for her job. To be able to create, one must know the qualities of the thing to be created and the functional relationships among the parts. The home furnishes unlimited opportunities for original creation in foods, table service, house planning, handicrafts, clothing, and human relationships. The home is the workshop where improved communication between men and women, adults and young people, and among young people themselves can be learned, providing the workshop leader—the homemaker—has the intelligence and skill in human relations to direct the participants in satisfactory learning experiences.

Studies of home economists indicate that they give credit to their college education for much of their success as homemakers. They feel that home economics has been of real benefit in preparing them for the career as homemakers which they have chosen to follow (9).

> We feel, that as college graduates in home economics, we are a fortunate group. Home economics trains every student for her personal life, for her job of potential homemaker, and at the same time recognizes the fact that most women need to become vocationally proficient. The woman absents herself from her professional life, but continues the performance of her skills. Her professional sisters are still interested in her activities, for it is to her that their advertising and research are directed. Her needs, her opinions are respected and sought after. She still associates actively with her professional societies. She never loses the feeling of belonging! Through her homemakers groups, she contacts people of similar experience, and her problems are made easier merely for the discussion. When she returns to her professional field, she is not behind the times, but behind her is the experience of a mature personality. For her there was little conflict between marriage and career. Home economists are never out of things; home economists never grow old!

Martha Van Rensselaer, in speaking of home economics in 1914, summed up what home economics education means to homemaking (16):

> The old methods of homemaking have not satisfied women's ability. Education of the past has not pointed out the home as a laboratory for science and art of the school, and woman has looked outside for her professional experience. Home economics unlocks a vast and interesting

laboratory and the result of the use of that laboratory is greater efficiency and a higher type of civilization, for "good citizenship is but an expansion of home ideals."

WHAT DOES THE JOB PAY?

Homemaking is an occupation—not a profession. The professions have established entrance criteria, usually based upon education and/or professional proficiency in the particular field. Unfortunately, there are no such requirements for entering home-making. The home economist in homemaking, however, should operate on a professional level in her homemaking even though she did not have to meet any educational qualifications or to be certified for entering the work.

Some may question the advisability of calling homemaking an occupation, for it is not found among the occupations listed in the census, nor is it defined in the *Dictionary of Occupational Titles.* This lack of recognition is justified only on the basis that homemaking is not a "gainful" occupation: whether or not the homemaker is paid in money for her services, she does produce economic goods and services through her activities in the home.

It is difficult for many reasons to assign a monetary value to the services of the homemaker. For example, there are no job specifications which homemakers are required to meet as they work in the home. Some perform at a high level of efficiency and turn out products and services of the highest quality, while the opposite is true of others. Homemakers do not compete with each other for jobs; they cannot be fired for poor performance, and promotions for exceptional service usually come in the form of better family relationships, a more stable family, and more appreciation from family members.

Granting these problems, an individual homemaker can estimate the value of her productive activities in wage terms. One method that has been suggested for doing this is to hire one or more workers to come into the home and perform all of the tasks, make all of the decisions, and assume all the responsibilities of the homemaker. These workers must perform at a level equivalent to that of the homemaker. The sum total of the earnings of these workers projected over a year may be assumed to be the annual earnings of the homemaker for home and household activities. Despite the many additional conveniences and resources available, today's homemaker spends as much time on household tasks as her counterpart did fifty years ago. The amount of time spent at individual tasks has shifted, though, because of changing family and social patterns (3). In Table 14-2 it will be noted that homemakers spend on an average approximately fifty hours a week working. The homemaker with four or more children averages over sixty-two hours per week in household tasks.

There are many hours of service which must be added to these totals. If there are small children in the home, the wages of an almost continuous baby sitter would

Table 14-2
Average hours per week spent at household tasks by homemakers in families of different sizes

household tasks	hours per family of no. of persons			average hours for all families
	2	3–5	6 or more	
Meal preparation	9.9	14.1	17.3	13.0
Dishwashing	4.5	5.9	6.8	5.5
Laundering	3.3	6.4	8.1	5.5
Sewing	1.8	1.9	1.2	1.8
House care	8.1	12.0	13.3	10.8
Yard work	0.5	0.7	0.4	0.6
Management and shopping	3.6	4.4	4.1	4.1
Transportation of others	0.5	1.6	3.2	1.4
Family care	2.3	8.8	7.4	6.4
Other	0.4	0.5	0.1	0.4
Total	35.1	55.7	62.2	49.3
Hours of hired housework	0.2	0.5	1.3	0.5

SOURCE: Florence Turnbull and Marguerite Paulsen Schroeder, "Time Spent on Household Tasks," *Journal of Home Economics*, vol. 62, p. 25, January 1970.

need to be added to the total previously calculated. In many families, again, the homemaker spends considerable time representing the family in the community and its organizations, and acting as the family hostess; this should also be added to her theoretical wages.

Another method of arriving at the homemakers' earnings is to base them upon what she could earn outside the home as a full-time wage earner. For example, if she could earn $90 a week as a full-time clerk, her yearly household income would be judged to be fifty-two times $90 or $4,680. If she could earn $150 a week as an office manager, her yearly earnings as a homemaker would be evaluated at $7,800. If she could earn $10,000 a year as a food-service director, her value as a homemaker would be considered the same. Obviously, this method has many pitfalls. The clerk, office manager, or food director is on duty only eight hours a day for a five- or six-day week, whereas the homemaker is on duty twenty-four hours a day for a seven-day week. Again, the woman who has the best earning capacity in the labor market may not be the most efficient household manager and worker.

A third method of estimating the earnings of the homemaker is to have the family members buy all the services she renders. The sum total of the cost of these services minus the cost of producing them at home would be the earnings of the homemaker. For example, if the homemaker made a dress for $10 which would cost $35 on the market, she would be earning $25. If the feeding of the family cost $40 per week when prepared and served at home by the homemaker, compared to $100 per week if purchased away from home, the earnings of the homemaker for this activity would be $60 per week. If a child were sick and needed a week of nursing care, the cost of a practical nurse for that time would be counted as earnings of the homemaker. In this way each activity carried on for the family by the homemaker would be priced in the market and the cost accredited to the homemaker's earnings. It can be seen that by this method the homemaker's earnings would be high, for it has been estimated that the homemaker performs twenty-seven different types of work in carrying on household activities.

Many home economists are faced with the question of whether it is better to give full time to homemaking or to carry the dual role of homemaking and paid employment outside the home. Often this cannot be answered purely on the basis of the homemaker's wishes or the preferences of her family. There is a great need for qualified home economists in the occupations and professions, and a good home economist is mindful of her community responsibility as well as that of her home. In terms of economics, many home economists have found that the value of their homemaking activities as full-time homemakers was similar to what they could earn as a full-time employed worker, provided they did not extend their work load as many working homemakers do.

SUGGESTED ACTIVITIES

1. In most communities there are several home economists in homemaking. Invite one of these to visit the class to discuss the following with the students:
a. In what ways has the home economics training received in college helped her in performing her job as a homemaker?
b. What do husbands think of home economics training as preparation for homemaking?
c. What are the advantages of being a trained home economist devoting full time to homemaking? What are the disadvantages?
d. What requests come to her from other homemakers and organizations in the community because she is a home economist?
2. The home economists who are combining homemaking and a paid career outside the home will be able to give the advantages and disadvantages of the dual role played by many women. One should be invited to discuss this dual role with the students.
a. How does home economics aid the home economists who carry homemaking and a profession outside the home?
b. What do the husbands and children think of homemakers working outside the home? What are the advantages and disadvantages of this dual role?
c. How does she arrange her schedule to carry both responsibilities equally well?
d. What advice does the homemaker who is pursuing a profession or occupation outside the home have for college students in home economics?
3. The students may be interested in studying the problems and needs of

homemakers in their community. In selecting the homemakers to be interviewed both home economics and non-home economics homemakers should be included.

a. What are the most important problems and needs of these homemakers?

b. What are the chief satisfactions that these women receive from homemaking?

c. What changes would they like to make in their careers as homemakers?

d. Are there any differences in the problems and needs, or satisfactions received by the home economics as contrasted with the non-home economics homemakers?

4. In evaluating the type of training needed for homemaking, the students will find it profitable to list all of the different jobs or types of responsibilities carried by the average homemaker during a week.

a. For how many of these will the home economics subject matter received in college courses give the basic information on which to base decisions?

b. For how many of these will home economics courses furnish some experience in performing?

c. To what extent will the student be better able to make application of the subject matter presented and experiences provided by being conscious of the types of responsibilities of homemakers?

REFERENCES

1. Bane, Juliet Lita, "Home Economists at Work," *What's New in Home Economics*, vol. 16, pp. 28–29, April 1952.

2. Gibbs, Mary, "Decision-Making Procedures by Young Consumers," *Journal of Home Economics*, vol. 55, pp. 359–360, May 1963.

3. Hall, Florence Turnbull, and Marguerite Paulsen Schroder, "Time Spent on Household Tasks," *Journal of Home Economics*, vol. 62, p. 23, January 1970.

4. Hughes, R. B., "Preparation for a Dual Role," *Journal of Home Economics*, vol. 61, pp. 350–358, May 1969.

5. Liston, Margaret, "Home Management Is an Evolving Field," *What's New in Home Economics*, vol. 31, p. 95, February 1967.

6. Mizi, Jessie J., Fern Tuten, and Joseph W. Simmons, "A Study of Sound Levels in Houses," *Journal of Home Economics*, vol. 58, pp. 41–45, January 1966.

7. Morse, Ellen A., Mary M. Clayton, and Lola DeG. Cosgrove, "Mothers' Nutrition Knowledge," *Journal of Home Economics*, vol. 59, pp. 667–668, October 1967.

8. Lehman, Ruth T., "The Home Economics Graduates in the Community," *Journal of Home Economics*, vol. 45, pp. 713–716, December 1953.

9. McGinnis, Esther, *The Homemaker Speaks*, p. 4, American Home Economics Association, Washington, D.C., June 1952.

10. National Manpower Council, *Womanpower,* p. 22, Columbia University Press, New York, 1957.

11. Todhunter, E. Neige, "Higher Education Challenges Home Economics," *Journal of Home Economics,* vol. 41, pp. 299–301, May 1949.

12. U.S. Bureau of the Census, *Statistical Abstracts of the United States,* 92d ed., 1971.

13. Van Rensslaer, Martha, "President's Address," *Journal of Home Economics,* vol. 7, p. 461, November 1915.

14. Wench, Dorothy A., "Employed and Non-employed Homemakers—How They Manage," *Journal of Home Economics,* vol. 59, pp. 737–738, November 1967.

15. Wilson, Mary Margaret, and Mina W. Lamb, "Food Beliefs as Related to Ecological Factors in Women," *Journal of Home Economics,* vol. 60, pp. 115–118, February 1968.

ADDITIONAL READINGS

Berg, Janice, "College Women Speak about Themselves and about Home Economics," *Journal of Home Economics,* vol. 57, pp. 627–628, December 1965.

DeAtley, Margaret, "Home Economics Based on Scientific Principles Is Concerned with Better Living," *What's New in Home Economics,* vol. 26, pp. 42–45, February 1962.

Donnelly, Jean, "Home Economics Sparks Unique Career," *What's New in Home Economics,* vol. 31, p. 20, September 1967.

Knoblock, Beverly, "Homemaking and the Family Role," *What's New in Home Economics,* vol. 29, p. 8, February 1965.

Searls, L. G., "College Majors and the Tasks of Homemaking," *Journal of Home Economics,* vol. 58, pp. 708–14, November 1966.

Stevens, Harriett A., and Margaret A. Osborne, "Characteristics of Home Economics Graduates," *Journal of Home Economics,* vol. 57, pp. 773–777, December 1965.

Surrette, Robert F., "Career versus Homemaking: Perspectives and Proposals," *Vocational Guidance Quarterly,* vol. 16, pp. 82–86, December 1967.

Swope, Mary Ruth, and Helen Sarck, "Employment Practices and Preferences of Homemakers in Two Central Illinois Communities," *Journal of Home Economics,* vol. 58, pp. 748–749, November 1966.

Walker, Katherine E., "Homemaking Still Takes Time," *Journal of Home Economics,* vol. 61, pp. 621–624, October 1969.

15
AFTER COLLEGE—WHAT?

At the end of her undergraduate college preparation, each home economics student must make a major decision as to her future course of actions. This decision not only will influence her welfare and happiness but is of major concern to society. Will she go immediately into professional work? Will she become a full-time homemaker? Or will she continue her education in graduate school? Some students may decide to combine two of these, namely, graduate study and professional work, graduate study and homemaking, or professional work and homemaking. A few of the very ambitious may try to combine all three.

While the students must make this decision for themselves, there are ways of getting very practical help with it. Most colleges have counselors or advisers who are able to assist students in evaluating the merits of the choices to be made, and the students' course adviser and department head or dean will be able to help them evaluate their qualifications for various positions. Through the placement service of the college, information can be obtained as to possible positions, salaries to be expected, and working conditions. Opportunities for graduate study in home economics, requirements for entering graduate schools, and fields of study available at different colleges and universities are items of information readily available to interested students.

In the foregoing chapters the various professional fields into which a home economics graduate may go have been discussed in some detail. Graduate study usually makes it possible for students to advance more rapidly in positions or professions and to render a higher level of service through their work; it is a requirement for many of the better positions.

GRADUATE STUDY

Organized graduate study in the United States had its beginning approximately 100 years ago. Before this time a few enterprising students did receive master's degrees' however, there were no special schools, departments, or faculties to supervise graduate as distinct from undergraduate study, and the standards and significance of graduate degrees were not clearly defined.

The first earned Ph.D. degree conferred by an American university was granted by Yale in 1861. Harvard instituted graduate work in 1863; however, its graduate department was not formally organized until some years later. In 1871, in addition to

Yale and Harvard, Princeton, the University of Michigan, and Lafayette College enrolled graduate students. In 1876 Johns Hopkins was established as an institution devoted exclusively to education and research *at the graduate level,* with Clark College following in 1887. Although this experiment as a college devoted solely to graduate work did not prove successful, it gave great stimulation to graduate-study development.

The growth in graduate study in the United States has been fairly rapid. The number of graduate students attending American colleges and universities for selected years is shown in Table 15-1 (3, 5).

Graduate study in home economics developed shortly after the turn of the present century. In 1914, Benjamin Andrews reported that there were twenty colleges and universities in the United States offering the degrees of master of arts and master of science in home economics, and at least one university, the University of Chicago, where a candidate could receive the doctor of philosophy degree in household administration (1). By 1914 these institutions had granted twenty-seven master's degrees in various phases of home economics. Of these master's degrees, 17 had been granted by three institutions, namely, the University of Chicago, Teachers College of Columbia University, and the University of Minnesota. Although only one doctor's degree had been granted in home economics by 1914, several home economists had done advanced study in fields related to home economics, such as economics, physiological chemistry, education, sociology, bacteriology, and physiology.

The demand for home economists with graduate degrees increases each year, and this demand is accompanied by the development of graduate offerings in departments and colleges of home economics and in graduate schools. In 1967–1968, 1,400 master's and 78 doctor's degrees were awarded in home economics (6). This figure includes the degrees given in home economics education.

Master's and doctor's degrees have become requirements for practically all college and university teaching positions, as well as for research in home economics. In addition, a graduate degree usually is required for all supervisory or specialist positions in home economics education and extension, and administrative positions; it is highly desirable preparation for major posts in dietetics, nutrition, institution

Table 15-1
Growth in graduate study in the United States

year	no. of graduate students
1871	44
1900	5,831
1920	15,612
1940	105,748
1960	314,349
1967	649,697

management, and those businesses or industries which provide products and services for the home. In other words, the home economist who wishes to qualify for the top positions in her profession must expect to do graduate study.

The subdivisions into which graduate study in home economics is ordinarily divided are: (1) foods and nutrition, (2) child development and family life, (3) family economics and home management, (4) textiles and clothing, (5) housing and household equipment, and (6) home economics education. In some colleges there are as many as ten subject-matter departments in the graduate school in home economics.

Students graduating in the upper 25 percent of their class should give serious consideration to graduate study, for the need for home economists with advanced degrees is very great. Unless a proportionate number of the present-day home economics students do advanced study, thus training themselves for college and university teaching, research, and positions of responsibility, the next generation of young people seeking higher education will be turned away from the colleges or taught by ill-prepared teachers. Furthermore, research designed to improve the health, welfare, and comfort of the family cannot go forward unless qualified home economists are available.

Home economics is not training enough personnel to staff the colleges and universities today, especially since most universities and many colleges are demanding doctor's degrees for their teachers and research personnel. Home economics is being pressured for both quality and quantity of personnel. When it is realized that professional employees in public institutions increased 40 percent between 1963 and 1966 and in private institutions the increase was 18 percent, the great need for people with advanced degrees becomes apparent.

The shortage of highly trained home economists is resulting in two trends, (1) increasingly, personnel from other disciplines are being recruited to fill home economics positions, and (2) home economists with lesser training than is true of other disciplines are holding home economics college and university positions. For example, 51 percent of all college and university teachers and research workers in 1966 held doctor's degrees, while only 19 percent of the home economics teachers and research workers did. There is little hope for improvement in the situation when

Table 15-2
Number of earned degrees conferred in 1967

field	bachelors'	masters'	doctors'
Agriculture	6,258	1,463	564
Education	120,879	55,861	3,529
Engineering	36,189	13,888	2,614
Home Economics	6,335	850	66

* Degrees in Home Economics Education are reported under Education.

one considers the small number of doctor's degrees being given in home economics.

From a financial standpoint, home economics students will find graduate study fairly easy. In a survey of ninety-seven colleges and universities in the United States giving graduate work in home economics, the fellowships, assistantships, and scholarships listed in Table 15-3 were available to home economics graduates (2).

In addition to the financial assistance obtained through colleges and universities, there are a number of scholarships and fellowships provided by private organizations, businesses, and industry. The American Association of University Women offers twenty-five fellowships annually to American women for advanced study and research. Although these are given to women studying in many different fields, home economists are eligible for them.

The American Home Economics Association administers thirteen fellowships and traineeships for members of AHEA to do graduate study (Table 15-4).

The Home Economists in Business Section of the American Home Economics Association has twenty fellowships with stipends of $3,000. Phi Upsilon Omicron provides a $500 annual scholarship for a foreign student majoring in home economics and a $1,000 scholarship biennially to a member who is an applicant for the doctor's degree in some phase of home economics. Information on the various types of fellowships, assistantships, and scholarships available to home economists for graduate study may be secured by writing to the headquarters of the American Home Economics Association.

In accepting a fellowship, scholarship, or assistantship, there are many factors which the students should consider. The fellowship or scholarship usually permits graduate students to give full time to study, although there may be some require-

Table 15-3
Educational aid for home economics students

subject-matter areas	number of awards
Administration	4
Applied and related art	39
Administrative dietetics internships	13
Child development and/or family relations	254
Family economics – home management	128
Foods, nutrition, food technology	379
Housing, design, and research	24
Houshold equipment	13
Home economics education	173
Institution administration and management	37
Public health and public health nutrition	10
Textiles and clothing	177
Extension	35
General home economics	23
Rehabilitation	9
Communications, journalism	5
Undesignated	86

Table 15-4
AHEA fellowships and traineeships

fellowship	no. of awards	stipend
Effie I. Raitt Fellowship	2	$4,000
Ellen H. Richards Fellowship	1	$3,000
Mildred Horton Fellowship	2	$1,500
Omicron Nu Research Fellowship	1	$1,500
Kappa Omicron Phi–Hettie Margaret Anthony Fellowship	1	$1,500
AHEA-Rsa Graduate Traineeships in Rehabilitation	6–7	$3,600

ments relative to their field of study or their service after study is completed. The assistantship is awarded in lieu of certain services returned to the college; so students should study carefully the conditions under which the award is made before accepting one. One's decision cannot be made on the basis of the size of the stipend alone: consideration should be given to the amount and type of responsibilities expected of the students in return for the financial award. Are the college fees to be paid by the student or waived by the college? What is the cost of living at the institution? What provisions are made by the college or university for the welfare of graduate students? The quality of the teaching and research staff with whom the student will work, as well as the general staff load, are important matters in determining the worthwhileness of an institution for graduate study. The size of the college and the newness of its facilities are less important than dedicated, well-trained, and sympathetic professors. The social as well as the academic atmosphere of the college will add much to or detract from one's education while pursuing graduate study. Graduate students should select graduate schools in full consciousness of their own personal problems, because some schools are in a position to administer to certain student needs better than others.

An advanced degree is not the only reward of graduate study—there are many personal satisfactions, as well. Many graduate students have the opportunity while they are studying to do part-time teaching or research, assist in laboratories, and work with college and university staff members in many ways, which can prove invaluable to the student who is truly seeking an education. The association with other graduate students, a select, alert group of young people, can be a very challenging and enjoyable experience.

The aim of graduate study in home economics is to help students discover and apply principles and clarify their understanding of the problems associated with family members and their living. It tries to educate scholars who, as a result of their more advanced knowledge, can produce improvements in the family and its members. This requires the creation of new methods of attacking problems and the development of new practices and understandings which contribute to the comfort, security, and enrichment of life.

Many avenues are open through which students may improve their thinking and fill in gaps in their knowledge, a process which provides new patterns of thought and a basis for clearer analysis. One of the major functions of graduate study is the extension of the frontiers of knowledge and the training of students for intellectual leadership.

ENTERING THE PROFESSION

What shall I be? What careers are there for me in home economics? For what am I best fitted? Sooner or later all thoughtful home economics students have to answer these questions. Some discover before they are out of high school that they have an intense interest in some occupation or profession, and some are still puzzled about what should be their life's work when they finish college.

Deciding upon a career is not something that one should be hasty about. It takes a great deal of thinking about the kinds of careers there are, the opportunities they offer, the time and money necessary to prepare for them, the aptitude one has for the various occupations or professions, the length of time one plans to spend on the job or in the profession, whether the work is to be full time or combined with homemaking, the ease of advancement in the occupation or profession, the part of the country in which one wishes or expects to live, and the financial rewards of the service.

The foregoing chapters have given much about the various areas in home economics, the personal and academic qualifications for entering them, and the interests of home economists in these fields. It now becomes the responsibility of the students to study themselves to ascertain the field for which they are best adapted and in which they can render the greatest service. Course advisers can be of much assistance in helping students make this self- and occupational appraisal. Also, they will be able to help students take the necessary steps to obtain satisfactory positions when their training is completed. Fortunately, many home economists find it fairly easy after college to move from one occupational field to a related one with little or no additional study. This is due to the general core of subject matter which most colleges require of all home economics students.

In making a professional or occupational choice, money or apparent security is not always a good criterion. Primary security lies today in one's ability to earn, good health, intelligence, adaptability, and willingness to work hard at the job. The long look ahead when choosing a career is very important, i.e., where will the job take one in ten or twenty years? To succeed in any job, one must be happy in the work itself and must feel that she is doing something worthwhile.

In home economics, all fields offer advancement, security, the respect of peers and associates, adequate salaries, opportunity for the use of personal ingenuity, and the chance to be of service. These can be found in all sections of the country as well as in foreign lands, and there are several levels of employment in all the areas which accommodate the beginner and facilitate advancement for one who is enterprising.

The student's responsibility is to decide upon the field for which she feels best adapted and in which her greatest interest lies. A successful and challenging career can be had in any of the fields of home economics, given the personal and academic qualities for success.

A HOME ECONOMICS EDUCATION MAY LEAD
IN MANY DIRECTIONS

The proof of the broadness of a home economics education is attested to by the wide range of professions, occupations, and services in which home economists are actively engaged. Some home economists deliberately choose to enter fields allied to home economics, others are sought out by agencies or businesses in recognition of their ability and training, while still others develop positions for themselves when employment in the field for which they are specifically trained is not available in their locality. Home economists today may be found in such diverse occupations as automobile designers, loan specialists for investment companies, stock brokers, public relations specialists, TV personalities, and ad infinitum. Let us look at a few of these numerous home economists who have found or developed very interesting and remunerative occupations for themselves—fields not usually thought of as home economics, yet for which home economics training undoubtedly prepared them.

THIS IS FRIEDA WALKER'S STORY

Today my position may seem unrelated to home economics. However, I can assure you that this is not the case. I am employed as a customer-relations consultant with a worldwide moving agency.

When I began my home economics studies, my primary desire was to help people, an interest that has remained with me. My four years of college education projected me into many subject-matter areas. In addition to the courses normally thought of as home economics, I explored in the fields of architecture, sociology, psychology, business, publicity media, public speaking, and the arts—the most of which were required for graduation in my curriculum. After I finished college, I immediately married, although I worked for a short time as a home economics extension agent. Soon afterward, I began my family, which consists of three girls and three boys ranging in age from ten to eighteen years.

A few years after marriage, my husband decided to return to the university for graduate study; with a rapidly growing family on a graduate fellowship, financial strain was inevitable. For short periods of time, I took part-time jobs, all in the field of home economics, to supplement the income. The work load of caring for small children and running a home plus the necessity of hiring some household help forced me to conclude that the income from part-time work did not justify my energy expenditure, despite the fact that I thoroughly enjoyed being "liberated," so to speak. I gave up the idea of outside employment until my youngest child was in school.

When the youngest child was four years of age, my husband accepted a foreign assignment which turned out to be an excellent experience for all members of the family. My home economics training again proved to be a lifesaver. During the two years overseas, I had to manage and train servants, assist the people in making the best use of available food for better health for their families, teach adult education classes, and even acted as a family counselor at times—all of this in addition to operating a school for five of my children (no suitable school was available in this area). Despite no previous teaching experience, my well-rounded education saw me through the teaching chores without too much difficulty.

When my last child entered school, I felt that I had some released time to return to the salaried society, although running a household of eight persons and all of the encompassing activities were enough to keep one occupied completely. As the cost of living increased as well as the demands of growing children, plus the expenses associated with a child entering college, I felt the need of a salaried position. In the small university community in which I live, eligible personnel far outnumbers the positions available. Most of the professors' and graduate students' wives have college degrees and many wish or need to work. Thus, the competition for a person with only a bachelor's degree is considerable, especially when this person must have flexible hours. Therefore, I sought to create a position for myself. First, I investigated a telephone answering service, especially for medical emergencies; there was not enough interest in the local medical profession to justify the expense of operation. Next, I considered an employment agency and later a rental agency, both of which, upon investigation, appeared impractical in this small community. Finally, after talking with the local representative of a worldwide moving agency, the opportunity of becoming a customer-relations consultant with this company evolved. The possibilities seemed both interesting and challenging, and the work would be part time, which seemed to fit my schedule. After some thought as to how my training and experience would equip me for this work, I decided to give the position a try. Within a few months, the position developed into a full-time job. However, by that time my family and I were organized to the point that full-time work was possible.

My responsibilities entail selling moves, estimating the cost of moves, settling claims, welcoming new people to town, and working with people in varied fields of business and professions. Now the question is—how did my home economics training prepare me for this work? I have found that much of the knowledge and insight that I acquired during my studies in home economics have stood me in hand at one time or another. A knowledge of public relations, family relations, housing, community development and relations, consumer economics, especially in the buying and management aspects, to mention only a few, are vitally useful when talking with people concerning their adjustment in a new community. My knowledge of household equipment and furnishings has been invaluable. My knowledge of children and home management have helped me to maintain a reasonably sane atmosphere at home while attempting to give my best performance to two full-time jobs.

Basically, the all around training one receives in home economics provides the necessary qualifications for many fields of work; one need not think that such training is useful only in the home and family. My success has convinced me that no field of study surpasses home economics in preparing individuals for whatever life offers to them.

THIS IS CAROL WALTON'S STORY

At the present time I am a free-lance consultant in my own business, HomEconomic Services, located in a large midwestern city—a business that grew out of my interest and training in art, my home economics education in college, and my work experience in home services with a public utility company.

My interest in home economics was evident even before I was aware of the professional field of home economics. As a child I enjoyed making doll clothes for myself and friends. This later advanced to making my own clothes and even to winning an award for fashion design from Cone Mills. Likewise, my interest in foods developed early. I have a very creative nature, and find a great deal of satisfaction in designing, building or putting something together myself. This interest has been invaluable in both my professional and personal life.

My first two years in college were spent in a well-known junior college where I received an associate arts degree in fashion design and illustration. From the junior college, I went to my state university, graduating with a bachelor's degree in home economics with a major in clothing and textiles and with minors in business and art. My first work experience was as a home economist in the home service department of a public service company, where my activities ranged from equipment demonstrations to recipe testing and consumer education. These programs were given for groups ranging from senior citizens to school children. The need for visual aids for presenting materials to these groups was soon evident, and so I started developing flannel boards, flip charts, caricatures for children's cooking schools, and posters.

After five years of home service work, I felt sufficiently confident in myself and my experience to venture into my own business—a free-lance consultant service in home economics. The city in which I lived had many businesses that could profit from the services of a professional home economist. However, the size of their businesses often did not warrant the employment of a full-time worker, and many of the heads of these businesses did not understand the contributions home economics had to offer to their operations. For promotion work, many businesses were using advertising agencies (oftentimes with little appreciation of the businesses special needs or their products' uniqueness) and models or the manager's wife to render the service which a home economist could render more satisfactorily.

As a free-lance home economist, I not only had to be able to render the service that agencies and businesses needed, I had to sell these firms on the belief that they could profit from such services. I am pleased to say that I have been very successful in this. My accounts now include, in addition to local firms, national appliance manufacturers, advertising agencies, food photography for television commercials or advertising posters, recipe testing, new product development, and many others. For example, a local sugar company was looking for new and different means of promoting its product without seemingly to promote the use of sweets by children. The idea of sugar molding and sculpture came to me—simple enough for the participation of children, yet challenging enough for the more sophisticated talent. The company bought the idea and are now preparing a booklet which will teach the procedures in sugar molding and sculpture ranging from the very simple to the more elaborate designs.

In my business, I often hire local home economists on a part-time basis; usually these are housewives with small children at home who are happy to have part-time work. It has been my experience that the business or agency is very receptive to the contributions of home economics if it is approached by a home economist who demonstrates knowledge of the firm or company, as well as a knowledge of its product or services.

My work has drawn me into many community activities and often these lead to rewarding business contacts. For example, in my state the home economists in business, in cooperation with the home economists in homemaking and extension, began a project of presenting home economics career talks to junior and senior high school classes. I was commissioned to create a set of flannel board aids and posters to be used in these talks. In two years. the demand for this illustrative material has doubled. As a result of this adventure, the home economics teachers asked for the development of "flip charts" to be used with their students. This has become a profitable sideline for me.

Not only are my business activities very challenging, through my art work I find a great deal of satisfaction in painting, researching for new visual aids, or working on a new promotional presentation. I am very content that home economics was the field that I chose to study. What I learned has been of great help to me both at home and in my profession. My professional work helps me to meet different people, work on their projects and problems, and since I am concerned primarily with promotion and advertising, this is a very creative outlet for me.

THIS IS VI LEONARD'S STORY

At the present time, I own and operate a fabric and needlework shop in the town where I live, a small rural town of 2,100 inhabitants. When I entered college, I had the idea of going into retail merchandising which would take me into the big city. However, my interest in a young man whose life was to be centered in a small rural community changed my plans.

My college degree was a bachelor of science in general home economics. It was not difficult for me to choose home economics as a major in college as I had always loved home economics in high school and 4-H club work. While in college, I became so fascinated with the whole field of home economics that I could not limit myself to one speciality, so I trained for extension work and took every course that I could in clothing and textiles. After finishing college, I spent one year as an extension home economist and then entered homemaking full time.

After about two years as a full-time homemaker, I began to feel the need to do something more. However, the presence of a small child precluded my leaving the home for work. Furthermore, there was little opportunity for employment in the traditional home economics fields in my small town. Since sewing and tailoring had always been my "cup of tea," I started my business career as a custom dressmaker. This brought in a reasonable income. However, there was no source in my area for buying quality fabrics. My earlier interest in merchandising and my knowledge of fabrics and finishes, as well as my sewing experience challenged me to open a fabric shop. I felt that I could give a type of service not available in other fabric shops. So I opened my shop which carries today a large selection of quality fabrics, quite unique for a town of this size.

The work that I am doing is very exciting. I view the lines in fabrics six months before they are on the market. My shop is small enough that I do my own buying, selling, teaching, and making of model garments. My enthusiasm has spread to the rest of the family and they help too. My business activities pull me out into the community where I give considerable service as well as receive the recognition which we all desire. I teach sewing classes, judge in fairs and other sewing contests, and am a 4-H club leader and consultant. I feel that I am considered the authority on all phases of textiles and clothing in my community. Certainly, I must give credit to my home economics training for preparing me to step out of the four walls of the home into an interesting and remunerative business.

THIS IS MARGUERITE ROBINSON'S STORY

At the present time, I am a consumer specialist with the U.S. Food and Drug Administration in the Chicago District. As a "liaison" between the Commissioner of the Food and Drug Administration and the consuming public, I interpret FDA's consumer programs to the public and in turn reflect consumer opinion to headquarters. My work covers a wide range of activities. In cooperation with the mass media, I appear on TV and radio interview programs, write and tape short radio spot announcements, and furnish material for radio and TV programs.

My department writes feature articles for newspapers, furnishes material for consumer articles, writes answers to questions received by consumer service columns, and reviews articles for professional magazines on subjects regarding the Food and Drug Administration. Answering consumer complaints is one of our major activities. These complaints are answered by phone, by letters, or by speaking directly to the consumer. Our consumer phones carry taped messages on topics of current interest to consumers. You may think that the above would be enough to keep my life interesting and more than busy. However, there are other areas in which I serve. I also give speeches for professional meetings, and oftentimes sponsor consumer workshops. We furnish kits of educational materials on consumer problems, develop visual aids, and appear on convention programs for professional and business organizations. Workshops for educators are given top priority. We give cooperation to those professionals who are working with low-income people, including public-aid case workers, nutritionists, and others.

The question arises, How did I get where I am or how did I prepare for this work? My training at the college and university level has been primarily in home economics. Like many home economists, my high school home economics teacher, who later became one of my college home economics professors, was a great influence in helping me to decide on a career in home economics. In my mind, home economics is the most satisfying and rewarding profession one can select. Training in home economics can lead to a wide variety of careers that are all exciting and challenging.

My first college degree was in home economics with additional majors in chemistry and education. Later I took a master of science degree in nutrition. When I finished college, I started teaching home economics in high school, and after completing my master's degree, I taught in college. Shortly afterwards, I became a home economist in business for the baking, milling, and dairy industries.

My home economics experiences and training have provided for me a great deal of travel and many interesting adventures. Since I enjoy meeting and working with people and like to travel, I have always chosen positions that provided these contacts. For example, during World War II, I was an aviation instructor at Keesler and Gulfport Fields in Mississippi, and later at the Escola Tecnica de Aviacao in Sao Paulo, Brazil. In this capacity, I trained soldiers for the United States and later the Brazilian Air Force.

In Brazil, my home economics training was put to good use. I lived in an apartment with two other American girls and our Brazilian maid. The everyday problems of getting a good diet, coping with the problems of food safety, and supervising a maid for three Americans in a foreign country required knowledge that no other training could supply.

Since I learned to speak Portuguese fluently, I was able to visit in many homes in the fascinating city of Sao Paulo and learned to understand and appreciate the family life in that city. In my travels to other Portuguese and Spanish speaking countries, I have conversed with the people and have gained an insight into their mode of living.

I have been very active and have held offices in service and professional organizations, among them, president, councilor, and legislative chairman of the Illinois Home Economics Association. Active membership and strong support of our professional organizations is very important if one is to succeed in a career in home economics.

THIS IS MIRIELLE THOMPSON'S STORY

My training in home economics has made my career with the world's largest electrical manufacturer my life's greatest challenge.

At present, I am supervisor-vendor documentation, design engineer, for the largest operation of heavy industry within this manufacturing concern. By now you are probably wondering, What does home economics have to do with vendor documentation in engineering? A great deal, because a supervisor works with *people,* and people have ambitions, desires, and needs. My courses in family relationships, child development, sociology, and guidance have all provided me with the basic tools for understanding their behavior and helping them meet their goals.

Other courses during my four years of college included mathematics, science, architecture, public speaking, art, and foods which proved to be very valuable assets in my career, particularly, as president of one of the company's employees associations and staging chairman of the state's apple festivals.

Shortly after college graduation, I married a lieutenant in the army. During my husband's four and a half years of active duty in World War II, we traveled extensively, and started a family, which consisted of a boy and a girl. After my husband's tour of active duty, we were faced with the decision of making the army a lifetime career or returning to his former position as a professor on a university campus. The decision was to return to the university.

After eight months, we began to feel the financial strain. We bought a home, and added my aging mother to the already growing family. The only alternative was for me to seek employment. I was fortunate in obtaining a position as mathematics teacher and guidance counselor in the local high school. Five years later, my home economics education paid off. I became head of a three-teacher home economics department, and manager of both the elementary and high school cafeterias. All my college courses were put to use. By this time my teacher's certificate was about to expire. Since a number of courses had to be taken for renewal, I decided to go for a master's degree. Thus, ten years after obtaining my bachelor's degree, I graduated with a master's of science degree. What a memorable day for my husband, children, and grandma! Little did I realize that this was only the beginning of a flamboyant career to follow.

Quite by accident, a friend dropped by to see us one weekend. He suggested that we should join him with the world's largest electrical manufacturer. We gave some thought to the idea, and then decided, What have we to lose? One month later, we found ourselves living in another state as new members of this company.

At this time I began my engineering career. At first, my work consisted of calculating Ido-Candela and foot candle curves in a photometric laboratory. Too much close work created a problem with my eyes. Since the company had nothing else to offer at this time, I almost ended my engineering career at this point. Before I had time to locate other work, the manager of marketing in the electrical company gave me the opportunity of my life . . . "Learn the product and sell it." Needless to say, I learned the product, traveled around the country, and sold it.

My knowledge of children and home management were invaluable to me in maintaining a "home atmosphere," even though I was "gadding" about the country and at the same time reaping the benefits of a most interesting career.

After eleven years in engineering and marketing with this company in the South, we moved to the North where my greatest opportunity was yet to come. Less than three years ago, I was made administrator in manufacturing for the largest operation of heavy industry within this manufacturing concern. As an administrator, I found myself again calling upon my background in home economics for help. In writing *Office Procedures Manual* for our secretaries, my home management knowledge was of tremendous help.

Recently, a tragic event occurred in our lives. A routine physical examination revealed that my husband has cancer and is now faced with a limited time to live. This incident has again brought to the fore the value of my home economics education. As a young girl in college, I had heard of things like this happening to people, but I never thought that it would happen to me!!

My leadership training obtained from one of industry's greatest teachers, coupled with my home economics background have opened many doors for me and have made it possible for me to achieve a reasonable feeling of success in these endeavors.

SUGGESTED ACTIVITIES

In most states, graduate study in home economics will be offered at one or more colleges or universities. The names of the institutions offering graduate study in home economics should be ascertained, and the students should be encouraged to make a comparative study of their offerings and requirements for degrees.

1. In what fields of home economics are master's degrees offered in the colleges of your state? Doctor's degrees?

2. What are the requirements for entering the graduate school? Are these the same at all of the institutions? Will the course of study which you are pursuing make you eligible for entering a graduate school in your chosen field?

3. What are the requirements for a master's degree in the various fields of home economics? Do some colleges or departments within a university require a thesis and others not? What are the values of doing a thesis when undertaking graduate work?

4. If there are graduate students on your campus, invite them to speak to the class. They could tell how they became interested in graduate work, how they happened to choose their field of study, and what they plan to do after they receive their degree.

5. Find out what fellowships, scholarships, and assistantships are offered by colleges and universities in your state for graduate study. What other aids are

available in adjoining states, or throughout the country? Invite a graduate student who is on a fellowship or assistantship to tell the class how she secured the aid and what she is doing in return for it.

6. Are there home economists in your locality who are engaged in professional, business, or service occupations that do not come under the usual label of home economics? Invite them to tell your class about how they got where they are.

REFERENCES

1. Andrews, Benjamin R., "Colleges and Universities," *Education for the Home,* part III, p. 98, U.S. Office of Education Bulletin 38, 1915.

2. "Graduate Opportunities for Home Economists—1968–69, 1969–70," *Journal of Home Economics,* vol. 60, pp. 114–126, February 1968.

3. National Science Foundation, *Graduate Student Enrollment and Support in American Universities and Colleges, 1954,* p. 132, NSF 57-17, U.S. Government Printing Office, Washington, 1957.

4. "1970–71 Graduate Fellowships and Traineeships," *Journal of Home Economics,* vol. 61, p. 594, October 1969.

5. U.S. Bureau of the Census, *Statistical Abstracts of the United States: 1969,* 90th ed., Washington.

6. U.S. Department of Health, Education, and Welfare, *Home Economics in Institutions Granting Bachelor's or Higher Degrees—1963–64,* p. 1, Office of Education, OE - 83014, October 1964.

ADDITIONAL READINGS

"Industry Contributes Funds for Home Economics Education," *What's New in Home Economics,* vol. 31, pp. 100–104, September 1967.

Miller, Francena L., "Womanpower," *Journal of Home Economics,* vol. 60, November 1968, pp. 693–696.

Monts, Elizabeth A., and Bernadine H. Peterson, "Graduate Teaching by Telephone and Radio," *Journal of Home Economics,* vol. 61, pp. 443–447, June 1969.

Ribbe, Marilyn, "Have You Considered Graduate Study," *Journal of Home Economics,* vol. 60, p. 137, February 1968.

Spuur, Stephen H., "The Graduate School," *Journal of Higher Education,* vol. 40, pp. 484–490, June 1969.

PART **3** INFORMATION
HOME ECONOMISTS
SHOULD HAVE

16 FEDERAL LEGISLATION AND HOME ECONOMICS

The activities of the federal government in promoting education for all citizens of the United States, especially since 1850, have done much to further home economics. Before this time and including the 1850s, woman's place was considered to be in the home, where higher education was thought unnecessary. Several state universities in the West had opened their doors to women students during the 1850s, and there were a few colleges for women, but most of these women's colleges were still on the junior college level.

THE MORRILL ACT

The first federal legislation of importance to home economics was the Land-Grant Aid of Colleges, better known as the Morrill Act. To understand the significance of this act, one must remember that around 1850 there was increasing demand for a new type of higher education, one that would differ from the traditional and classical concepts which were held by the colleges of the day. This new education was to be for the sons and daughters of the classes who earned their living from agriculture and industry.

In 1857 Justin Smith Morrill of Vermont introduced into the Congress a bill for the establishment of state colleges for the teaching of agriculture and the mechanic arts. Although the bill was passed by Congress in 1858, it was vetoed by President James Buchanan. It was introduced again in the next Congress, passed, and signed into law by President Abraham Lincoln in 1862.

The purposes and provisions of the Morrill Act were stated as follows (10):

> There is granted to the several states . . . an amount of public land, to be apportioned to each State a quantity equal to thirty thousand acres for each Senator and Representative in Congress to which the States are respectively entitled by the apportionment under the Census of 1860. . . .
>
> All money derived from the sale of [these] lands . . . shall be invested . . . in [a] . . . manner . . . that such funds shall yield a fair and reasonable rate of return. . . . Provided, That the moneys so invested or loaned shall constitute a perpetual fund, the capital of which shall remain forever undiminished . . . and the interest of which shall be inviolably appropriated, by each State . . . to the endowment, support, and maintenance of at least one college where the leading object shall be, without excluding other

scientific and classical studies and including military tactics, to teach such branches of learning as are related to agriculture and the mechanic arts . . . in order to promote the liberal and practical education of the industrial classes in the several pursuits and professions in life.

In the second Morrill Act of 1890, additional money was appropriated for the endowment and maintenance of these colleges, and also funds to be applied "only to instruction in agriculture, the mechanic arts, the English language, and the various branches of mathematical, physical and natural, and economic sciences, with special reference to their application to the industries of life. . . ."

Women quickly applied for admission to these colleges, and many of them were open to women from the beginning. With women in their midst, the colleges were forced to find something to teach to suit their needs and interests. This led to the first offerings in what is now known as home economics, a field in which the land-grant colleges were indisputably the pioneers (4).

Home economics fitted well into the pattern of these land-grant institutions, for it was designed to promote the *scientific and economic advance of the home for the mass of citizens.* Home economics grew as the land-grant colleges grew, and by 1890, four land-grant colleges had home economics departments, namely, Iowa, Kansas, Oregon, and South Dakota.* By 1905, twenty-two land-grant colleges offered a four-year program in home economics (9).

The organization of the land-grant institution is unique. Each college or university has three major divisions, frequently referred to as its "three arms." These major divisions or parts are (1) academic instruction, (2) extension service, and (3) research service. Home economics has a major program in each of the three branches: the home economics students attending the land-grant institutions are being instructed in the academic division; the 4-H club, youth, and adult education programs are carried by the extension division; and much of the research which supports these two programs is provided by the research service.

The land-grant colleges and universities are the major training centers for college students in the United States (10). Of the students attending the 2,230 institutions of higher education in 1966, 20.4 percent were enrolled in the land-grant institutions. In other words, in numbers the land-grant institutions represented less than 4 percent of the institutions of higher education and had 20.4 percent of the students (10). The proportion of home economics students and graduates is even more in favor of the land-grant institutions.

SMITH-LEVER ACT

The Smith-Lever Act of 1914 represented the first organized attempt by the United States government to carry on adult education. Furthermore, it was the first specific

---

* Illinois Industrial Institute opened its home economics department in 1874; however, the work was allowed to lapse after 1880 and was not reinstated until 1900.

legislation for the home by the federal government. It made available a sizable sum of money for promoting home economics work and placed home economics on the same level as agriculture for federal support. The significance of the bill was emphasized by Isabel Bevier, who said at the time of its passage, "No single legislative act has brought to home economics either so great opportunities or such serious obligations."

The purpose of the Smith-Lever Bill was stated as follows (11, p. 570):

> In order to aid in diffusing among the people of the United States useful and practical information on subjects relating to agriculture and home economics, and to encourage the application of the same, there may be inaugurated in connection with the college or colleges in each State receiving the benefits of [Land-Grant Aid to College] . . . agricultural extension work which shall be carried on in cooperation with the United States Department of Agriculture.

The cooperative extension work was defined as "the giving of instruction and practical demonstrations in agriculture and home economics to persons not attending or resident in [land-grant] . . . colleges in the several communities" (11, p. 508). The service was designed to provide rural people with the latest experimental findings, technical advice, and successful methods of farming and homemaking which would help to make them well-informed citizens.

In the years that followed, additional appropriations were made by Congress to better finance and enlarge the extension service, and the work was expanded to include the 4-H club and older, out-of-school youth programs, and the families in the villages, towns, and cities. The eagerness with which the states adopted the extension program is shown by the fact that in 1915, one year after the passage of the Smith-Lever Bill, all the states had accepted its provisions (5).

The development of the extension program in home economics has been phenomenal. In less than sixty years, the program has grown to the point that home economics education is available to homemakers, boys and girls, and teen-agers in practically every county or subdivision of every state and territory of the United States. Its personnel has enlarged from two part-time workers in 1910 to 4,054 county home demonstration workers in 1967, plus 180 supervisors (6, p. 6). In addition, there are over 500 subject-matter specialists and leaders or administrators servicing these county workers (6, pp. 29–109). Local volunteer leaders totaling over 500,000 help extend the teaching of the home economics extension staff.

Some idea of the influence of the cooperative extension program in home economics on the families in the United States may be gained by studying Table 16-1(1).

The extension program for young men and women is directed to young people approximately eighteen to thirty years of age, whose interests and needs have matured beyond the 4-H club program but who have not yet effectively been absorbed into adult extension programs.

Table 16-1
Summary of extension teaching and other activities of extension home economists

activity	total number
Home and out-of-office visits·	794,229
Office calls	1,696,398
Telephone calls	3,241,340
Newspaper articles and stories	217,867
Broadcasts made—radio	114,141
television	8,809
Publications distributed to the public	16,143,651
Meetings held—adult work	13,851,242
youth work	426,064
persons attending meetings	24,927,568

In 1971, 4-H club work reached an enrollment of nearly 4 million boys and girls in more than 96,000 4-H clubs.

Home economics extension programs differ by states and counties, depending much on the problems, needs, and interests of the people living in the area, and their economic and social status.

Thus, through the aid and stimulation brought by the original Smith-Lever Act, a very extensive program of home economics education for homemakers, youth, and boys and girls has developed. The influence of this program today not only reaches to all corners of the United States and its territories but is also helping raise the level of living in many countries of the world.

HOME ECONOMICS IN THE OFFICE OF EDUCATION

The Office of Education was created in 1867, "to collect such statistics and facts as shall show the condition and progress of education, to diffuse such information as shall aid the people of the United States in the establishment and maintenance of efficient school systems, and otherwise to promote the course of education (14, pp. 334–335). It is the principal agency of the federal government responsible for formulating educational policy and coordinating educational activities at the national level.

By 1915, home economics in the schools of the United States had developed to the point that two specialists in home economics were appointed in the Office of Education, which was then known as the Bureau of Education. The persons chosen for this new work were Mrs. Henrietta Calvin and Miss Carrie M. Lyford. The importance of these new posts to home economics is well expressed by an editorial which appeared in the October 1915 issue of the *Journal of Home Economics* (2):

> Both the United States Bureau of Education and the Home Economics world are to be congratulated upon the wise and thorough way in which

Mrs. Calvin and her associate Miss Lyford are beginning the important work that lies before them as specialists in Home Economics of the Bureau of Education. . . .

Home Economics teachers who have found themselves too busy to observe the work of others to any extent will be glad to know that Mrs. Calvin hopes that "in time we shall be a central station for the gathering and distribution of material. With our larger opportunities we may be able to discover new and interesting efforts and convey this information to teachers meeting similar problems."

The work of home economists in the Office of Education has grown as home economics has grown in the schools. Home economics in the public schools was greatly stimulated by the passage of the Smith-Hughes Act of 1917.

SMITH-HUGHES ACT

Government-sponsored vocational education in home economics owes much of its development to the passage of the Smith-Hughes Act of 1917 and the later expansion of the act through additional appropriations, and home economics in the public schools was greatly stimulated by its provisions.

The beginnings of vocational education had been established long before the passage of the Smith-Hughes Act. Practical work in cooking and sewing developed early in the public schools for girls and by 1900 was fairly well recognized, and a similar type of practical shopwork had developed for boys through the manual training movement, which had its beginning in 1886. In addition to the work in the schools, farmers' institutes had developed throughout the states, and some extension work for farmers and boys and girls was getting under way. By 1906, these vocational activities had grown to the extent that the Society for the Promotion of Industrial Education was formed. At the insistence of this new society, in 1914 Congress authorized a commission to study the needs for industrial education and the part the federal government should take in this venture; Senator Hope Smith of Georgia was made chairman of this commission, with Senator Dudley M. Hughes as a hard-working member.

The commission found able leadership in Congress in the persons of these two gentlemen. Senator Hughes had been very active in the farmers' institutes for some years and had served on a committee in 1905 to develop ways of extending agricultural clubs into the rural schools (7). He saw the United States as a great agricultural and industrial nation, leading the world in the production and consumption of goods and services and setting a new high in the standards of living of the masses of people. He believed firmly that "when man's mind is trained and his hand is left unskilled, he is only half educated" (7).

The findings of the Commission on Industrial Education led to the passage of the Smith-Hughes Act of 1917. This act authorized an appropriation of over 7 million dollars for education in the fields of agriculture, home economics, and trades and industry, which was to be a cooperative enterprise between the states and the federal government. The vocational education act of 1946, usually referred to as the George-Barden Act, provided for further development of vocational education and authorized an annual appropriation of $29,267,081. An amendment to this act in 1956 extended and improved practical nurse training and authorized vocational education in the fishing trades, in industry, and in their distributive occupations (14, pp. 251–252).

Vocational education was defined as training for the common wage-earning employments. It could be given to boys and girls who, having selected a vocation, desired preparation for entering it as trained wage earners; to boys and girls who, having already taken up wage-earning employment, sought greater efficiency in that employment; and to wage earners established in their trades and occupations who wished, through increase in their efficiency and wage-earning capacity, to advance to positions of responsibility (12). This new type of education could be given in all-day, part-time, and/or evening schools. At least one-half of the instruction time had to be given to practical and useful work, and, in order to ensure high-quality work, the Smith-Hughes Act required that teachers of vocational subjects have at least four years of college training in their special fields—a high standard for the day in which the bill was passed.

Many problems were encountered in putting the Smith-Hughes Act into effect. It required states to organize home economics and agricultural and industrial education on a state-wide basis. This was difficult in many areas, for facilities were limited and teachers of these specialties were scarce; furthermore, some states had had little experience with vocational education. In spite of this, vocational education made great strides after the passage of the bill, and by 1929 the work had developed to the point that Congress felt justified in passing the George-Reed Act, which was followed in 1934 by the George-Ellzey Act and in 1937 by the George-Deen Act, all of which authorized additional appropriations for vocational education in home economics, agriculture, and industry and trades.

Home economics in the vocational education program owes much to the influence of Mrs. Dudley M. Hughes, who, like her husband, was very much interested in improving the lot of her fellow man. She has been given credit for standing at the shoulder of her husband when he sat down to author the legislation to provide Federal aid for vocational education in the public schools and reminding him to remember the girls: "Don't leave out the homemakers," she said (7). Mrs. Hughes is known as the unofficial mother of the Future Homemakers of America, a national organization of high school home economics students.

To illustrate the effect of the Smith-Hughes Act upon vocational education it is only necessary to point out that in approximately 40 years since its passage, 65 percent of the high schools in the United States and its territories have come to offer vocational education, and there are approximately 3½ million youths and adults enrolled (3).

HOME ECONOMICS RESEARCH

After the land-grant colleges were established, it soon became evident that a body of scientific information must be built up as a basis for teaching in the new fields which these colleges were to promote, as well as for the development of a progressive agriculture. The authorization of the agricultural experiment stations came through the Hatch Act of 1887.

This authorization states (11, p. 508):

> In order to aid in acquiring and diffusing among the people of the United States useful and practical information on subjects connected with agriculture, and to promote scientific investigation and experiment respecting the principles and applications of agricultural science, there shall be established, under direction of the college or colleges or agricultural department of colleges in each State or Territory . . . a department to be known and designated as an "agricultural experiment station."

Although the original object of the agricultural experiment stations was to conduct research in physiology of plants, fertilizers, grasses, farming practices, and other questions bearing directly on the agricultural industry, interest soon began to develop for research on human nutrition and problems relating to the family and the home. For the next twenty years, however, only limited home economics research was carried on. It was the passage of the Purnell Act in 1925 that brought home economics research to the forefront. The Purnell Act authorized funds for (11, p. 508):

> . . . conducting investigations or making experiments bearing directly on the production, manufacturing, preparation, use, distribution, and marketing of agricultural products and including such scientific researches as have for their purpose the establishment and maintenance of a permanent and efficient agricultural industry, and such economic and sociological investigations as have for their purpose the development and improvement of the rural home and rural life. . . .

The crises of the First World War, with the necessity for food conservation and preservation, brought into focus how little actually was known about foods and their nutritive value. Home economists were asked to help with the problem of feeding and caring for a nation at war, a responsibility which brought respect and dignity to home economics and highlighted the need for home economics research. The Purnell Act made it possible to assign federal funds to home economics research, and by 1931 approximately 95 percent of the home economics research programs were supported by Purnell funds (4).

Another notable expansion in the home economics research programs in our land-grant institutions came in 1946 with the passage of the Research and Marketing

Act. This act gave formal support for regional research and was responsible for the regional housing and nutritional status studies of the 1950s, as well as some research in textiles and clothing, and family economics and marketing.

Today, home economics research extends into all fields of home economics. The chief problem is that there is not enough home economics research being carried on and the research is not evenly distributed through the various areas. In 1967, 685 theses and research projects were reported from the land-grant colleges and universities. Three-fifths of these studies were in the areas of child development and family relations, food and nutrition, and home economics education. The federal and state funds for programs in research in home economics departments, schools, and colleges of land-grant institutions in 1961–1962 were distributed as follows: 53 percent to foods and nutrition; 12 percent to child development and family relations; and only 3–8 percent in each of the other areas (8). Home economics research, like all areas in home economics, has been challenged by problems resulting from the changing patterns of life in the United States and the world. The future holds almost limitless possibilities for research work.

The influence of the federal government upon the development of home economics has been very far-reaching. Not only has it provided the necessary funds for many of the programs, but the stimulation and often the leadership for home economics development and expansion in research, in education at the high school, college, and adult levels, as well as in the vocational and trade areas.

SUGGESTED ACTIVITIES

There are several ways by which students may appraise the help of federal funds and leadership to home economics in their states.

1. Write to the supervisor of home economics in the state department of education to secure the following information:

   a. In how many high schools in the state is home economics, especially teachers' salaries, partially or totally financed by federal funds?

   b. How much money is contributed by the federal government to supervisors' salaries and other expenses?

   c. What is the total amount of money received in the state from federal funds for the promotion of home economics education in the schools?

   d. What other types of help does the federal government furnish in the state to home economists and home economics generally?

2. The director of extension at the land-grant college in the state can give the student the following information:

   a. How many home demonstration agents, specialists, and district agents are there in the state?

   b. How much money does the federal government furnish to the state to help support the extension service?

c. What other services in home economics does the Federal Extension Service furnish in the state?

3. By writing the director of the agricultural experiment station at the land-grant college, the federal government's contribution to research in home economics and related fields can be learned.

a. How many home economics research projects receive federal support?

b. In what fields of home economics are these research projects?

c. What questions are these studies trying to answer?

d. How many home economists are employed by the experiment station?

4. Where is the land-grant college of the state? How large is the department or college of home economics? When was home economics introduced into the land-grant college or university?

A trip to the land-grant college would give the student a chance to visit the "three arms" of the land-grant college, namely, college instruction, cooperative extension service, and the experiment station. Studying the work of the home economists in each division will give a good picture of home economists in the land-grant college.

5. Are there other ways by which the federal government furthers home economics in the state? The Governor's office could furnish information on other federal funds and activities in which the state shares which would be of interest to home economists.

REFERENCES

1. *Activities of Cooperative Extension Service,* Federal Extension Service Circular, No. 555, Washington, March 1964.

2. "The Bureau of Education and Home Economics," *Journal of Home Economics,* vol. 7, pp. 433–434, October 1915.

3. *Digest of Educational Statistics, 1968,* United States Department of Health, Education, and Welfare.

4. Eddy, Edward Danforth, Jr., *Colleges for Our Land and Time,* pp. 62, 171, Harper and Brothers, New York, 1957.

5. Hurt, Mary Lee, "Expanded Research Programs under Vocational Education," *Journal of Home Economics,* vol. 57, pp. 173–177, March 1965.

6. Mast, C. L., Jr. and Associates, *Count Agent Directory,* 54th ed., Florsman, Ill., 1969.

7. Mobley, M. D., "Dudley M. Hughes: A Man with a Vision," *American Vocational Journal,* vol. 30, pp. 29–31, November 1955.

8. Personius, Catherine, "Home Economics in the National Scientific Effort," *Proceedings: National Seminar and Workshop for Home Economics Research Administrators,* Nebraska Center for Continuing Education, University of Nebraska, Lincoln, April 5–7, 1967.

9. True, Alfred C., *A History of Agricultural Education in the United States,* 1785–1925, p. 286, U.S. Department of Agriculture, Misc. 36, July 1929.

10. U.S. Bureau of the Census, *Statistical Abstracts of the United States, 1969,* 90th ed., p. 124.

11. *United States Code, Title 7, Agriculture,* Pars. 301–304, 341, 362, 1953.

12. *United States Code, Title 20, Education,* p. 3662, Par. 21, 1959.

13. *Statistical, 4-H Club Work and Work with Young Men and Women, 1961,* p. 1, United States Department of Agriculture, Extension Service Circular 540, Washington, July 1962.

14. *United States Government Organizational Manual 1958–59,* National Archives and Records Service, General Services Administration, Federal Register Division, 1968.

17 NATIONAL ORGANIZATIONS OF HOME ECONOMISTS

Professional organizations render two types of services to their members: they recognize outstanding service and ability and provide ways by which members of the profession may further group interests through member participation and support. Usually these are organized nationally or internationally and have chapters or local groups in states, cities, or countries.

PROFESSIONAL ASSOCIATIONS

The American Dietetic Association

The American Dietetic Association is the professional organization of qualified dietitians and nutritionists. It is to the dietitian, the nutritionist, or the food-service manager what the American Medical Association is to the physician. It was founded in 1917 by a group of fifty-eight women who had the vision to foresee the growing need for persons educated in the science and trained in the art of feeding people (1).

The objectives of the association are threefold: to improve human nutrition, to advance the science of dietetics and nutrition, and to promote education in these and allied fields. To obtain good positions in foods and nutrition often requires membership in the American Dietetic Association, because this membership serves as a certification that one has met its qualifications through high-standard training.

There are academic as well as general requirements for membership. Students majoring in foods and nutrition will do well to check their curricula against the current academic requirements of the association. (See Chapter 9, page 137 for ADA membership requirements.)

One of the chief activities of the American Dietetic Association is the establishing of high professional standards through determining the academic requirements for membership in it and the supervision of approved dietetic internships. Another of its activities is providing programs and workshops to help members keep up with the latest in food and nutrition theory and practice. It also maintains a placement bureau where professional records of registered members are assembled, kept on file, and made available to prospective employers upon request.

The official organ of the association is the *Journal of the American Dietetic Association;* it is issued monthly and features articles on the latest developments in food administration, nutrition, diet therapy, public health, research, and educational methods.

A loan library is maintained for members of the association to dispense information on hospital diets, outlines of plans used in school and college eating units, out-patient clinics, public health organizations, and general information of interest to the dietitian or nutritionist.

One of the more recent services of the association to its members has been the establishment of a loan fund for graduate study. In addition, it has a fellowship fund available to members on a competitive basis.

The membership of the American Dietetic Association is approximately 18,600. The highest percentage of the members is employed in hospital food service, but others are employed as nutritionists in federal, state, city, county, or private agencies, college teaching, school-lunch programs, and commercial food service (2).

The official headquarters of the American Dietetic Association is located at 620 North Michigan Avenue, Chicago, Illinois.

The American Home Economics Association

The American Home Economics Association is the official association of all home economists, irrespective of their field of specialization. Among its members may be found the highly trained scientist, the high school teacher, the adult educator, the nursery school teacher, the business home economist, the homemaker, and many others. The common denominator in all of these groups is an interest in the promotion of family well-being through home economics. Membership in the association requires a college major in home economics or a related field.

The purpose of the association, as stated in its constitution, is as follows (2):

> The object of this Association shall be to provide opportunities for professional home economists and members from other fields to cooperate in the attainment of the well-being of individuals and of families, the improvement of homes, and the preservation of values significant in home life.
>
> Specifically, the Association shall work toward this object by encouraging and promoting (1) wider and better understanding of the value of home economics to individuals and to nations; (2) understanding of the significant place of homemaking in our society; (3) cooperation with other community, national and international groups concerned with family well-being; (4) improvement of the standards of preparation and of continued professional growth of its members; (5) application of the physical, biological, and social sciences and of the arts to homemaking; (6) investigation and research important to the family and to the institutional household; and (7) legislation designed to aid in the improvement of home and family life.

The American Home Economics Association was organized December 31, 1908, as an outgrowth of the Lake Placid Conferences. Mrs. Ellen H. Richards of

MIT was its first president and Benjamin R. Andrews of Teachers College, Columbia University, its first secretary-treasurer. In the years since its organization it has experienced phenomenal growth: beginning with a membership of 700, the membership today approximates 29,000. It has affiliated associations in fifty-seven states and foreign countries. In addition there are 387 college clubs affiliated with the national organization (2, p. 450). Membership in the association is open to persons with (6):

1. A bachelor's degree or an advanced degree with a major in home economics or in a specialized area of home economics from an accredited university or college in the United States or Canada.
2. A bachelor's or advanced degree from an accredited college in the United States or Canada with a major in a specialized subject-matter area related to home economics with a minimum of two years experience in home economics.

Membership in the association may be obtained by applying directly to the national headquarters, through membership in an affiliated state association, or through membership in homemakers' groups or college clubs.

The work of the association is carried on through its affiliated state home economics associations, its elected officers and paid staff, its professional and subject-matter sections, and its special and standing committees. Although the American Home Economics Association actively participates in many areas of family living needing leadership and improvement, its major activities have been in consumer interests, legislation, educational standards, nutritional programs, and international cooperation, particularly in recent years. The association and its committees cooperate at both the national and the international level with various technical, research, and educational organizations in furthering families' interests and well-being.

The association renders special service to its members through its publications, its fellowships and scholarships, its information service, and its promotion of workshops and conferences in professional and subject-matter areas. A list of the publications available from the association can be obtained by writing directly to its headquarters.

The official organ of the association is the *Journal of Home Economics,* which has had continuous publication since 1909.

The official headquarters of the American Home Economics Association is 2010 Massachusetts Avenue, N.W., Washington D.C. 20036

The Department of Home Economics
of the National Education Association

The Department of Home Economics was organized in 1927 as the National Education Association Department of Supervisors and Teachers of Home Economics, but in 1939, the name was changed to the Department of Home Economics. Its membership is made up primarily of home economics teachers and supervisors in the elementary and secondary schools but is open to anyone concerned with home economics education. It has approximately 3,700 members (2, p. 450).

The purposes of the department are to encourage the growth and development of home economics education in school programs and to foster cooperative studies for the improvement of home economics instruction.

The department has an annual convention. Also, it publishes a bulletin and newsletter series annually that are concerned with improving home economics teaching.

The Home Economics Division of the American Vocational Association

The American Vocational Association came into being in 1906. It was first organized as the National Society for the Promotion of Industrial Education, but the name was changed in 1917 to the National Society for Vocational Education, and in 1925 the name American Vocational Association was adopted at the time of the merger of the National Society for Vocational Education and the Vocational Education Association of the Middle West.

The purposes of the association are as follows (2, p. 450):

> To promote the improvement and expansion of vocational and practical arts programs throughout the country; to protect and stabilize these phases of education through legally constituted school authorities at national, state, and local levels; to facilitate the professional growth of its members; to encourage a cooperative spirit and understanding among the workers in all phases of vocational and practical arts education; and to furnish up-to-date information about these educational fields for both educators and the general public.

The American Vocational Association has five major divisions, one of which is that of home economics education. The Home Economics Education Division provides opportunities for teachers, teacher trainers, and supervisors of home economics to work together in studying and helping to solve important problems related to providing education for wholesome family life through meetings, communications, research, publications, and legislation. It is the official channel for coordinating the programs of vocational homemaking education with the activities of other educational and home economics groups (4, 5).

Membership in the American Vocational Association is open to all persons interested in the specific purposes of the association; in 1970 the membership was 45,000 (2).

The official organ of the association is the *American Vocational Journal,* and its official headquarters is located at 1010 Vermont Avenue, N.W., Washington, D.C. (2, pp. 663–664).

The National Association of Extension Home Economists (NAEHE)

The National Association of Extension Home Economists, formerly known as The National Home Demonstration Agents' Association, was founded in June 1931. It is an organization of extension agents actively engaged in home demonstration work in counties and cities, and honorary members approved by the executive board. The object of the organization (2, p. 442) is to provide a permanent national organization for home demonstration agents of the United States and Territories whereby:

1. Professional standards may be raised.
2. Fellowship among its members may be promoted.
3. A centralized means for the exchange of ideas may be provided.
4. Cooperation among State Home Demonstration Agents' Associations may be stimulated.
5. The organization of State Associations of Home Demonstration Agents may be encouraged and developed.

The association meets annually, and one of the special features of the meeting is the recognition ceremony for agents who have rendered outstanding service.

The association provides two fellowships of $500 annually, known as the Grace Frysinger Fellowships. These are awarded to home demonstration agents on the basis of merit to provide an opportunity to study and observe home demonstration work in another state or states.

The association has a membership of approximately 3,600, with affiliated associations in forty-nine states and in Puerto Rico. Its central office is now located at Gallatin, Missouri (2, p. 287).

American School Food Service Association

The American School Food Service Association (ASFSA) was founded in Chicago in 1946 through the merger of the Food Service Directors Conference and the American School Cafeteria Association. The membership of the association is made up of persons engaged in school food service or related activities in public or private schools, colleges, and universities. The ASFSA is a professional organization with affiliates at the local, state, and regional levels; its membership exceeds 48,000 (2, p. 442).

All ASFSA services and activities are directed primarily toward achieving the following goals outlined in the association bylaws:

1. To improve the health and education of school children through nutritionally adequate and educationally sound, nonprofit food service programs.
2. To maintain and further develop high standards for school food service programs.
3. To encourage and promote between school personnel and the general public such unified efforts as will assure for every school child adequate school food services.
4. To promote legislation designed to foster adequate school food service programs.
5. To promote interest in the recruitment and training of school food service personnel and to improve and protect their status.

The organ of the association is the *School Lunch Journal* with ten issues per year, and its headquarters are in Denver, Colorado (2, p. 442).

The National Association of Vocational Homemaking Teachers

This is a professional society of homemaking teachers who are members of the American Vocational Association. It holds an annual meeting. Its permanent headquarters address is 1025 15th Street, N.W., Washington, D.C. 20005 (2, p. 450).

National Association of Home Economics Supervisors

The membership of this association is made up of supervisors of home economics in each state and members of state home economics staffs whose major responsibility is supervision of in-service home economics education programs. Its purpose is to strengthen and improve home economics education in the public schools. It is a section of the Home Economics Education Division of the American Vocational Association. It had a membership of 280 in 1968 (2, p. 450).

PROFESSIONAL SOCIETIES

Kappa Omicron Phi

Kappa Omicron Phi is a professional fraternity for women in home economics. It was founded December 11, 1922, at the Northwest Missouri State Teachers College in Maryville. Affiliated with the national organization are forty-one active chapters, with a total membership of 8,566 (2, p. 564).

The preamble to the constitution states the following:

The purpose of this organization is to further the best interests of Home Economics in four year colleges. We realize the World needs women who have attained an intellectual, a spiritual, ethical, and aesthetic poise. Therefore, in order to develop women with higher ideals of sane living, with deeper appreciation of the sanctity of the American Home, with broader social and higher intellectual and cultural attainments we do adopt this constitution.

The governing body of the fraternity is the national council, which calls the organization to meet in conclave every two years.

Membership is open to home economics students in their sophomore year. Members must maintain a "B" average in their home economics courses and possess such desirable qualities as honesty, leadership, a professional attitude, and promise of outstanding achievements.

An efficiency plaque is awarded every two years to the chapter having the highest rating, and each chapter presents an award yearly to the most outstanding senior.

The official organ of the fraternity is *The Distaff*, published each fall and spring. Its headquarters' address is Rural Route 1, Box 268 A, Williamsburg, Pennsylvania 16693.

Phi Upsilon Omicron

Phi Upsilon Omicron is a professional home economics fraternity founded at the University of Minnesota in 1909. The purpose of the organization, as stated in the constitution, is, "to establish and strengthen bonds of friendship; to promote the moral and intellectual development of its members; and to advance and promote Home Economics" (2, p. 567; 7).

Affiliated with the national organization are forty-six active chapters in colleges and universities and sixteen alumni chapters (2, p. 626), which are organized into seven districts, with a district counselor in charge who visits the active chapters in her district every other year. The business of the organization is carried out at the national conclave, held biennially, to which each chapter is entitled to send a delegate with expenses paid by the national council.

Election to membership is based on scholarship, professional attitude as shown by service to home economics and to the college, character, leadership potential, and demonstrated leadership on the college campus. Any girl in the upper two-fifths of her class scholastically is eligible to join during her junior and senior years.

The official magazine of the organization is *The Candle*, which is published each spring and fall.

HONOR SOCIETIES

Omicron Nu

Omicron Nu is an honor society for women and men in home economics; it is devoted to the recognition and promotion of scholarship, leadership, and research as a part of the worldwide home economics movement. It was founded in 1912 at Michigan State Agricultural College, now Michigan State University in East Lansing (2, pp. 663–664).

Membership in Omicron Nu is based upon high scholarship and promise of future achievement (2, pp. 663–664): only persons from the highest 20 percent of their class are eligible for membership, and election is not permitted earlier than the fifth semester or eighth quarter of the college course.

There are forty-three active chapters in colleges and universities throughout the United States affiliated with the national organization, as well as three alumni chapters.

The chief activities of the fraternity center around the promoting of graduate study in home economics. This is carried on by acquainting Omicron Nu members and others with graduate opportunities in home economics, by awarding biennially two international scholarships of $1,000 and one research fellowship in the amount of $1,000.

The total national membership of Omicron Nu is over 25,000. The national organization meets in conclave every other year, and each chapter sends a delegate.

The official organ of the fraternity is the *Omicron Nu Magazine,* which is published semiannually. The business office of the national organization is in the Home Economics Building, Michigan State University, East Lansing, Michigan 48823.

SUGGESTED ACTIVITIES

1. When was the Home Economics Association in your state founded? Who is the president? How many home economists belong to the state association? What are some of its major activities?

2. Is there a college home economics club on your campus? Who is the president? What are the major activities of the club? Is it affiliated with the American Home Economics Association?

3. Is there an organization of the American Dietetic Association in your city? In your state? How many home economists in your state are members of the American Dietetic Association? How many members of your college home economics staff are members of the American Dietetic Association?

4. Is there a home economics professional or honor fraternity on your campus? What are the requirements for membership? In what activities is the fraternity engaged?

REFERENCES

1. *Dietetics as a Profession,* pp. 26–28, The American Dietetic Association, Chicago, 1951.

2. *Encyclopedia of Associations,* 6th ed., vol. I, National Organizations of the United States, Gale Research Company, Detroit, 1970.

3. *Home Economics Education Division,* American Vocational Association, Inc., Washington, D.C.

4. Lawson, Dorothy S., and Martha Creighton, "Fifty Years of Progress in Home Economics Education," *American Vocational Journal,* vol. 31, pp. 67–74, 104, December 1956.

5. "Membership Facts and Application," *Journal of Home Economics,* vol. 61, p. 395, May 1969.

6. *National Education Association, Addresses and Proceedings, 1957,* pp. 333–334, vol. 95, National Education Association, Department of Home Economics, Washington, 1957.

7. Robeson, John, ed., *Baird's Manual of American College Fraternities,* 18th ed., George Banta Company, Inc., Minosha, Wis., 1968.

18 A LOOK TO THE FUTURE

Each college student should ask the questions, What will I be doing twenty-five years from now? How well will I be doing it? What changes in family living are to be expected, and how best can one prepare to meet the new challenges? There is no "crystal-ball gazer" capable of answering these questions, but certainly life will be lived differently when the children of the present-day college students are ready for college than it is today.

A writer in *Changing Times* (4) suggests that if one were projected into the 1980s, he would pass through an era of scientific achievement unequaled in history. He would discover countries and civilizations unknown today. Time and distance will have shrunk to the point where they will mean almost nothing. The population will have increased materially: in the United States alone, the next twenty-five years will witness an increase of over 80 million people, which is the same as adding one city approximately the size of Chicago every year.

It is predicted that in the next decade (2):

1. The world population will double, with great concentration in the urban areas. Three-fourths of the population of the United States will live in 200 densely populated cities on 10 percent of the land.
2. There will be increased physical and mental stress.
3. There will be mounting environmental pollution, with pure air becoming one of scarcest resources.
4. There will be considerable ocean farming and the use of synthetic protein.
5. There will be more "people problems."
6. Family competence will be stressed more than family adjustment.
7. There will be a soaring gross product which will make possible high consumption.
8. Education will be increasingly important due to the massive technological advances.
9. The work week will be shortened.
10. Unemployment, among the unskilled particularly, will increase.
11. Natural resources will be scarcer.
12. Life will be longer.

Home life will be different in the 1980s, also. One may wake up in a bedroom that is round instead of square. In the summer, a blanket may be used to keep cool; in the winter, perhaps no blanket will be used at all. A dome over the bed will emit warming rays. There will be blankets that take your temperature. The electric blanket will sense your temperature and automatically adjust to the right degree. A blanket manufacturer has come up with an idea to get the most persistent sleeper out of bed on frigid mornings—an electric blanket that is hooked up to an alarm clock. Ten minutes before the alarm goes off, the blanket automatically shuts down. If that chill fails to wake you, the alarm sounds (5).

Perhaps the refrigerator will have lost its importance by the end of the next quarter of a century, since most foods will not need refrigeration. Cooking will be fast, cool, and effortless. Housewives will push a button to cook, to raise or lower a shelf, to get a recipe, or to get rid of waste. An automatic server will bring food to the table and return the dirty dishes to the dishwasher. The ultimate is expected to be a kitchen-sized Univac. The housewife will insert a coded card, push a button, and presto!—the food for the next meal will be prepared. We are told that already a dual unit consisting of an electric oven connected by a conveyer system to a food freezer is available that automatically transfers frozen food from the freezer into the oven.

Breakfast will consist of bacon and eggs that have been kept in the house for weeks, fresh as ever, thanks to atomic sterilization. Processed food will look and taste as fresh as the day it was picked.

With all this advance, food choices will increase many times. It was estimated in 1960 that the housewife had to choose from 5,000 food items, one-third of which were nonexistent twenty or thirty years ago. If this rate of growth continues, the homemaker in the 1980s will have approximately 8,000 items from which to choose.

In all probability, houses will be built with movable partitions, detachable rooms, and walls that will slide or fold up like an accordion. Color will be everywhere, and if the color of an interior wall becomes tiresome, it will be replaceable with a wall of another color. Windows will be so designed that when it rains, they will close automatically. TV screens will hang on the wall like a picture and provide babysitting and house intercommunication facilities, as well as entertainment. People will more and more live in group-owned property and in apartments.

Dishes may be cleaned in a few minutes with a jet of air. Electrostatic dust gatherers will keep the house shiny, and self-operating polishers, vacuum cleaners, and floor scrubbers will do the dirty work. Pushbuttons on the TV will deliver immediately any advertised product.

Not only will there be a revolution in the food and housing industries during the next twenty-five years but the textile industry of the future may bear little resemblance to the present. The prophets say (19):

> Dressing the family—what a delightful and rewarding experience it will be in the year 2000 to 2025. All the genius of modern science will have made beauty and function synonymous. There will be no hesitation as to fabric performance because all the desirable properties will be built-in. Clothes will be cleaned quickly and efficiently in a closet wired with supersonic

sound. At the touch of a button, all soil will be released, caught on a floor trap. Alterations and exchanges will be outmoded since the new fabrics will have an elasticity that permits them to expand and contract to individual measurements. Clothes can be as light as air and still be capable of warmth or cooling, whichever is desired. . . . With climate control fabrics, fashions will be sold to wear year around. . . . Fabrics will be designed for specific purposes to meet the needs of highly diversified activities. . . . By the year of 2025, the idea of weaving fabrics may be a thing of the past. . . .

Portions of every wardrobe may well be disposable. There will be more fabrics of non-woven paper. Our fabrics may well start from liquid form and be "poured," "extruded," or "rolled." The making and grading of clothing patterns may be simplified into an IBM type of operation with no sewing required, seams merely bonded by heat or pressed together.

Shopping for clothes will be easier. You may no longer have to spend hours in the dressing room to find what you want. A new garment in a store-installed "fashion-mirror" will reflect your neck and head and, through a series of slides, show to you how you will look in the store fashions. If you like what you see in the mirror, you ask for the actual garment to try on (8).

Many are the changes that will take place in the next three decades, and they will occur in all places and in all areas of life. The advance in medicine and drugs will be just as startling as in housing, food, and clothing. Certainly, medical science today is saving many patients who would have died a decade ago. We have machines today that can print out in twelve minutes the findings of twelve chemical tests of a sample of blood. A doctor can bounce ultrasound through a patient to spot patterns of abnormality. A surgeon can implant an artificial heart-assist device and substitute blood vessels. A scientist can show how spare parts might be made from animal protein. It is predicted that by 1984, the transplantation of artificial organs run by electric parts will be common. By 1995, there will be wholesale immunization against bacterial and virus diseases. And by 2,000, we may have chemical control of hereditary defects by manipulating molecules of genes (8).

Not only will people have better health, longer life, and more leisure in the next generation, they will have more opportunities for education and more access to the good things of life. The computerized classrooms and talking typewriters will exist to help students to learn and to "beef up" their skills in reading, arithmetic, social studies, foreign languages, speech, typing, etc. School buildings will be round or hexagonal, air-conditioned, and carpeted, with walls and furniture that are movable to create learning areas of various sizes. More and more libraries will offer the use of programmed teaching machines to learn a new language or study some other subject.

There will be televisions that fight fires, care for the sick, teach school, and explore the world. The day will come, TV engineers confidently predict, when your TV set will provide you with electronic mail delivery, shopping service, all manner of links to banks, libraries, and other institutions (6). To aid in personal cleanliness, there will be individually wrapped low-priced toothbrushes to be used and thrown away, sold via vending machines. The bristles of the brush will be coated with a water-soluble dentifrice. All the user will do is moisten, brush, and throw the brush away (7). Whether the people will have more satisfaction in life resulting from all of the new gadgets and services in the next decades will depend upon the extent to which these changes are used for living creatively and favor a finer sense of values.

Tomorrow's homemaker may find herself in a rather different environment from that of today. How will she react to these changes? Will she be able to remain secure in the midst of the great array of choices? How will all of these changes affect the family? What will be the place of homemakers or women in general in the new communities which are to develop? No doubt, in the new automatic age, machines may do much of the work, but they cannot do the thinking necessary for wise choice-making, planning, and guidance.

Young persons who are graduating today in home economics will have the responsibility not only of living adequately and creatively in this rapidly changing world but of guiding others along this path. To do this, home economics, hand in hand with other disciplines, must meet the *real living needs* of families and do it in a way that fits a fast, changing time. Home economists of the future must understand science, art, mechanics, and human relationships in a way never dreamed of today. It is important that they be at least as concerned with the outside world as they are with the home. This concern will carry home economists increasingly into industry, where the products to be used in the home are produced. Home economists need to be a part of the creation and manufacture of products, for they have the responsibility to see that these products are so designed and constructed that creative, healthful, and satisfying home life is easier to attain.

The number of choices in the use of time and money within the family will also increase many times. Competition for these family resources will increase the pressure on individuals and families. Better education in management and consumer buying must keep pace with this growing competition if consumers are to be able to behave rationally and intelligently in the marketplace.

Social, economic, and political issues will increasingly involve home econo-mists. When one lives in a world where men travel at a speed of 18,000 miles an hour and where men go to other planets, all people in the world become neighbors. Increasing attention must be given by home economists to the development of a society which promotes the good life for all families and to the reduction or elimination of those factors which produce illness, crime, disease, war, and broken homes. It is not enough to help families adjust to the environment in which they live; home economists must set out to improve this environment. Community housekeep-ing must increasingly include understanding and even leadership in state, national, and international affairs.

The desire for a better standard of living, plus the need for workers, will continue to push more and more women into the labor force (2, 16). Since the majority of these working women will be homemakers, home economists must devise improved ways of housekeeping and homemaking which conserve energy and time so that the working homemaker can carry the two jobs without strain. This may require a shifting of values concerning household tasks and the traditional ways of doing them and a reevaluation of many family activities and functions in light of the new way of living. It will highlight the idea that education is a continuous process which does not end with formal schooling. The need for continuing education will be accentuated by the fact that women are marrying very early, many before they have finished their formal education. In order to keep pace with their better-educated husbands, as well as to meet the challenges of the new day, they must seek educational opportunities as adult women to a much larger extent than they are doing today.

Home economists may have to play a much larger role in family-life education than they have in the past. No doubt, the rapid social and economic changes will create a greater gap than ever before between the generations. This may make marital and parent-child relationships more difficult. Home economists will have to know more about what it takes to have a good home environment for healthy growth and development of both children and adults and to find better methods of getting widespread understanding by the general population.

In addition to the expansion of the traditional fields, home economics is destined to play a major role in rehabilitation and job education for the handicapped and culturally deprived in the next decade. Home economists have always been interested in this work. However, the new concern of the federal government and its recognition of what home economics can contribute are offering many new challenges to and demands for service from home economists.

The changes going on in our society that highlight these needs for new types of service as well as the expansion of the old are shown in the following statement (20):

> The next two decades will see us as a nation with a rapidly increasing population, with an increasing percentage of its population either older people or youth, a nation of restless, moving people, a nation with an increasing high standard of living, but, with a disturbing large number who do not share the wealth, a nation of workers with high wages but with a disturbing large number of people who do not seem to fit in anywhere, a nation of urban dwellers with all of the problems that urbanization brings.
>
> We shall continue to have the sick, the physically impaired, the mentally ill and retarded, the addict, children from broken homes, delinquents—both youth and adults—the poor, the aged, and the unemployed.
>
> The problems in the years ahead will be intensified by the conditions under which people live.

Home economists, as never before, have the opportunity to make a measureable contribution to the solution of these problems through social and rehabilitation services, welfare and public health agencies, in the elementary, secondary, and adult education programs, through youth services, agencies for the aged and dependent, etc.

Work with the handicapped will increasingly tap the resources of home economics. Today, it is estimated that there are 2.2 million individuals with physical disabilities (18). Each year 425,000 more are added to this group through accident and disease. Women with physical disabilities, approximating 12 percent of the 40 million women with homemaking responsibilities, are the major responsibility of home economists. Home economists are involved, also, in many other areas of rehabilitation such as helping with the selection and designing of specially designed and adapted clothing, planning such things as home entrances, kitchen and bathroom arrangements for the disabled, training these individuals for independent everyday living and the acceptance of their disability.

Legislation is already reflecting the trend toward family-centered rehabilitation, and the home economist with her family-centered approach is especially fitted for this work (13). Increasing numbers of home economists are serving as full-time staff members or consultants in rehabilitation programs (12). At the present time the demand for home economics teachers for the handicapped is far beyond the supply. In addition, the Vocational Amendment of 1968 may be expected to give impetus to better training for the handicapped adolescents and adults, as well as job training for the culturally deprived which will strain further the short supply of home economists.

It is increasingly apparent that the national war on poverty must include a mighty battle against poverty of the spirit. This is a tremendous opportunity for home economists. Home economists must be the bridge of communication between the consumer and management; between those who sell and those who buy; those who need and those who supply; between those who purchase and those who produce (9). Furthermore, home economics must direct its attention to evaluating accepted values and ways of living and promote new and better functioning ones.

Certainly, values and the behavior and attitudes associated with these values are changing and will continue to change. However, change in itself is not important. It is the end result of the change that will determine the success or failure of the future way of life. The basic values of human life, such as freedom, love, human dignity, equality of opportunity, need for law and order, to mention a few, are even more basic today than formerly, and man will always strive toward the fulfillment of the ideals that these values express. It has been true in the past and will be true in the future that the road to success is never a straight line; many errors are made in moving toward the ideal, and sometimes behavior develops on the part of individuals or masses that destroy the very goal they hope to achieve. For example, some feel that the present-day promiscuity, commune living, women's liberation movement, etc., may threaten the very foundation of the family. No doubt these movements may shake the present foundation on which the family is anchored during the process of shaking off old shackles and obsolete laws and experimenting with new attitudes and ways of doing things. However, the family will survive, changed, and no doubt, better suited to meet the needs of human beings.

Ours is a society with a basic and enduring faith in education. We believe that education can point the way to new hope for all. The world today is one that needs to be filled with leaders who are enthusiastic over the challenges it faces, who possess creative leadership, and have compassion and deep social consciousness and committment. They must be far-sighted leaders who are able to set the pace for new patterns of living and break the deadlock of the past.

If we as home economists truly believe that our discipline can make a vital contribution to our society, we must do more than believe--we must act. We must be willing to have home economics change as other facets of our social order changes in order to better serve humanity. If home economics grows with the new challenges presented to it, the need for what home economics has to offer will increase with every.new development of science and society. Home economics has always been a rewarding field, but never before have the challenges, the excitement of rapid development, or the opportunities for creative careers been so great. It is a wonderful field for the bright, able, and creative student.

THE NAME "HOME ECONOMICS"

In addition to all the pulls on and demands for service from home economists in the next decades, the name of our profession will continue to receive its share of attention. No one, today, would defend the idea that the name "home economics" truly delineates the areas in which home economists serve. However, to date, no one has come up with a better suggestion.

The name "home economics" was a fairly adequate selection on the part of our founders, for it quite ably described the field at that time. The word "home" referred to the place of residence of one's family. The word "economics" came from the Greek compound term (1): *oikos* meaning household property or estate; and *nomos* meaning the management of the household property or estate; and when the two words were used together, they referred to the management of the family, its members, relationships, activities. and possessions.

As time has moved on and society has become more complex and urban, economics has become to be thought of as a science related to the production, distribution, and consumption of goods, and their interrelationships with government and public and private agencies. A number of branches of economics have developed, such as industrial economics, production economics, agricultural economics, household economics, consumption economics, land economics, welfare economics, managerial economics, microeconomics, etc. Thus, the term which originally referred to the total activities and relationships of the large household, now has a much narrower meaning.

Much thought has been given over the last decade to finding a better name for all the subject matter and activities that are a part of home economics. Certain universities have substituted new names for the college administering the home economics work, although to date, none of them appear as good as the name we have.

"Family living" or "family life" is the nomenclature most frequently substituted. The catalog of one university using the name "family living" says: "The college contributes to the total university community by offering courses designed to develop insight and understanding about various aspects of family life. . . . Much of the work that was at one time confined to the home has moved out into the community and has resulted in highly specialized professional services to all homes and families." The implication appears to be that as a result of this phenomenon there is less need of home economic services in the homes.

It is true that a portion of the production aspects of the large household has moved out into the community and larger political division. However, the selection and decision-making activities have greatly increased. The homemaker today needs the services of the home economist as much as ever. She is a very busy person with many production, consumption, distribution, and decision-making activities to perform. The study of Hall and Schroeder (14) of 1,200 homemakers made in 1969 in Seattle showed that these homemakers averaged 49.3 hours per week in household activities. When there were six or more persons in the family, the number of hours devoted to household work by the homemaker increased to 62.2 per week—a long work week for anyone. It is true that there have been shifts in the importance of household activities. However, food preparation, meal serving and cleaning up, and home maintenance and cleaning are still the big consumers of the homemakers time.

The majors or specializations of the college of family living of the university cited are the traditional ones for home economics: child development and family relationships, clothing and textiles, food and nutrition, home economics education, and housing and management (2).

Family living as a name for the work of home economists has other limitations. There are many interests and activities of home economists that cannot be covered by the term family living, and there are other disciplines that have a stake in the family. For example, the sociologist feels that the study of the structure, origin, and function of the family, and later the welfare of the family is his domain, and sociology can take credit for developing the early courses in family relationships and marriage, and at the present time is offering the major part of these courses at the college and university level. Likewise, the psychologist feels that human development as a field of study is his.

Rather recently, one college of home economics changed its name to the College of Human Ecology (10). According to the college catalog, "The focus of the program . . . is on the study of human development and the quality of the human environment. . . . The College seeks to enhance the well-being of individuals and families through research, education, and application of knowledge in the physical, biological, and social sciences, and the humanities. . . . The College is particularly concerned with problems of human welfare and family-well-being." The five departments of the college are community service education, consumer economics and public policy, design and environmental analysis, human development and family studies, and human nutrition and foods.

When one analyzes the term "human ecology," granting that this is a popular term today, it becomes evident that it is perhaps more limiting than the term "home economics." It is true that the word ecology also comes from *oikos* meaning home or estate. However the subject matter and activities associated with ecology do not parallel those traditionally known as home economics. Ecology is that branch of science concerned with the interrelationships of organisms and their environments. The environment includes the influence of other plants and animals present as well as those of the physical features, which include land, air, and water. The field of human ecology is interested in the evolution of our species by interaction, pressures, and genetic variation; dynamic phenomena, such as natality and mortality; competition with other populations; population growth and regulation; and environmental and cultural factors influencing the structure of populations. In reality, economics and sociology might be thought of as the "ecology of man in the broad sense" (9). These two disciplines are interested in the relation of man to his environment, both physical and social. Thus human ecology cuts across the domains of several disciplines that are as well known as home economics, and have well-developed fields of service, teaching, and research in human ecology. Furthermore, universities already give courses in human ecology that have nothing to do with home economics. Human ecology does not emphasize many of the interests of home economics and loses sight of the family emphasis so important to home economics.

At still another university, the college of home economics has become the college of human development (17). According to the catalog of this university, "The College of Human Development is a professional college designed to prepare people for the expanding field of *human services*. Its purpose is to develop ways both of resolving and preventing problems in such areas as child development, youth, aging, family relations, community development, health, administration of justice, mental health, consumer affairs, and industrial administration." The college operates through four academic divisions, namely, biological health, community development, individual and family studies, and man-environment relations. Thus, in one sweep it takes over much of the areas of psychology, sociology, economics, law, health sciences, social work, and human ecology. Such a college might be justified in order to promote a closer working relationship between the above-mentioned disciplines. However, it certainly is not home economics. Interestingly enough, in the above mentioned university there are departments of sociology, economics, health sciences, psychology, to mention a few, and the college of liberal arts gives as one of its primary functions "to promote specialized training, both graduate and undergraduate in the basic disciplines of the humanities and the social and behavioral sciences." The college of human development in stating its major purpose "to develop ways of both resolving and preventing problems" would disturb many home economists who would not wish to see home economics accept a problem approach. A former dean of the college in a public address said, "In such a college, students undoubtedly will specialize, each choosing one human need to study deeply and one profession through which to serve that need, just as engineers specialize. And as in medicine, some students in such a college will prepare as generalists. These will look at the whole spectrum of human needs and their inter-relatedness and they will invent new promising avenues for action" (15). Several questions can be raised about the above statement. To many home economists, home economics has always been an applied field of the arts and sciences, as have other applied fields, such as engineering, agriculture, and medicine. However, the focus of the application of the principles of the arts and sciences differ. The major focus of home economics has been the *improvement of the home and family and its relationships.* Some home economics students have been generalists. However, none, no matter how well educated, would feel qualified to "look at the whole spectrum of human needs and their inter-relatedness." This would require the knowledge of many disciplines and perhaps several lifetimes of study. The majority of home economics students today choose one area of subject matter to study in depth and train for a professional career. They also realize that human needs represent different levels of complexity. Some can be met by professionals in one field while others require the cooperative efforts of professionals from many fields.

Home economics since its inception has had a major interest in and contribution to make to the improvement of many aspects of the family, its home, its members, the environment in which it lives, and to human development. No doubt these interests will continue and expand in the future. Not only will home economics expand its traditional fields in the future, through cooperation with other disciplines and agencies, it will expand into other fields and enlarge its contribution. Cooperation between disciplines is the pattern for the future.

When one considers the new names that have arisen and the many facets of the problem, home economics remains the best term to date for the fields of endeavor now known as home economics. In the first place, government research, extension, and special programs use the name "home economics" and to change the name in these agencies would be difficult. The federal government, public and private agencies, foreign governments, and leaders in other disciplines have at long last begun to recognize the breadth of the field of home economics and the tremendous contributions that home economists are making, not only to the people of our society, but to the peoples of the world. The American Home Economics Association, after some study recently, decided to continue to use the name "home economics."

It is important that all home economics colleges and universities use the same nomenclature, and their trained personnel think of themselves as home economists. Varied nomenclature confuses the home economists, and it confuses even more those outside the profession.

Home economics throughout its history has adjusted to change and has no peer as a profession for women (11). Also, it has increasingly challenged men to prepare for professions through its disciplines. The founders and leaders of home economics through the years deserve high praise for creating this inspired way for men and women to contribute uniquely to the needs of the world. The home economics college and university students of today must accept the challenge and leadership that those of the past have laid down, for it is· up to them to see that the next generation can say in truth, *home economics has no peer as a profession for those truly interested in improving the home and family living in the state, the nation, and throughout the world.*

REFERENCES

1. Andrews, Benjamin R., *Economics of the Household,* p. 2, The Macmillan Company, New York, 1928.
2. Byrd, Flossie M., "A Definition of Home Economics for the 70's," *Journal of Home Economics,* vol. 62, pp. 411–415, June 1970.
3. Brigham Young University Bulletin, *Catalogue of Courses 1968–1970,* pp. 96–97, Brigham Young University, Provo, Utah.
4. *Changing Times: The Kiplinger Magazine,* vol. 11, p. 25, June 1957.
5. *Changing Times: The Kiplinger Magazine,* vol. 21, p. 6, February 1967.
6. *Changing Times: The Kiplinger Magazine,* vol. 23, p. 33, June 1969.
7. *Changing Times: The Kiplinger Magazine,* vol. 21, p. 5, February 1967.
8. *Changing Times: The Kiplinger Magazine,* vol. 23, p. 5, November 1969.
9. Clarke, George L., *Elements of Ecology,* p. 1, John Wiley & Sons, Inc. New York, 1954.
10. Cornell University Announcements, *New York State College of Human Ecology, 1970–71,* vol. 62, p. 15, Ithaca, N.Y., 1970.
11. Dieken, Gertrude, "Where Should Home Economics Be Twenty-five Years from Now?" Symposium, Nov. 13, 1957, Home Economics Division, Association of Land-grant Colleges and Universities, Denver, 1957.
12. Eckhardt, May Elizabeth, "Progress Since '63," *Journal of Home Economics,* vol. 61, pp. 410–412, June 1969.
13. Fisher, Gerald H., "Challenge of Field Service by '75," *Journal of Home Economics,* vol. 61, p. 417, June 1969.
14. Hall, Florence Turnbull, and Marguerite Paulsen Schroder, "Time Spent on Household Tasks," *Journal of Home Economics,* vol. 62, pp. 23–29, January 1970.
15. Henderson, Grace, *Home Economics in a Changing World,* A Lecture Delivered before College Chapter of the American Home Economics Association, Virginia Polytechnic Institute and State University, Blacksburg, May 1968.
16. National Manpower Council, *Womanpower,* pp. 31–34, Columbia University Press, New York, 1957.
17. *The Pennsylvania State University Bulletin, 1970–71,* vol. LXIV, University Park, May 1970.
18. Trotter, Virginia Y., "Dimensions of Home Economists in Rehabilitation," *Journal of Home Economics,* vol. 61, pp. 405–407, June 1969.
19. Tucker, Beryl, "Fashions in Their Future," *Parents' Magazine,* vol. 32, pp. 155–159, October 1957.
20. Whitten, E. B., "Rehabilitation Philosophy of Today and the 1970's," *Journal of Home Economics,* vol. 61, pp. 405–407, June 1969.

PART 4 APPENDIXES

1 WHAT TO EXPECT IN COLLEGE

Students begin a new phase of their lives when they enter a college or university. It can prove to be very stimulating and worthwhile, or a disappointment to both the student and his parents. The outcome depends upon the student's preparation for college, his interest in and desire to make good grades in college, the eagerness and efficiency with which he goes about his work, and his ability to handle the various challenges confronting him on the modern day campus. College and university students have always been a privileged group. Furthermore, today's students will have the chief responsibility for the welfare of our nation during the next two or three decades. Thus, the emphasis in the educational process must be on developing students into mature, sensitive, and responsible adults (35).

In the United States today, there are approximately 7.5 million young people in colleges and universities between the ages of eighteen and twenty-one years—55.5 percent of this age group. It is predicted that by 1975, the number in colleges and universities between eighteen and twenty-one will be 10.5 million (25).

The growth of the community junior college is partially responsible for the soaring numbers in college. The junior college enrollment for the fall of 1968 topped that for 1967 by 14–46 percent and reached a total of approximately two million (29).

Not only are a larger proportion of the young people entering college today than formerly, more of them are getting degrees. The number of degrees granted by institutions of higher education in 1969 was over 900,000 as compared with slightly less than 500,000 in 1950 (33). Thus, a college degree is not as distinctive as it once was, and increasingly it is becoming a requirement for entrance to a vocation. On the other hand, it is believed that this degree is becoming increasingly difficult to get due to the competition for college entrance. The day may soon be at hand when large numbers of well-qualified young people will be refused admission to college because the campuses are too crowded to accommodate them. Some educational leaders question the ability of the colleges and universities to expand at the required rate to accommodate those who are clamoring to get in. Dr. Bruno Bettleheim told Congress recently that colleges and universities have expanded too fast and have increased their enrollment beyond all reason. He feels that today there are many students in college with little interest, ability, or use for a college education. "Students who do not know what they are preparing for, and why, lead revolts. There are no militants in medicine, engineering, and the sciences. Militant leaders are bright, but emotionally fixated at the age of the temper tantrum" (16).

The number of women seeking admission to colleges and universities is increasing slightly more rapidly than that of men (25). Of all freshman students for 1968–1969, 44 percent were women, an increase of 5.8 percent above the previous year. The increase for men during the same year was 4.3 percent. If the trend continues, by 1980 the total number of women in colleges and universities may well equal that of men (23).

It may be of interest to see where the women are enrolled. In 1969, women comprised the following percentages of all students in the following fields:

Agriculture	15.5 percent
Arts and sciences	46.3 percent
Business	23.2 percent
Home economics	99.0 percent
All others	45.6 percent

Although the proportion of all bachelor's degrees given to women has steadily increased over the last ten years, and will probably continue to increase, this has not been the trend for master's and doctor's degrees. Less than one-third of all master's degrees are given to women and only 11 percent of the doctor's degrees (27). These proportions have remained relatively constant over the last ten years and probably will change little in the next decade.

Table A 1-1
Earned degrees from 1957–1958 to 1977–1978

year	bachelor's degrees			master's degrees			doctor's degrees		
	number granted	men percent	women	number granted	men percent	women	number granted	men percent	women
1959–1960	394,889	65	35	74,497	68	32	9,829	89	11
1969–1970*	752,000	57	42	190,700	67	33	26,500	89	11
1977–1978*	989,000	54	46	274,000	68	32	43,900	89	11

* Estimated.
SOURCE: *Projection of Educational Statistics to 1977–1978*, 1968 ed., p. 127, Department of Health, Education, and Welfare, Office of Education, Washington, D.C.

Thus, women are not holding their own against men when education beyond the bachelor's degree is concerned.

Home economics recognizes the occupational demands of women in the modern world and therefore emphasizes training for wage earning and careers, as well as for living. This is wise, for there has been a steady increase in the percentage of the labor force in the United States that is "womanpower." In 1920 women constituted only 20 percent of the total labor force in the United States, while in 1970 the proportion of women had risen to 38 percent (24). This same trend holds for married women. Whereas, only 24 percent of the married women worked outside the home in 1920, 56.6 percent do so today. For a woman to have an income of her own has become the way of life in the United States. In 1967, the proportion of women 16 years of age and over with personal income approximated 71 percent. A direct relationship exists between the educational attainment of women and labor force participation. The more education a woman has received, the greater the possibility that she will be engaged in paid employment, and employed in the higher status and better paid positions. When working women have four years of college, 73 percent are in professional and technical positions; when they have five years of higher education, 87 percent are in professional and technical occupations (20).

WHAT THE COLLEGE OFFERS

The college or university has much to offer students in both preparation for living and earning a living. It may be hard to prove that higher education makes better mothers, wiser voters, or more enlightened citizens, but it seems reasonable to assume that it does. It is equally difficult to prove that a college background enables one to live a fuller, richer life, but there is sufficient positive evidence to justify the decision that anyone of high intelligence who fails to go to college will miss a great deal and will find it difficult to gain equivalent experience elsewhere (37).

College students come into contact with many of the best minds of the past and present. Under the influence of these minds in the classroom, library, laboratory, and formal and informal discussions, new worlds to be explored come before the students. College will furnish the opportunity to acquire knowledge and develop habits of thinking which will provide a basis for leadership and the solution of problems. It can help young people find meaning and purpose in life. Also, there are many adults on the college staff, in the churches, and in the communities where colleges are located who are able and willing to advise college students.

The college experience can help students discover major interests and aptitudes. It can help them develop goals in life and start them on the road toward the achievement ol these goals. It will acquaint students with issues and problems in society. It will furnish new and interesting associations among peers and superiors. Yes, college has much to offer, but it places many challenges before college students. They will find that the greater the opportunities for education, growth, and development, the more will be expected of them in service and leadership.

College provides many opportunities for independent choices. The college environment may furnish many young people their first real opportunity to exercise rather complete direction over their lives. This is a special privilege, but it has pitfalls. Upon entering college, most students must accept the responsibility of getting up in the morning and getting ready for the day. In college, no one is going to see that the student gets to class on time and regularly. Colleges do not furnish supervised study halls, so the responsibility of when and where to study is the

Fig. A-1 The students are discussing some campus problems with the president of the university. (Courtesy of the Virginia Polytechnic Institute and State University)

students'. They may find that the college dormitory is not as conducive to study as their rooms at home, and this may be their first experience in living among a large group of young people. There will be many young people from whom to select friends, and seldom is a college student completely away from his fellows.

College offers a multiplicity of extracurricular activities from which to choose. No one can participate in all the activities available on any college campus, so choices must be made. This requires the ability to determine the amount of time which can be freed from study and class attendance for activities. The wise student will select activities which will stimulate growth in all areas of his personality. Some activities should contribute to social and emotional growth; some should serve intellectual, cultural, and spiritual ends; and certainly some should improve one's health and physical well-being. Along with participation in all these activities, the student must keep uppermost the major goal in college: that of satisfactory academic achievement.

Reasonable participation in extracurricular activities seems to be associated with success in college. Higher achievers not only participate in more college activities, they also have more hobbies (31, 32). No doubt this participation helps the student to acquire a better-rounded education and to live a fuller and more creative life. Some students do have a tendency to get involved in activities to the point that grades suffer. A wise student, when planning for study and activities, can detect when there is not enough time left for academic work. Also, trying to do too many things produces unnecessary fatigue.

Fig. A-2 Many students work while in college to help defray some of their college expenses. (Courtesy of the Virginia Polytechnic Institute and State University)

KNOWING THE COLLEGE

It is important to know one's college. Students need to be given a clear indication of what the college stands for, what it expects, and what it will demand of them before they enter. Unfortunately, "students today see distressingly few significant differences among the majority of colleges" (28).

Knowing a college presupposes an understanding of its purposes, its facilities, and its general organization. The student should be aware of fields of specialization in her department or college. In most colleges or departments of home economics there are several areas of emphasis. The requirements of the various majors and the opportunities which they open to the student should be studied.

The traditions of the college should be understood, and the unique attributes of the college should be sought out. These may be due to research, faculty-student relationships, the alumni, or the winnings of the football team. Most colleges are proud of their history, and students should acquaint themselves with it.

A student should become familiar as soon as possible with the student organizations and activities at her school. From this knowledge, extracurricular activities can be chosen on the basis of which ones will be most profitable. The cultural and broadening activities made available by the college should be investigated. The policies of the student-government organization should be studied in order to assure compliance with the rules and regulations of the college. The student should also explore the library facilities, for a good library is an essential provision for an education.

If the college has a student handbook, many of these facts can be learned from it, and other information can be obtained from the catalog. The student's dean, department head, or course advisor will be interested in supplying her with the information and necessary orientation to help her become a loyal and happy student.

HOW WELL DO YOU KNOW YOUR COLLEGE?

Complete the following statements for your own college or university.
1. The college was founded in the year of _____.
2. The college is supported by _____.
3. The president of the college is _____.
4. The chief purposes of the college are _____
_____.
5. The president of the student body is _____.
The president is majoring in _____.
6. The student body is composed of _____ students.
7. The colors of the college are _____.
8. The college song is _____ and was written
by _____.
9. The president of the alumni association is _____.
10. The dean of the college or the head of home economics is _____
_____.
11. There are _____ home economists on the staff of the college.
12. In home economics a student may prepare for _____ occupations
or professions. These occupations or professions are as follows: _____
_____
_____
_____
13. Some of the outstanding home economics alumni of the college are _____
_____
_____
_____

14. They have made their names in the following types of work: _____

_____

15. The president of the home economics club is _____.
16. Home economics students who achieve high standards of scholarship and/or leadership may become members of the following honorary societies:

_____

_____

17. To graduate in home economics a student must have completed _____ _____ units or credits with an average grade of _____.

EFFICIENCY IN COLLEGE

With the growing demand for college entrance today, colleges and universities have found it necessary to use various selective devices to screen out the possible academic failure and drop-out before he is admitted. In spite of all these efforts, about one-half of all freshmen entering American colleges each fall will drop out before graduation (7). Although the drop-out rate is high, there is no evidence that the attrition rate of college students has risen in the past forty years (13). Furthermore, many of these drop-outs return to college at a later date. A study made of the students entering the University of Illinois in 1952 showed that of the 50.3 percent who dropped out of college before graduation, 70.2 percent came back to college sometime during the ten years after matriculation, and 54.9 percent went on to graduate (13). Another 5.1 percent returned to school and graduated after a longer lapse than ten years.

Good mental and physical equipment are assets to any college student; however, the most successful students are not always the ones with the highest IQ or the best physique. Students today are familiar with college admission and scholarship tests before they enter college. Upon admission to college they will receive another battery of tests administered by the college. Among these will be intelligence and educational aptitude tests. Most of these tests give a percentile score which indicates what percentage of the students tested rated lower than the individual taking the test (15). For example, if the student's aptitude rating is 75, this score would indicate that 75 percent of the entering freshmen had less aptitude for college or the specialized field of work than did he. Usually students below the twenty-fifth percentile are advised not to enter college (5, 23). In general, aptitude and intelligence test scores indicate the general level of academic work to expect from a student in her college career.

Intelligence and aptitude tests may not reflect the true potential achievement of some students (2, 18). Tests based upon the number of correct responses in a given length of time place the "slow-motion" student at a disadvantage. Since there is no scientific evidence to indicate that speed of reaction is associated with intelligence (26), the slow person is handicapped in all tests based upon time. Also, some tests measure many environmental factors, and students do not come from equally rich backgrounds.

Living away from home usually means living with other students, and no matter how much a student has heard about college beforehand, surprises await him. He can never be completely prepared for the many new things going on, the new experiences that occur. Most freshmen face competition for grades that is far sharper than anything they have experienced before. "Freshman shock" usually does not occur until the first grade reports come out. Many students receive their first C's, D's, and F's in their freshman year. This should not be too upsetting, because high schools and colleges may be very different worlds with very different grading standards (30).

Financial barriers to higher education are crumbling. However, some students do find finances a handicap, especially if they come from an economically deprived background. If the student has the ability that college work requires and obtains the money to attend, home background will not be a serious handicap. The student may, however, have to work harder at the beginning of her college career than the student who comes from a home where good English has been spoken, where good books and magazines were read, and where the arts and sciences have been topics of general conversation.

Students who have chosen home economics as their field of concentration face the additional problem of selecting one of many diverse specializations. There are occupations in home economics for almost every type of interest, from those based primarily upon the biological, physical, or social sciences, to those dependent upon the arts.

Good study habits are of the greatest value in college achievement (9, 22). These include knowing how to study, as well as putting adequate time and concentration into one's studies. (Good study habits will be discussed in detail in Appendix B.)

Previous school success, as shown by high school grades, is possibly the most important single indicator of how well a student may be expected to do in college (20). The quality of high schools varies, however, so that high grades in one may not indicate any greater achievement than average grades in another. If a student has done well in high school, this usually indicates that she has the ability for academic work, that she knows how to study, and that she is able to apply her knowledge.

Achievement in college will also be influenced by the student's expectancies. Individuals go to college for various reasons. Some may go because all their friends are going, that is, because it is the customary thing to do. For others it may be easier to go to college than to go to work to make a living. Still others go to college because it is a family tradition, or because it is the road to the right type of contacts for business or social success. Fortunately, there are others who go to college for the great opportunities which college has to offer.

In making a self-analysis, each student should ask, What are my reasons for going to college? What do I expect to get from college? It is believed that what one receives from an experience is greatly influenced by what he is seeking. If the student's reason for going to college is to prepare for a vocation, interest and energy will be directed toward this goal. If the chief reason for being in college is to meet the "right type of people," social activities may become uppermost. Not knowing what to expect from college may cause some students difficulty in getting sufficient singleness of purpose to achieve anything worthwhile. Goals are necessary for college success, for satisfaction usually results when one's expectations have been met.

The college will be able to contribute more to some students than to others. All students are not at the same stage of development when entering college; some may be better developed intellectually, while others may be more advanced socially, emotionally, or physically. Also, within the individual student, all phases of personality may not be equally developed. Some who have the ability to get along well with others may not be sufficiently well equipped academically to ensure the best use of their college years. Others may not have learned how to handle their bodies in order to have enough energy to meet all the demands placed upon them. Still others may feel handicapped in the social areas, including associating with other students, dating, and engaging in college activities. Others may have spiritual needs. All phases of personality must be developed equally if one is to become a well-rounded student and if the maximum from the college experience is to be received.

It is advisable to be aware of one's own progress in the various phases of development when entering college. In other words, if students are eighteen years of age chronologically at this time, they should strive to become eighteen years of age intellectually, emotionally, socially, physically, and spiritually. How is developmental age judged in the various phases of personality? This is not easily determined, since there are no standardized behavior scales for each age period against which one can measure behavior and ideas. If what characterizes satisfactory behavior at eighteen years of age were known, freshmen or sophomores could compare their customary ways of behaving and their ideas with this scale to see how well they compare.

Some students have learned to use their potential to a much greater degree than others (32). These students may not score as high on an intelligence test, but because of good work habits and consistent study, their accomplishments may be greater than some with more apparent ability. One who does not work to capacity frequently is referred to as an "underachieving" student.

Some capable students do not do as well as they should because they are unable to judge what satisfactory college work requires. Horrocks describes the problems of these students as follows (19):

> On the other side of the picture is the bright child who has always received high grades and copious praise for doing work that is ridiculously easy for him. He finds that he is seldom challenged intellectually and comes to assume that "sloppy" work (still superior when compared to the efforts of the less bright) is all that is required of him. He comes to feel that he has a right to receive high grades and high praise, although in terms of his true

ability he has done little to merit them. When he enters college and has to compete against his intellectual peers, he often finds himself totally unaccustomed to the efforts that are required of him. Many such individuals are unable to adjust to these new demands and grow resentful, feel inferior, and often leave college.

Below is a list of behavior items which a freshman class in home economics considered necessary for making the most successful beginning in college. It may be interesting to check oneself on the Self-Analysis Chart for Home Economics College Freshmen. Perhaps the class members would enjoy revising and adding to this list to make it apply more closely to the college they are attending. If a student can truthfully answer "Yes" to all of the statements below, she can expect college to be a glorious adventure in living and growing; those which cannot be answered "Yes" may indicate the points at which work in self-improvement should be started.

SELF-ANALYSIS CHART
FOR HOME ECONOMICS COLLEGE FRESHMEN

On the right-hand side are three columns headed "Yes," "Sometimes," and "No." Place a check in the column which describes your behavior for each statement.

	yes	sometimes	no
1. My class assignments are done thoughtfully, regularly, and on time.	___	___	___
2. My activites are planned so as to have a good balance between work and play.	___	___	___
3. I attend the educational and cultural programs of the school and community.	___	___	___
4. I attend classes regularly and punctually.	___	___	___
5. I am attentive in class and ask questions concerning materials not understood.	___	___	___
6. I review daily class notes before going to class as an aid in better understanding the new material to be explained.	___	___	___
7. I review my class notes and assignments at regular periods in preparation for tests.	___	___	___
8. I try to set up a satisfactory environment for study before undertaking the preparation of my lessons.	___	___	___
9. I am able to stay away from home without getting homesick.	___	___	___

	yes	sometimes	no

10. I am able to discriminate between friends of good and bad influence.

11. I know how to take care of myself in various situations.

12. I know what is expected of me by the college and my family.

13. I am able to live with others outside my family smoothly and easily.

14. I respect the rights and property of others in the classroom and dormitory.

15. I am able to abide by college rules and regulations.

16. I am able to buy the things I need on the money I have available.

17. I am successful in making friends with many people.

18. I am able to choose between the many extracurricular activities available to me.

19. I enjoy giving a helping hand to someone in need.

20. I seek out the social contacts and activities which I need for growth in personality.

21. I enjoy the social activities provided by the college.

22. I am able to accept criticism constructively.

23. I do not pretend to be what I am not.

24. I am honest in the statements which I make about myself, my family, and others.

25. I try to be unselfish and fair in my dealings with others.

26. If I have a problem which seems more than I can master, I go to a qualified person for help.

27. I am generous with praise and sparing of criticism in dealing with others.

28. I usually can see more good than bad in the persons whom I meet.

29. I do not put others in embarrassing situations or talk about their shortcomings.

	yes	*sometimes*	*no*
30. I always carry my share of the load.	___	___	___
31. I usually feel satisfied with my accomplishments.	___	___	___
32. I get sufficient sleep each night to feel rested the next morning.	___	___	___
33. I make sure that I get an adequate diet each day.	___	___	___
34. My dress is adapted to the demands of the weather and the activities of the day.	___	___	___
35. I take necessary precautions to maintain good health.	___	___	___
36. My clothes are kept clean and in order so that I make a good appearance.	___	___	___
37. I follow diligently the rules of hygiene, including habits of regular hours of sleep, proper elimination, and sufficient exercise.	___	___	___
38. I participate in and enjoy the activities provided for college students.	___	___	___
39. I usually have a feeling of well-being and peace.	___	___	___
40. I support the church of my choice and attend its services regularly.	___	___	___

THE COLLEGE INVESTMENT

A college education is an investment in money, time, and energy. In dollars, this investment will be roughly $8,000 to $16,000 for the four years, depending upon the type of college attended and the spending habits of the student. The cost of attending college has been rising steadily since 1956 and probably will continue to rise over the next decade. In fact, it is rising about $200 per year in public institutions (3, 17). The student must consider carefully how to use these resources while in college because future success and happiness may be largely dependent upon them. Certainly the soundness of the investment does not depend upon the amount of money spent or the social standing of the college; it must be weighed against what happens to the student in preparation for future work and in ability to live the good life.

The amount of money needed to attend college varies greatly from one to another. Private colleges usually are more expensive than state-supported schools; private women's colleges are usually more expensive than private coeducational colleges; Eastern schools usually are more expensive than those in the Midwest, West, or South.

Table A 1-2
Average basic charges per full-time student in institutions of higher education

year	total cost	public 4-year			total cost	private 4-year		
		room	board	tuition & fees		room	board	tuition & fees
1955–1956	$ 846	$170	$478	$198	$1,404	$243	$522	$ 639
1965–1966	1,011	289	444	278	2,014	348	498	1,168
1975–1976*	1,222	412	434	376	2,663	458	489	1,716

* Estimate.
SOURCE: "Average Basic Charges Per Full-time Student in Institutions of Higher Education," *American Education,* vol. 3, p. 33, July–August 1967.

The cost set by the college or university is not all. It is estimated that the total cost for a year in a college or university for the average student is twice the amount charged by the institution.

Financing a college education has become an increasingly complex and expensive process. Sound planning of a program to finance a college education requires information about: (1) total college costs, (2) personal and family resources, (3) types of financial assistance available, and (4) sources of financial assistance. Almost all financial aid to college undergraduates, other than that which comes from the family, falls into the categories listed below (14):

I. SCHOLARSHIPS
    A. State scholarships
    B. Scholarships from civic and service clubs (Lions, Elks, Kiwanis, etc.)
    C. National Merit Scholarships and other corporation scholarships
    D. Scholarships offered by private organizations and individuals for students in their community
    E. Scholarships offered by colleges and universities
    F. Scholarships offered by clubs and organizations for their members (4-H, Boy and Girl Scouts, etc.)
    G. Scholarships offered by companies to children of employees; awards offered by unions to children of members
    H. Scholarships offered by denominational groups
II. LOANS
    A. National Defense Student Loans
    B. State guaranty student loans
    C. Bank loans
    D. Loans for church members in church-related institutions
III. STUDENT EMPLOYMENT
    A. In the college, department, or local business
IV. SPECIAL
    A. Assistance grants for children of deceased or disabled veterans
    B. Nursing school loans
    C. Federal grants in special areas
    D. National Achievement Scholarship Program for Outstanding Negro Students

During the 1967–1968 school year, 1,175,000 students received aid from the National Defense Student Loans, Educational Opportunity Grants, and the Guaranteed Loan Programs. The total value of these undergraduate assistance programs was more than 1 billion dollars (8, 34). This figure does not include the many scholarships and loans provided by private organizations, businesses, individuals, and the colleges and universities themselves.

The amount of money individual students borrow varies greatly. While some borrow small amounts, others borrow to cover all college expenses. In a study of 86,304 college borrowers in the fall of 1960, it was found that 30 percent of the students borrowed all of their college expenses, 29 percent borrowed three-fourths, and 26 percent borrowed at least half (11). Of the borrowers in this study, 60 percent were men and 40 percent were women. Eighty percent of the borrowers depended on the student loan funds at their institution as their source of loans. For generalized information on scholarships and other financial aid available at various institutions, the following publications should be helpful:

Babbidge, Homer D., *Student Financial Aids: Manual for Colleges and Universities.* American College Personnel Association, Washington, 1960.

Cox, Claire, *How to Beat the High Cost of College,* Random House, New York, 1964.

Fine, Benjamin, and Sidney A. Eisenberg, *How to Get Money for College,* Doubleday & Company, Inc., Garden City, N.Y., 1964.

Feingold, S. Norman, *Scholarships, Fellowships and Loans,* vol. 55, Bellman Publishing Co., Cambridge, Mass., 1962.

Moon, Rexford G., *Student Financial Aid in the United States: Administration and Resource,* College Entrance Examination Board, Princeton, N.J., 1963.

Student Assistance Handbook: Guide to Financial Assistance for Education beyond High School, U.S. Library of Congress, Legislative Reference Service, Rev., U.S. Government Printing Office, 1965.

Study Abroad International Scholarships, Educational Exchange, vol. XVII, 1968–69, 1969–70, United Nations Educational, Scientific and Cultural Organization, Paris, 1968. (Available in the United States, UNESCO Publications Center, New York.)

Students should consult with their dean for information on scholarships and other financial aid available at their institution.

In addition to borrowing funds for college expenses, many students carry part-time jobs (16). It is not known how many students earn money while attending college; however, it has been estimated that from one-third to one-half of the present-day college students earn or receive from military service all or part of their expenses (36). In fact, more students earn part of their expenses by on-campus jobs than have scholarships. Typically, the student workers average between eleven and twenty hours a week (21).

The effect of working while in college is not clear, but the following conclusions appear to be sound. The students who work more than twelve hours a week have to forgo many social activities and seem to use the college hospitals somewhat more than the nonworking students, but there is no clear-cut evidence that their grades are affected (4, 31). The grades of working students appear to be just as high as those of nonworking students.

Students who need financial aid should consult the dean of the college or the head of the department in which they are enrolled to ascertain the resources available. These administrators are in a position to advise concerning what type of aid is available and most suitable to each student, as well as the procedures for obtaining it.

SUGGESTED ACTIVITIES

1. Through class discussion, develop acceptable behavior criteria for college freshmen in home economics in the following categories: social, emotional, physical, intellectual, and spiritual. The students should decide what the college has a right to expect of freshmen or sophomores in each respect and what the student has a right to expect of the college. Should the college expect more from home economics students than others? Why?

2. What are the major problems of college freshmen? If the students list the problems which they are having, solutions to the problems may be found through class discussion. To what extent are the problems similar for all students? Do these problems result from inadequate preparation for college, inadequate facilities in the college, or are they due to other factors?

3. Prepare a report on the advantages of adequate preparation for college to be delivered to a high school class. The points that should be stressed in the report may be developed through class discussion.

4. What are the class members' major reasons for attending college? Are their reasons for going to college the same as their parents' reasons for having them go? To what extent are the reasons similar or different for the members of the class? How will these reasons affect the success of the various students?

5. Each student should think through her plans for the future. How definite are these plans? What do the students expect to get from college? How do they plan to go about achieving these expectancies?

6. What are the extracurricular activities in which the students are engaging? To what extent will these activities produce a well-rounded college life? Are the students engaging in activities to develop the aspects of their personality which need most development?

7. What will the first year of college cost? Make a plan for spending during the first year. This should include board and room, tuition, incidentals, textbooks and supplies, and personal expenses. The personal expenses should include

travel, clothing, personal care, amusements and recreation, gifts, dues, etc. It will be interesting to see how the proposed plans compare for the students in the class.

8. How many students in the class have scholarships, Are working part time, Have loans? What scholarships, loans, and work opportunities are available to home economics students? How many of the students will need financial aid to graduate? Ways of obtaining financial aid by home economics students should be discussed.

9. What background in homemaking or home economics have the students brought with them to college? A survey of how many of the students have sewed, prepared and served meals, had the responsibility for the care of children, earned money, bought household supplies and equipment, managed a home, traveled by themselves, carried responsibilities in clubs or civic organizations will present the experience background of the students. Of what help do they feel these experiences will be in being successful in college?

REFERENCES

1. Aiken, Lewis R., "Rank in High School Graduating Classes of Various Sizes as a Prediction of College Grades," *Journal of Educational Research,* vol. 58, pp. 56–60, October 1964.

2. Astin, Alexander, "Personal and Environmental Factors Associated with College Drop-outs among High Aptitude Students," *Journal of Educational Psychology,* vol. 55, pp. 267–273, August 1964.

3. "Average Basic Charges per Full-time Student in Institutions of Higher Education," *American Education,* vol. 3, p. 33, July–August 1967.

4. Baker, Darald B., "The Working Student and His Grades," *Journal of Educational Research,* vol. 35, pp. 28–35, September 1941.

5. Bernard, Harold W., *Toward Better Personal Adjustment,* 2d ed., pp. 115–137, McGraw-Hill Book Company, New York, 1957.

6. Bettleheim, Bruno, "Too Many Misfits in College," *U.S. News and World Report,* vol. 66, p. 3, April 7, 1969.

7. Bord, Bernard, "College Students: Why They Drop Out," *The Kiwanis Magazine,* vol. 53, pp. 22–25, 42, September 1968.

8. *Borrowing for College: A Guide for Students and Parents,* U.S. Office of Education, 1965.

9. Brown, William F., Norman Abeles, and Ira Iseve, "Motivation Differences between High and Low Scholarship College Students," *Journal of Educational Psychology,* vol. 45, pp. 215–223, April 1954.

10. Crawford, Mary M., Stanley Steinkamp, and Edward L. Housewald, *"Student Spending, Indiana University, 1951–1952,"* Bulletin of the School of Education, Indiana University, Bloomington, Ind., November 1955.

11. *Digest of Educational Statistics,* 1968 Ed., p. 78, U.S. Offfice of Education, 1968.

12. Dolan, Eleanor F., "Higher Education for Women," *Higher Education,* vol. 20, p. 5, September 1963.

13. Eckland, Bruce K., "College Graduates Who Came Back," *Harvard Educational Review,* vol. 34, pp. 402–420, Summer 1964.

14. *Financing an Undergraduate Education,* pp. 1–16, U.S. Office of Education, 1965.

15. Grantlund, Norman E., *The PTA Magazine,* vol. 62, pp. 8–10, March 1968.

16. Hall, Robert C., and Stanton Craig, *Student Borrowers: Their Needs and Resources,* pp. 2–3, U.S. Office of Education, 1962.

17. "High Cost of College," *U.S. News and World Report,* vol. 66, pp. 48–49, April 14, 1969.

18. Holland, John L., "The Prediction of College Grades from Personality and Variables," *Journal of Educational Psychology,* vol. 51, pp. 245–254, October 1960.

19. Horrocks, John E., *The Psychology of Adolescence,* p. 243, Houghton Mifflin Company, Boston, 1951.

20. *Journal of Home Economics,* vol. 58, p. 707, November 1966.

21. MacGregor, Archie, "Part-time Work—Good or Bad?" *Journal of College Placement,* vol. 26, pp. 127–132, February 1966.

22. MacLochlan, Patricia S., and Collins W. Burnett, "Who Are the Superior Freshmen in College?" *Personnel and Guidance Journal,* vol. 32, pp. 345–349, February 1954.

23. McKinney, Fred, *Psychology of Personal Adjustment,* pp. 40–42, John Wiley & Sons, Inc., New York, 1960.

24. Miller, Francine L., "Womanpower," *Journal of Home Economics,* vol. 60, p. 697, November 1968.

25. Parker, Garland G., "Statistics of Attendance in American Universities and Colleges, 1968–1969," *School and Society,* vol. 97, p. 43, January 1969.

26. Plant, James S., *Personality and the Cultural Pattern,* p. 81, The Commonwealth Fund, New York, 1937.

27. *Projection of Educational Statistics to 1977–78,* 1968 ed., p. 127, U.S. Office of Education.

28. Sandeen, C. Arthur, "The Meaning of a Bachelor Degree," *School and Society,* vol. 96, pp. 101–102, Feb. 17, 1968.

29. *School and Society,* vol. 97, p. 137, March 1969.

30. Scott, John Finley, "So You're Going to College," *Public Affairs Pamphlet,* No. 394, October 1966.

31. Smith, Donald E., and Roger L. Wood, "Reading Improvement and College Grades: A Follow-up," *Journal of Educational Psychology,* vol. 46, pp. 151–159, March 1955.

32. Smith, Leland, "Significant Differences between High Ability Achieving

and Non-achieving College Freshmen, as Revealed by Interview Data," *The Journal of Educational Research,* vol. 59, pp. 10–12, September 1925.

33. *Statistical Abstracts of the United States, 1971,* 92nd ed., pp. 131 U.S. Department of Commerce, 1971.

34. Trimble, LaValle, "How to Get Money for College," *American Education,* vol. 3, p. 9, July–August 1967.

35. Vaughn, Maurice S., "Creativity and Creative Teaching," *School and Society,* vol. 97, p. 231, April 1969.

36. Wilkins, Theresa Birch, *Financial Aid for College Students: Undergraduate,* p. 2, U.S. Office of Education, Bulletin No. 18, 1957.

37. Woodring, Paul, *The Higher Learning in America: A Reassessment,* pp. 199–214, McGraw-Hill Book Company, New York, 1968.

ADDITIONAL READINGS

"American Youth: Its Outlook Is Changing the World," *Fortune,* vol. 79, pp. 59–60, 1969.

Cox, Claire, *How to Beat the High Cost of College,* Random House, Inc., New York, 1964.

Dressel, Paul L., "The Meaning of a College Education," *The Journal of Higher Education,* vol. 39, pp. 481–489, December 1968.

Egan, Mary C., "To Serve Is to Know," *Journal of Home Economics,* vol. 61. pp. 13–16, January 1969.

Feingold, S. Norman, *Scholarships, Fellowships, and Loans,* vol. 4, 1st ed., Bellman Publishing Company, Cambridge, Mass., 1962.

Garraty, John Arthur, and Walter Adams, *A Guide to Study Abroad,* 1962, 1963, ed., Channel Press, Inc., Manhasset, N.Y., 1962.

Ginzberg, Eli, *Life Styles of Educated Women,* Columbia University Press, New York, 1966.

Hill, Helen, "In Defense of the Underachiever," *The Delta Kappa Gamma Bulletin,* vol. 34, pp. 16–26, Summer 1968.

Student Assistance Handbook: Guide to Financial Assistance for Education beyond High School, rev., U.S. Library of Congress Legislative Reference Service, U.S. Government Printing Office, 1965.

Swope, M. R., "How Short Is the Shortage? Facts of Home Economics Personnel in Higher Education," *Journal of Home Economics,* vol. 59, pp. 765–768, November 1967.

Todd, F. J., G. Terrell, and C. E. Frank, "Differences between Normal and Underachievers of Superior Ability," *Journal of Applied Psychology,* vol. 46, pp. 183–191, June 1962.

U.S. News and World Report, "High Cost of College," vol. 66, pp. 48–49, April 14, 1969.

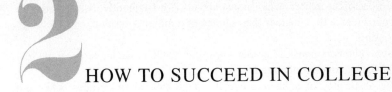
HOW TO SUCCEED IN COLLEGE

Look at the students in college; they vary greatly in their approach to college work. Some are very eager for knowledge and put forth great effort to learn more than is required. Others regard college courses as necessary hurdles for entrance into professional or business careers. There are others who see the need of doing well in their college courses, but because of their poor academic background, or personal and emotional problems, seem unable to do so. Finally, there are the playgirls, the drifters, the social butterflies, the protesters, and the students who are too interested in other things to put forth the effort to make good grades.

It pays to make good grades in college. Studies of various businesses and professions indicate that success in scholarship and extracurricular activities are closely related to success in later life (1). Certainly not all the successful men and women graduate in the upper tenth of their classes, but there is a definite tendency for those who are better students in college or have more education to have the better paying or the more influential and responsible positions later in life (9, 10).

The successful home economics student must be able to do high-quality work in a rather wide range of subject-matter courses. Furthermore, these courses will be scattered through the arts and sciences. To become a good student in home economics requires the same qualities of dedication and self-discipline necessary for success in any field. High scholarship in college can be achieved by understanding the characteristics of good students and then developing these traits as rapidly as possible.

CHARACTERISTICS OF GOOD STUDENTS

There are measurable differences between high-ranking and low-ranking students (13, 25, 27).

1. High achievers have done significantly better work in high school and spend more hours studying than do low-ranking students.
2. The high achievers are more concerned with cultural aspirations while nonachievers are more concerned with status, money, and the "good" life.
3. High achievers participate in a greater variety of extracurricular activities, and possess more hobbies than do nonachievers.
4. High achievers report fewer personal problems.

5. High achievers are generally satisfied with their department and their choice of subject matter, while nonachievers are frequently dissatisfied with the department staff, consider their choice of a major poor, and tend to change departments.

6. High achievers consider grades important while nonachievers usually feel that grades are overemphasized.

7. The associates of achievers usually make satisfactory grades, while the associates of nonachievers tend to do unsatisfactory work.

8. The achievers are usually independent, purposive, and efficiently organized individuals.

9. The high achievers are more willing to postpone immediate gratifications to achieve distant goals than are the nonachievers.

10. High achievers have stronger motivation for studying, tend to be more self-confident, and appear to have greater capacity for working under pressure. The under achievers show a marked tendency to procrastinate and tend to rely upon external pressure to complete assignments.

Good students *usually* have good study habits. Poor students *frequently* have poor study habits. Many students finish high school without having learned to study effectively, while others have habits which are actually detrimental to their progress (10, 11, 12, 18). On entering college, one should evaluate his study habits as objectively as possible. This survey will reveal several types of information. How is the study work planned for each evening, for the day, for the week, and for the quarter or semester? How does the student get ready to study? How much time is spent in getting ready to study? How is each study period organized and attacked?

The good student has a plan for studying. The old saying, "Time and tide wait for no man," is true of college life. Students have twenty-four hours daily at their disposal—time that can be used wisely or foolishly. In spending time, the student must realize that an hour wasted is gone forever. There is enough time in the day for the average student to meet all study and work needs, social and activity interests, and health and personal requirements if these activities are planned carefully around the time available. Time, like money, if invested wisely brings good returns in knowledge, creative experiences, satisfying friendships, a healthy and rested body, and abilities and skills to carry on life's work.

In order to plan for the wise use of time, one must know the demands to be made upon it. Students may say that this is impossible, but is it? The specific demands to be made may not be known, but they can be classified rather easily and time budgeted for them. A time plan should be built around the academic work. The plan will show at what time each course is to be studied through the week and the periods set aside for review and unusual assignments. It will provide time for reports, term projects, and examinations. It will set aside time to be devoted to recreation, rest, and personal care. The time for meals and other duties will be scheduled. It will allow "free time" to do as one pleases, with other time for reading for personal interest. In addition, it will provide adequate time for sleep.

When the schedule is planned, it should be kept in mind that the more difficult subjects should be studied at hours of peak efficiency. Students must test themselves to learn their own periods of greatest efficiency, but usually the early-morning hours are most productive; efficiency tends to drop toward the end of the morning. Comparative efficiency is similar for the afternoon hours; however, efficiency is lower in the latter part of the afternoon (12). No doubt the same picture would be found for the evening. Thus, for most students, the hardest subjects should be studied in the morning, soon after a light lunch, or directly following a rest period and dinner.

The schedule should be arranged to prevent wasting time between classes. Books or materials to be studied during an hour between classes should be carried along, so that the student may sit down in the first quiet place she can find and make good use of the hour.

It does not take a specialist to make a study and activity plan. To begin, list the names of the courses and the number of hours to be spent in lecture and laboratory for each subject during the week. Suppose the student's courses were as in Tables A 2-1 and A 2-2.

Table A 2-1
Student course program

courses	hours to be spent weekly in	
	lecture	laboratory
English composition	3	0
Algebra	3	0
Biology	2	3
Principles of art and design	1	6
Elementary nutrition	2	3
Physical education	0	3

After listing the courses, the next step is to set up a schedule form similar to the one in Table A 2-2. This should have spaces for each hour of the day and for all of the days of the week. On this form should be written the class hours for each of the courses listed in Table A 2-1. The next step is to determine the amount of time necessary to prepare for each class and the time at which the preparation can be done most effectively. Study periods should be labeled specifically, such as "study English," "study algebra," etc. Merely to write in "study" does not furnish a definite enough guide. Unless the subject to study is specified, the student may waste time trying to decide what to study or use too much time on some subjects to the neglect of others.

It is customary in most colleges for instructors to expect two hours of preparation for each class lecture. In other words, if the English class meets three hours each week, the student will be expected to devote six hours of preparation to English during the week. Some subjects may need more than two hours per class period for preparation, and there may be a few subjects which require less. Usually

Table A 2-2
Student schedule form

Term _____ 1st _____   Name _____ Jane Doe _____

Hour	Monday	Tuesday	Wednesday	Thursday	Friday	Saturday	Sunday
7:00	Dress	Dress	Dress	Dress	Dress	Dress	
7:00– 8:00	Breakfast and leave for class						Dress
8:00– 9:00	Biology		Biology		Room care	Study algebra	Break-fast
9:00–10:00	English	Prin. of art & design labora-tory	English	Prin. of art & design labora-tory	English	Prin. of art & design	Sunday school and church
10:00–11:00	Study English		Ele. nutri.		Ele. nutri.	Study biol.	
11:00–12:00	Ph. ed.	Algebra	Phys. ed.	Algebra	Phys. ed.	Algebra	
12:00– 1:00	Lunch						
1:00– 2:00	Study algebra	Biology labora-tory	Study algebra	Ele. nutri. labora-tory	Study prin. of art & design	Study biol.	Dinner
2:00– 3:00							
3:00– 4:00	Study biol.		Study prin. of art & design		Study algebra	Free	Study English
4:00– 5:00	Free reading or study						
5:00– 6:00	Free						
6:00– 6:30	Dinner						
6:30– 7:00	Curricu-lar clubs	Free					
7:00– 8:00		Study English	Study art	Study nutri.	Free		
8:00– 9:00	Study biol.		Study English				
9:00–10:00	Study nutri.	Write letters		Write letters			
10:00–11:00	Personal care						
11:00	Sleep						

there is no outside preparation for a three-hour laboratory class, but if the instructor requires it, time must be allowed in the plan.

The exact time one studies for each course may vary with the whims or wishes of the individual, but there are rules that one may use for guidance. As stated before, the courses which are the most difficult to master should be studied when the student is most alert. Preparation time should be allowed before each class period, if possible, so that daily assignments can be taken care of. Unbroken periods of several hours for study prevent the waste of time in getting started and in putting materials away for short periods. *Special time,* including considerations such as quietness in the dormitory, lack of crowding in the library, and rooms with good ventilation or lighting, should be taken advantage of when making a study schedule.

The Student Schedule Form (Table A 2-2) suggests one way to plan a weekly schedule. It should be noted that the study periods are so arranged that the student will have two hours for study before each class period. In addition to the study periods, on each day there is at least one hour given to *free study or reading.* This is not time to be wasted; it is to be used where additional study is needed for a subject or for reading of special interest to the student.

Daily, the hour before dinner and the half hour after dinner are marked *free time.* This is time that students may use as they please. Personal care is allotted an hour each day because personal appearance is important, and this aspect of life should not be neglected. Most students find that they can have three evenings a week for dating or other recreation without endangering their time for study. Students should strive to be in bed by eleven o'clock if possible. Late studying does not pay good returns in achievement, because fatigue is detrimental to rapid learning and clear comprehension (7, 8, 12).

If the student is working part time to help finance school expenses, these work hours should be placed on the schedule along with the class hours. If the work consumes more than ten hours a week, it is usually advisable to carry fewer credit hours during each session, unless the hours of work come at a time allotted normally to free time (20). It is better for the student not to tie up all free time in work activities, since associations with fellow students in recreational activities are helpful in becoming a better-rounded person.

Some students, especially those working or engaging in extracurricular activities, maintain that they cannot use a schedule because of the unforeseen interruptions, but it is these students who cannot afford to be without a schedule. If there are unforeseen interruptions, an analysis of the schedule will show immediately where there is free time to do the work that could not be done because of the interruptions.

After the schedule is planned, it should be tried out for at least a week. Changes necessary for more efficient use of time should be noted on the schedule. As soon as possible, the schedule should be stabilized and followed carefully. This does not mean a rigid compliance, for a schedule is only a guide. However, the student who has not learned to budget time will need to stay very close to a schedule at the beginning.

Good students make every effort to improve their learning ability (12, 22). Certainly learning is an individual matter, and no two students will learn the same way. However, for most students similar ingredients make for success in learning. The first prerequisite is that the student *must want to learn* (2, 6). Each course and class must be approached with a positive attitude and a desire to get as much from it as possible. The student who goes into a course fearful, or with the idea that it has nothing to offer, is defeated from the beginning. A good student attacks assignments creatively and accepts them as an opportunity to partake of new ideas or knowledge.

To learn most effectively, students must realize that they are themselves responsible for their own education. Study is hard work, and "half effort" brings little reward. The statement that genius is 5 percent inspiration and 95 percent perspiration is very true. Students will retain more of what they read and hear if they are interested in the material being discussed.

As the student enters a new course, she will make more rapid progress if she gives thought to what is to be gotten from the course and the best procedures for getting it. One's best learning does not come from sitting back peacefully and letting the teacher or the textbooks do all the work. Students will learn more if they participate actively in the class. It has been said that you can lead a student to a classroom or a textbook, but you can't make him learn.

As soon as possible, a good student makes application of the new knowledge by finding examples of general principles or problems discussed in class or in reading. These general principles are to be applied in making decisions. For example, if in physics the student learns that under heat gases expand, she recognizes the fact as the principle operating in leavening agents in cakes, breads, etc. If in textiles the fact is stated that a satin weave does not hold up well under abrasion, the unsuitability of materials with the satin weave for chair seats or for any use where there would be much rubbing becomes apparent.

Using good judgment in studying improves learning ability. Decisions as to what materials need to be memorized, analyzed, or simply understood should be made deliberately. Much effort can be wasted and actual learning hindered by trying to memorize materials of which only an understanding is expected. Items to be memorized should be those that are used frequently by the student as she pursues her studies. For example, the reading material may list trends in clothing production, and the number of clothing manufacturing firms from 1850 to 1960 may be given. By analyzing the data, the student may gain the knowledge that commercially made clothing has been in existence a little over 100 years. At first it dealt with men's and later women's coats and suits. Little children's clothing was made in factories prior to 1900. After 1900, the growth in the clothing industry was very rapid. Other similar ideas should remain in her mind. There is little likelihood that the instructor would expect a student to memorize the number of establishments in each decade, for such information would be of little general use to her. The same applies in other subjects. In chemistry, for example, too often students memorize formulas when they should seek to understand how the formulas were devised and learn to reconstruct them.

The good student knows what is expected. She never leaves the classroom before she has a clear understanding of the next assignment. Since assignments frequently are given at the beginning of the class, it is important to come to class on time. Furthermore, a good student is regular in class attendance, for it has been shown that good class attendance is associated with good grades in college (3, 14, 16). If a class is missed because of illness, or something else outside the student's control, the work should be made up as soon as possible.

Assignments prepared regularly and accurately are associated with good grades, for every lesson is important. One failure a week may mean failure in the end. The better student does not limit the day's preparation to the assignment but will push on into new avenues of knowledge which the assignment may suggest. Also, the lesson or material to be learned is reviewed before each class.

The good student works independently and economically. Help is asked for only when it is needed, and such tools as a dictionary, the necessary reference books, and other equipment for efficient and good work are at hand. A good student is a steady worker who approaches her studies with confidence, courage, and determination. The recognition that it is important to do one's best is always before the good student.

QUALITIES OF GOOD READERS

Good reading ability is an essential attribute of a good student. College work is greatly dependent upon one's ability to learn through reading. Studies of college students' reading abilities suggest that a large number of students are attempting to do successful college work with low reading ability; it has been estimated that one-fourth of all college students have reading deficiencies (14, 20). Many colleges and universities maintain remedial reading classes or reading clinics, where students may have their reading abilities analyzed and where, if necessary, they may attend special classes in which their reading habits are examined and improved (21).

A good reader usually is a rapid reader with a high degree of concentration (7, 28). Good comprehenders adjust their rate of reading by slowing down as the material increases in difficulty. Poor comprehenders apparently read easy and difficult material at much the same rate. Intelligence, purpose for reading, opportunities for referral, and continuity of context influence the effectiveness of the reader. For many slow readers, erratic thoughts crowd in upon the mind and prevent full comprehension of what is read. This requires rereading, which consumes time. Furthermore, the slow reader finds it difficult to form meanings rapidly, so that they fuse and give rise to larger meanings. One test of the quality of one's reading is to quiz oneself on the materials as soon as they are read. This can be done by summarizing the ideas presented or asking oneself questions about them.

Articulation and lip and throat movements tend to reduce speed in reading. The eyes can perceive much more rapidly than the lips can articulate. For this reason, sight reading is almost twice as fast as oral reading.

A good reader should be able to read 300 or more words a minute. If the student's reading speed is below this, efforts to improve reading speed should be set in motion. The following suggestions should help (17, 24, 26):

1. Before starting to read a book or article, note the author and title. Use the table of contents to find the specific assignment instead of leafing through the

book (5). Determine the relationship of the assigned chapter to the rest of the book. Read any introduction or summary accompanying the chapter.

2. Skim boldfaced or italicized headings and illustrations. Turn headings into questions by asking who, what, when, and why.

3. Read by phrases and paragraphs. Pick out the topic sentence in the paragraph—the topic sentence fits the main point of the paragraph. The remaining sentences usually explain or amplify the topic sentence. Keep the mind active, and read for ideas, not words.

4. Read against time. Check reading time for a page in the textbook. Then, with complete concentration, try to read the page in less time. Read just as rapidly as possible, while still understanding the meaning. The extent to which reading speed can be improved with a continuation of this procedure is amazing.

5. Adjust reading speed and general approach to the kind of material being read. If the reading material has considerable detail, read slowly enough to comprehend the detail. If the purpose of the reading is just to get the main ideas, then speed up the reading rate and concentrate on the main ideas.

6. Do not skip over new words. If new words are found, look up their meaning. It is wise to have a notebook handy in which to write down new words and their meaning. A regular review of these words and practice in using them will increase reading speed and comprehension and at the same time build vocabulary.

7. Read all assignments with the idea of getting new ideas or seeing new relationships. This approach will aid in increasing the ability to concentrate.

8. When reading textbooks, underline sentences that are worth remembering. If the statement is very important, also place a check mark in the margin. Make brief legible notes on the reading in your own words. This procedure is of inestimable value to a student when attempting to review for a test.

9. Try to retain as much of the information as possible. Good readers have more retentive ability and more information at their command.

10. When reading, stop periodically and ask questions about what has been read. Integrating these materials or ideas with past learnings leads to new meanings.

11. Review what you have read. Recite orally the materials checked and your notes.

Improving ability to concentrate is the mark of a good student. Concentration depends upon motivation and attention (18). Practically everyone recognizes that a *motivated* or *interested* person is more attentive, but it should also be recognized that *skill in paying attention builds motivation.* Because of the far-reaching effects of this knowledge, many college students should reexamine their mental habits and attention ability. Comprehension and learning result in part from the habit of keeping the mind active and *thinking about the topic as one reads about it.* One of the best ways to promote concentration is to have a purpose. Interest in the subject being read about or discussed and appreciation of its value are also aids to concentration. The poor student is characterized by a lack of decisiveness of action, a tendency to procrastinate, and perhaps an unwillingness to conform to academic requirements, routines, and regulations. One will be better able to concentrate if reading is done with the idea of reciting or writing down what has been learned.

In so far as possible, one should try to eliminate distracting factors. If a dripping faucet is distracting, either turn it off or move to a place where the dripping cannot be heard. If students passing by the table prove distracting, find a place to study which is away from the traffic of the library.

It will be impossible to eliminate all sounds and factors that may prove distracting. For this reason, it is advisable to plunge into studying and block out all of the stimulation which might prove annoying under other conditions. This takes practice, but the mind can be trained not to react to many stimuli that may prove distracting to others.

PREPARING FOR EXAMINATIONS

A good student methodically prepares for examinations and tests each day of the term. She seeks an acquaintance with the different types of tests and the specialized knowledge and abilities necessary to score well on each type. In order to prepare for a specific test, the student should inquire as to the type of examination to be given and what the examination will cover.

A good student will thoroughly learn the subject matter day in and day out, with regular reviews. In reviewing for a test, the main points of the text or texts, reading and lecture notes, laboratory manual, and outside reading references should be studied, assimilated, and compared for reliability and thoroughness.

A few hours with other students in a question, answer, and problem-solving session may prove very valuable. Good students may find it more profitable to carry on a question-and-answer session by themselves if the other students are not equally prepared.

The ability to listen attentively is one aid to learning. William Armstrong makes the following suggestions for better listening in class (1):

1. Get ready to listen as soon as the bell has rung.
2. Watch the teacher closely. Listen to every word he says, ignore all other sounds, and keep your eyes on the teacher.
3. Have your ear ready for directions. Your work can be lightened greatly by following the teacher's *directions;* he is working for you and is trying to help you.
4. Listen to other students when they recite. Hear what they say, note the good points, spot the words, and be ready to supply information they lack.

5. Take notes. Writing is one of the best ways to train yourself to listen. In order to write, you force yourself to listen.
6. Adapt yourself to each teacher's methods.
7. Think ahead of your teacher. This will substitute active listening for passive absorption.
8. Check every tendency toward mind wandering.
9. Listen critically, thoughtfully, and understandingly.

Before attempting to answer questions on an examination, read all questions through carefully. Many students do not do as well as they might on tests because they do not understand just what the question asks. Pages of good material written on an examination will be of no value if they do not answer the questions.

After reading through the questions, divide the time allowed on the examination among the questions in order that they all may be answered in the time available. Before beginning the answer to a question, outline the answer mentally or on paper. This not only saves time but makes for a better-organized and more complete answer.

A relaxed student usually does better on an examination than one who is tense. If a student has studied conscientiously and has reviewed well for the examination, a good night's sleep before the examination and a feeling of confidence are assurances of good performance.

Good students are made, not born. They must want to learn, and they must plan their lives so that they have time for the various demands made upon them. They must know their strengths and weaknesses and daily strive to improve their power of concentration and reading skill. They must study effectively and prepare earnestly for the various testing periods of the term. All students can become better students, but this requires knowing what good study habits are, being willing to abide by the rules for efficient study, planning for the most effective use of time, and putting forth the necessary effort to achieve.

QUALITIES OF A GOOD STUDENT

Below are listed ten qualities of good students. Check the appropriate column to the right to indicate the extent to which you possess each quality.

	usually	sometimes	seldom
1. Class assignments are done conscientiously and to the best of my ability.	_____	_____	_____
2. Materials are classified as to those needing to be memorized, those to be analyzed, and those simply to be understood.	_____	_____	_____
3. Assignments are understood and recorded systematically before leaving the classroom or laboratory.	_____	_____	_____

	usually	*sometimes*	*seldom*
4. Errors on daily assignments or on test papers are noted and corrected.	_____	_____	_____
5. Class and laboratory notes and textbook materials are reviewed regularly.	_____	_____	_____
6. Good attention is maintained throughout class periods.	_____	_____	_____
7. Promptness and regularity in class attendance are maintained. Time in laboratories is used efficiently.	_____	_____	_____
8. A special effort is made to understand what is expected by each teacher in each class.	_____	_____	_____
9. Study periods are approached in a businesslike manner.	_____	_____	_____
10. An effort is made to sit in a seat near the front of the room or where there are few distractions.	_____	_____	_____

Any student who can check "Usually" for each of the items above has many of the qualities of a good student. "Sometimes" or "Seldom" markings indicate some needs for self-improvement.

SUGGESTED ACTIVITIES

1. Each student should plan a weekly activity schedule as suggested in Table A 2-2. Afterward, the strengths and weaknesses of the various plans may be brought out through class discussion.

2. The students might discuss some of the problems they are having in preparing their college assignments. How many of the problems are student-centered and how many are college-centered? What conditions make for good study practices; for poor study practices? How can the distracting factors be removed or lessened?

3. To what extent are the students entering into campus activities? How many are finding it difficult to decide among the numerous activities on the campus? Why? How many have not had as many opportunities for social activities as they need or desire? What suggestions do the class members have for helping these students?

4. Is college life conducive to good physical habits? To what extent are the students becoming fatigued? Is this due to lack of sleep, poor planning, too much noise in the dormitory, or other reasons? What suggestions do class members have for reducing fatigue? Are the students eating a well-balanced diet? What dietary problems are they finding? Are the students finding their clothes suitable for college life? What part of their wardrobes seems to be the least adequate? What advice would they give to high school seniors in selecting their college clothing?

5. To what extent does each student have the qualities of a good student, suggested earlier? How can these habits be built up? What helps are available on the campus to the students who wish to improve their study habits?

6. What are the chief "time wasters" among the students? How can they be eliminated? Is the college program responsible for some of them? In what ways?

REFERENCES

1. Armstrong, William H., *Study Is Hard Work,* pp. 122–125, Harper and Brothers, New York, 1956.

2. Anikeeff, Alexis M., "The Relationship between Class Absences and College Grades," *Journal of Educational Psychology,* vol. 45, pp. 244–249, April 1954.

3. Argyris, Chris, "Some Characteristics of Successful Executives," *Personnel Journal,* vol. 32, pp. 50–55, June 1953.

4. Astin, Alexander, "Personal and Environmental Factors Associated with College Drop-outs among High Aptitude Students," *Journal of Educational Psychology,* vol. 55, pp. 267–275, August 1964.

5. Botel, Morton, *How to Teach Reading,* 4th ed., pp. 34–38, Follett Educational Corporation, Chicago, 1960.

6. Brown, William F., Norman Abeles, and Ira Iseve, "Motivation Differences between High and Low Scholarship College Students," *Journal of Educational Psychology,* vol. 45, pp. 215–223, April 1954.

7. Carlson, Thorstein R., "The Relationship between Speed and Accuracy of Comprehension," *Journal of Educational Research,* vol. 42, pp. 500–511, March 1949.

8. Clark, R. E., *The Effect of Sleep Loss on Performance of a Complex Task,* U.S. Department of Commerce Publication 20286, OSRD Report 3153, 1943.

9. *Digest of Educational Statistics,* 1968 ed., p. 15, U.S. Office of Education, 1968.

10. Gist, Noel P., C. T. Pihbald, and C. L. Gregory, "Scholastic Achievement and Occupations," *American Sociological Review,* vol. 7, pp. 752–763, December 1942.

11. Hill, Helen, "In Defense of the Underachiever," *The Delta Kappa Gamma Bulletin,* vol. 34, pp. 16–26, Summer 1968.

12. Hoeflin, Ruth, and Ralph E. Bender, *Problems and Concerns of College Freshmen,* Ohio Agricultural Experiment Station Research Bulletin 757, Wooster, Ohio, February 1955.

13. Hummel, Raymond, and Norman Sprinthall, "Underachievement Related to Interests, Attitudes, and Values," *Personnel and Guidance Journal,* vol. 44, pp. 388–395, December 1965.

14. Jackson, Robert A., "Prediction of the Academic Success of College Freshmen," *Journal of Educational Psychology,* vol. 46, pp. 296–301, May 1955.

15. Kilby, Richard W., "The Relation of a Remedial Reading Program to Scholastic Success in College," *Journal of Educational Psychology,* vol. 36, pp. 513–534, December 1945.

16. Kersting, K., "Absences and Averages," *School and Community,* vol. 53, p. 17, February 1967.

17. LeCount, Samuel N., *How to Improve Study Habits,* Pacific Books, Palo Alto, Calif., 1953.

18. Lum, Mabel K., "A Comparison of Under- and Overachieving Female College Students," *Journal of Educational Psychology,* vol. 51, pp. 109–114, June 1960.

19. McKinney, Fred, *Psychology of Personal Adjustment,* 2d ed., p. 127, John Wiley & Sons, Inc., New York, 1949.

20. McKinney, Fred, *Psychology of Personal Adjustment,* 3d ed., pp. 41–42, John Wiley & Sons, Inc., New York, 1960.

21. Morgan, Clifford, and James Deese, *How to Study,* McGraw-Hill Book Company, New York, 1957.

22. Netchinsky, I., "Reading Improvement Program at the State University Urban Center in Brooklyn," *Journal of Reading,* vol. 11, pp. 362–366, February 1968.

23. Richards, James M., John L. Holland, and Sandra W. Lutz, "Prediction of Student Accomplishment in College," *Journal of Educational Psychology,* vol. 58, pp. 343–356, December 1967.

24. Roberts, Helen Erskine, "Factors Affecting the Academic Underachievement of Bright High School Students," *The Journal of Educational Research,* vol. 56, pp. 175–183, December 1962.

25. Robinson, Francis, *Effective Study,* rev. ed., Harper & Row, New York, 1961.

26. Smith, Leland, "Significant Differences between High-ability Achieving and Non-achieving College Freshmen As Revealed by Interview Data," *The Journal of Educational Research,* vol. 59, pp. 10–12, September 1965.

27. Thalberg, S. P., "Reading Rate and Immediate versus Delayed Retention," *Journal of Educational Psychology,* vol. 58, pp. 373–378, December 1967.

ADDITIONAL READINGS

Braam, L. S., and Allen Berger, "Effectiveness of Four Methods of Increasing Reading Rate, Comprehension, and Flexibility," *Journal of Reading,* vol. 11, pp. 346–362, February 1968.

Harris, Albert J., *How to Increase Reading Ability,* 4th ed, David McKay Company, New York, 1961.

Kelly, Ingra K., and Dorothy Mich, "The Relationship between College Reading Laboratory Experience and Gains in College Grade Point Average," *Journal of the Reading Specialist,* vol. 7, pp. 50–54, December 1967.

Preston, Ralph C., and Morton Botel, *How to Study and Study Habits Checklist,* rev. ed., Science Research Associates, Chicago, 1967.

Ray, Darrel D., and Mavis D. Martin, "Gains in Reading Achievement," *Journal of Reading,* vol. 10, pp. 238–242, January 1967.

Shafter, Harry, *Faster Reading Self-taught,* Simon and Schuster, Inc., 1959.

3 VISUAL AND AUDITORY AIDS IN HOME ECONOMICS CAREERS

1. A new look at home economics careers.   Color   78 Frames   12 Minutes

Describes college preparation for home economics careers and shows the many opportunities in a variety of career areas. (1964)
Source: American Home Economics Association, 2010 Massachusetts Avenue, N.W., Washington, D.C. 20036

2. AHEA tapes.

Offers selected recordings from special AHEA events including annual meetings, national workshops, and conferences.
Source: Public Relations Department, American Home Economics Association, 2010 Massachusetts Avenue, N.W., Washington, D.C. 20036

3. Career posters.

Presents a new series of 15 black and white posters, 22 in. × 32 in., suitable for framing or mounting. (1969)
Source: American Home Economics Association, 2010 Massachusetts Avenue, N.W., Washington, D.C. 20036

4. Careers with a double future.   Color   15 Minutes

Describes the double opportunities open to young women who can serve as home economics instructors while preparing for marriage and personal homemaking.
Source: California Home Advisory Board, University of California Press, Berkeley, California.

5. Be involved—be a home economist.   Color   36 Slides   25 Minute Script

A new series with 36 color slides of young home economists on the job.
Source: American Home Economics Association, 2010 Massachusetts Avenue, N.W., Washington, D.C. 20036

6. Better living through research.   Color   21 Minutes

Shows research by the U.S. Department of Agriculture at the Institute of Home Economics, Beltsville, Maryland, in the fields of food, textiles, and housing.
Source: Du Art Film Labs., Inc., 245 West 55th Street, New York, New York

7. Home economics—a double career.   Color   14 Minutes

Explains that a knowledge of home economics fundamentals is important to every young woman, whether she uses this knowledge for homemaking, her career, or both.
Source: Consolidated Film Industries, 959 Seward Street, Hollywood, California

8. The home economics story.   Black and white   25 Minutes

Depicts various aspects of college home economics and the major careers open to college trained home economists.
Source: Iowa State University, Film Production Unit, Alice Norton House, Ames, Iowa

9. Why study home economics.   Black and white   10 Minutes

Presents two teen-agers as they learn about homemaking and vocational opportunities in home economics.
Source: McGraw-Hill Textfilms, 1221 Avenue of the Americas, New York, New York

10. Yours to choose.   Color   23 Minutes

Shows many aspects of home economics, including nutrition, testing consumer goods, designing, and sewing.
Source: Encyclopedia Britannica, Educational Corporation, 1150 Wilmette Avenue, Wilmette, Illinois

11. The costumer designer.   Black and white   10 Minutes

Shows the costume designer's importance to the production of a film in creating costumes that are appropriate historically, geographically, and dramatically.
Source: Teaching Film Custodian, 25 West 43d Street, New York, New York

SUPPLEMENTARY AIDS

1. College dropouts.   Color   60 Frames

Parl 1. Explores many of the freshman year pressures showing why college freshmen drop out.
Part 2. Shows why college education is part of a national goal. Lists famous people who never went to college.
Source: Guidance Associates Division, Harcourt Brace Javanovich, Box 5, Pleasantville, New York

2. Financing your college education.   Color   41 Frames

Shows various ways of earning money for college expenses.
Source: McGraw-Hill Textfilms, 1221 Avenue of the Americas, New York, New York

3. Health careers.   Black and White   15 Minutes

Surveys careers in health work, showing various activities of health workers.
Source: Equitable Life Assurance Society of United States, 1285 Avenue of the
Americas, New York, New York

4. Careers in restaurant management.   Color   16 Minutes

Relates how Jim Welty gets the university training he needs to start a restaurant of
his own. Outlines the various courses and field experiences offered by the university.
Source: Ohio State University, Motion Picture Division, 1885 Neil Avenue, Columbus, Ohio

5. Helping teachers to understand children (Pt. 1).   Black and white
   21 Minutes

Presents the story of the work of the Institute for Child Study at the University of
Maryland.
Source: Du Art Film Labs., Inc., 245 West 55th Street, New York, New York

6. How to get a job and keep it.   Color   39 Frames

Explains the best ways to find a job and to move ahead in a career.
Source: Essential Education, Box 968, Huntsville, Texas

7. How to investigate vocations.   Color, Black and white   11 Minutes

Considers how to interpret vocational guidance tests and to apply this information;
and how to raise questions related to specific jobs.
Source: Coronet Films, Coronet Building, Chicago, Illinois

8. How to make a career decision.   Color   39 Frames

Shows how early counseling can help people to make wise decisions.
Source: Coronet Films, Coronet Building, Chicago, Illinois

9. How to study occupations.   Color   40 Frames

Stresses the importance of studying job opportunities and relating them to one's
interests and abilities.
Source: Popular Science Publishing Company, 239 West Fairview Blvd., Inglewood,
California

10. Marriage and career.   Color   45 Frames

Compares life patterns of girls today with those at the turn of the century and
discusses preparation for woman's dual role.

Source: Popular Science Publishing Company, 239 West Fairview Blvd., Inglewood, California

11. Mental health careers. Color, Black and white 20 Minutes

Follows a teen-ager as she interviews individuals in the community and discusses vocations in the mental health field.
Source: Rustin Film Association, 5910 Wayzata Blvd., Minneapolis, Minnesota

12. Personal qualities for job success. Color, Black and white 11 Minutes

Outlines the elements for job success.
Source: Coronet Films, Coronet Building, Chicago, Illinois

13. Planning for success. Color, Black and white 11 Minutes

Points out how to set goals and then match them to one's ability.
Source: Coronet Films, Coronet Building, Chicago, Illinois

14. Planning your career. Black and white 16 Minutes

Offers three basic steps for planning a career and requirements for selected vocations.
Source: Encyclopedia Britannica, Educational Corporation, 1150 Wilmette Avenue, Wilmette, Illinois

15. Teaching by television. Color 51 Frames

Shows how to use TV in the classroom and to teach over TV.
Source: Baker Science Packet, 650 Concord Drive, Holland, Maryland

OUT OF PRINT BUT MAY BE FOUND IN STATE AND UNIVERSITY LIBRARIES

Home economists and dietitians. 48 Frames

Gives an overview of the work of dietitians and selected home economists. Produced by: Society for Visual Education, General Precisions Corporation, 1345 Diversey Parkway, Chicago, Illinois

INDEX

Cooking schools:
  Philadelphia, 9, 10
Cooperative Extension Service, 78
  advantages and disadvantages, 86
  development of, 256–258
  interest checklist, 87–88
  number of home economists
    employed, 257
  positions for home economists, 78,
    126
    qualifications for, 83
    salaries, 80
  program aids, 79
  Smith-Lever Act, 257–258
Corning Glass Works, 174, 175
Cost of attending college, 298–299
Counseling:
  in family life, 100–101
  home economics teacher and, 63–
    64
County home economists in
  extension, 79–82
  number of, 79
  qualifications for work, 79–82
Creative food careers, 142
Cutter in clothing manufacturing,
  116

Dame schools, 4
Decisions in homemaking, 228
Degrees in home economics, 72,
  238–239, 287
Department of Home Economics,
  National Education
  Association, 267–268
Designer in clothing and textiles,
  112–115
Designing of clothing:
  employment opportunities, 110,
    112–115
  free-lance designers, 115
Dewey, Annie G., 14

Dewey, Melville, 14
Dietetics:
  American Dietetic Association,
    265–266
  definition of, 134–135
  interest checklist, 148
  positions in, 132–133
    qualifications for, 134–138
    salaries, 147
Dietitians:
  activities of, 134–138
  administrative, 135
  army and air force, 135
  hospitals and clinics, 132
  number of, 133
  requirements for membership in
    American Dietetic Association,
    137
  therapeutic, 135
Disadvantaged, work with, 62
Distaff, The, magazine, Kappa
  Omicron Phi, 271
Distribution of clothing, positions,
  110–111
District agents, extension, 83–84
Dodge, Grace, 7
Domestic Receipt Book, 7
Domestic science and art, schools of,
  12–13
Domestic science curriculum at
  Illinois Industrial University,
  12–13
Draper in clothing and pattern
  production, 116
Dual role, training for, 45, 51

Education in home economics:
  aims, 61, 66
  interest checklist, 74
  positions in, 61
    advantages and disadvantages,
      68–70

Fellowships for home economics
students, 240–242, 269, 272
Films and slides for home economics
careers, 318–321
Financial aid for college students,
298–300
Financial problems of college
students, 300–301
Financing college education:
cost of, 298–299
sources of students funds, 299–300
students earning while in college,
300–301
Finishing schools, 5
Food and Agricultural Organization
(FAO), 208, 217–218
Food service, 140–142, 181
commercial, 180–182
positions for home economists in,
132, 141
salaries, 147
school-lunch program, 140–141
Food specialists, 142–144
Food technology, 145–146
Foods and nutrition:
consultants, 142–144
creative foods careers, 142
development of, 32
dietetics, 134–138
food managers, 140–142
food specialists, 142–143
food technology, 145
institution administration, 141–142
interest checklist, 148–150
number of home economists in,
133–134
nutrition, 138–140
positions, 132–151
salaries, 147
research and testing, 145–146,
192–193
Ford Foundation, 209, 220

Foreign service, opportunities for
home economists, 207–223
Fulbright-Hays Act, 211–215
nongovernment agencies, 218–221
Peace Corps, 215–217
qualifications, 221–222
United Nations programs, 218–
221
4-H club specialists in extension,
82–83
4-H clubs, 79, 98–99, 82, 85, 257
number of, and members, 83, 258
purposes of, 82–83
Framingham State Normal School, 15
Free-lance designers, 115
Frysinger, Grace, fellowship, 269
Fulbright-Hays Act, 208, 211–215
Future Homemakers of America, 64,
68
membership, 61, 64, 260

General education and home
economics, 50
General Foods Kitchens, 133, 144
George-Barden Act, 260
George-Deen Act, 260
George-Ellzey Act, 260
George-Reed Act, 260
Gloucester high school, 69
Good Housekeeping magazine, 10
Good students, characteristics of,
305–311
Good study habits, importance of, 294
Graders in clothing production, 116
Graduate study in U.S., 237–238
Grants for foreign service, 208–211

Hale, Nathan, 4–5
Hall and Schroeder, study of
homemakers, 281
Handicapped, work with, 278–279

Hatch Act, 261
Hemenway, Mary, 7, 28
Henery, David, 39
High schools (*see* Secondary schools)
Home catering, 142
Home economics:
  aims of, 38–40
  as applied science and art, 49
  beginnings, 3, 6
  Isabel Bevier, 23–25
  development of, 11–14, 256
  Henrietta Willard Calvin, 31–32
  coeducation and, 5, 6
  combines liberal arts and sciences,
    41
  definition and scope, 41–45
  early scientists and, 10
  finding place in, 49–55
  Mary Tileston Hemenway, 7, 28
  Lake Placid Conferences, 14–16
  land-grant colleges and, 11–14
  legislation affecting, 255–262
  Abby Marlatt, 27–28
  name changes, 280–284
  in public schools, 6
  related movements, 7
  Ellen H. Richards, 8–9, 20–23
  Sara Tyson Rorer, 9–10
  Martha Van Rensselaer, 25–26
  Edna Noble White, 34
Home economics curriculum,
    beginnings in college, 11–12
Home economics degrees given in
    colleges and universities, 72,
    238–239, 287
Home Economics Division, American
    Vocational Association,
    268–269
Home economics magazines, early, 10
Home economics students and
    college, 287–288
  expenditures in college, 298–299

Home economics students and
    college:
  responsibility for selecting
    profession, 51–52
Home economists:
  need for, 44–46
  number employed, 54
  services rendered, 171
Home management:
  administrative positions, 156–158
  careers, 155–169
    interest checklist, 165
    qualifications for positions, 158
    residence houses, 25, 31
    salaries, 164–165
Home service:
  directors, 162–164
  opportunities in, 175–180
  salaries, 164–165
Homemaking, 225, 234
  clothing the family, 229
  community life, 230–232
  feeding the family, 229
  management, careers in,
    72
  occupational categories of
    homemaking activities, 227
  as a profession, 225–235
  remuneration, 232–234
  self-expression, 230–232
  working outside the home, 45
Honor societies, 271–272
Horrocks, John E., 295
Horton, Mildred, fellowship, 241
Hospital dietitians, 132–134
House furnishings, 155–169
Household economics and
    management, careers in, 72
Household equipment positions,
    162–164
  interest checklist, 166
  research in, 195–196

Household equipment positions:
  salaries, 164–165
Housekeepers, executive, 158
Housing, 53, 160–170
  interest checklist, 166
  research, 195–196
  salaries, 164–165
Howard University, 212
Hughes, Senator Dudley M., 259–261
Hughes, Mrs. Dudley M., 259–261
Hunt, Caroline L., 8
Huntington, Emily, 7
Hutchins, C. B., 43

Illinois Industrial Institute, 12, 34, 39
Illustrator in designing, 112–115
Industrial Education Association, 7,
  260
Industry and commercial agencies,
  foreign service opportunities
  in, 209–210
Institute of International Education,
  220
Institution housekeepers, 158
Institution management and
  administration, 141–142
Interest checklists:
  business and communications,
    185–186
  child development and family
    relations, 103–106
  clothing and textiles, 126–128
  extension, 87–88
  foods and nutrition, 148–151
  home economics education, 74–75
  home management and family
    finance, 165–166
  housing and household equipment,
    166
  research, 203–204
Interior decoration, 53, 161–162

International Farm Youth Exchange
  program, 209, 220
International service agencies
  employing home economists,
    153, 207–223
Iowa State University, 63

Jones, Nellie Kedzie, 27
Journal of Home Economics, 267
*Journal of the American Dietetic
  Association*, 265
Journalism for home economists, 54,
  111, 182–183
Junior colleges, 287

Kansas State University, 12
Kappa Omicron Phi, 270–271
Kindergarten education, 8
Kitchen-Garden Association, 7
Knowing one's college, test for,
  291–293

Lake Placid Club, 14–16
Lake Placid Conferences, 14–16, 266
Land-grant institutions, 11–14, 253
  Morrill Acts, 255–256
  students attending, 256
Langworthy, C., 23
Leaving college, students' reasons for,
  293–294
Legislation affecting home economics,
  255–262
Lincoln, Abraham, 255
Lyford, Carrie M., 258
Lyon, Mary, 5

Management positions, 156–158,
  227–228

Scholarships, assistantships, fellowships, and loans, 240–241
School Lunch Journal, 270
School-lunch program, 8, 9, 23, 140, 270
  qualifications for positions, 140
Schools for girls, early, 4–5
Scientists, early influence of, 10–11
Secondary schools:
  activities of home economists in, 61–63
  advantages and disadvantages of position in, 68–70
  qualifications for, 65–67
Self-analysis for students, 296–298, 314–315
Shaw, Mrs. Quincy, 8
Smith-Hughes Act, 25, 259–260
Smith-Lever Act, 25, 78, 256–258
Smith-Mundt Act, 25
Social welfare, home economists in, 101–102
Society for Promotion of Industrial Education, 259–260
Space buyers, 122
Sparkman, John, 62
State home economics leaders in extension, 83–85
Stewardess, work for home economists, 221
Student financial aid, 299–300
Study abroad, 211–215
Style, meaning, 111–115
Success in college, factors affecting 293–296
Swallow, Ellen Henrietta (*see* Richards, Ellen H.)

Talbot, Marian, 15
Teachers College, Columbia University, 7

Teaching home economics (*see* Careers and professions; Education in home economics; Opportunities for home economists)
Technical schools, 125–126
Television, 183–185
Test kitchens, 145–146
Testing, 145–146
  (See also Research in home economics)
Textile and clothing careers, 53, 110–131
  degrees granted in, 72
  research in, 193–195
Therapeutic dietitians, 135–138
Thompson, Benjamin (Count Rumford), 10
Thwing, Carrie, 11
Thwing, Charles, 11
Time schedules in college, planning, 304–308
Timing in designing, 112
Todhunter, E. Neige, 230
Training directors in clothing production, 116
Travel programs for teachers, 69–70
Treatise on Domestic Economy, 7

UNESCO, 208
UNICEF, 208
United Fruit Company, 210
United Nations:
  Food and Agricultural Organization (FAO), 208, 217–218
  opportunities for home economists, 208–209, 217–218
  World Health Organization (WHO), 217–218
U.S. grants for foreign service, 207–217
U.S. Air Force, dietitians in, 135